The Saturated Society

Theory, Culture & Society

Theory, Culture & Society caters for the resurgence of interest in culture within contemporary social science and the humanities. Building on the heritage of classical social theory, the book series examines ways in which this tradition has been reshaped by a new generation of theorists. It also publishes theoretically informed analyses of everyday life, popular culture, and new intellectual movements.

EDITOR: Mike Featherstone, *Nottingham Trent University*

SERIES EDITORIAL BOARD
Roy Boyne, *University of Durham*
Nicholas Gane, *University of York*
Mike Hepworth, *University of Aberdeen*
Scott Lash, *Goldsmiths College, University of London*
Roland Robertson, *University of Aberdeen*
Couze Venn, *Nottingham Trent University*

THE TCS CENTRE
The *Theory, Culture & Society* book series, the journals *Theory, Culture & Society* and *Body & Society*, and related conference, seminar and postgraduate programmes operate from the TCS Centre at Nottingham Trent University. For further details of the TCS Centre's activities please contact:

The TCS Centre
School of Arts and Humanities
Nottingham Trent University
Nottingham Trent University
Clifton Lane, Nottingham, NG11 8NS, UK
e-mail: tcs@ntu.ac.uk
web: http://sagepub.net/tcs/

Recent volumes include:

Informalization: Manners and Emotions Since 1890
Cas Wouters

The Culture of Speed: The Coming of Immediacy
Jom Tomlinson

Consumer Culture and Postmodernism
Mike Featherstone

Advertising in Modern and Postmodern Times
Pamela Odih

The Saturated Society

Governing Risk and Lifestyles in Consumer Culture

Pekka Sulkunen

Los Angeles • London • New Delhi • Singapore • Washington DC

SAGE Publications Ltd
1 Oliver's Yard
55 City Road
London EC1Y 1SP

SAGE Publications Inc.
2455 Teller Road
Thousand Oaks, California 91320

SAGE Publications India Pvt Ltd
B 1/I 1 Mohan Cooperative Industrial Area
Mathura Road, Post Bag 7
New Delhi 110 044

SAGE Publications Asia-Pacific Pte Ltd
33 Pekin Street #02–01
Far East Square
Singapore 048763

Library of Congress Control Number: 2008933210

British Library Cataloguing in Publication data

A catalogue record for this book is available from the British Library

ISBN 978-0-7619-5941-0

Typeset by C&M Digitals (P) Ltd, Chennai, India
Printed in Great Britain by the MPG Books Group
Printed on paper from sustainable resources

Contents

Foreword

This book sets out to address a simple question. Why is it so difficult to implement preventive policies on lifestyle problems such as alcoholism, smoking or other health-endangering practices in contemporary societies, even though we know the risks, and we know how policy can minimize them? At first, the answer seemed simple and obvious: neo-liberalism. The regulation of alcohol use, nutrition, physical exercise, sexuality, mobility, housing and other relevant choices, would interfere with the free market, and also with consumers' freedom. In the political circumstances in which we live, this would be highly controversial and would raise objections not only from the industries concerned but also from consumers. Market forces seem to have too much power against the public interest; there is no health lobby strong enough to weigh them out. The free market is a fundamental doctrine of the European Union, the World Trade Organization and other powerful institutions, and any attempt to contradict them in this matter will be doomed to failure no matter how good the intentions. This is how it seems.

As is often the case when simple questions invite simple answers, the questions that arise next are so much more complex. Why, if there is public interest, does it not take effect *through* the market? Why do governments spend so much money and energy trying to persuade consumers and citizens, to commit themselves through policy programmes, partnerships, plans, contracts, empowering advice and other means, which intuitively make sense but, according to most experts, have little effect?

To answer these questions, and to write this book, took several years longer than I had foreseen. Not only did I feel the need to gain a much more detailed understanding of the mundane ways of reasoning on these matters among policy-makers, prevention workers, treatment experts, and actual and potential risk-takers themselves, it was also necessary to review what academic social science and dominant policy ideologies had to say about justifying public intervention in private life in modern societies. These two interact and influence one another in a way that makes the understanding of one necessary for the understanding of the other.

As a result of these studies, I can now offer the reader a new perspective on how modern industrial society has turned into consumer capitalism. Arguments that can be used to justify – or to challenge – public policy in lifestyle regulation have changed. The modern ideals of progress, universal individualism and the nation have become saturated. These ideals have justified policies on central aspects of living in modern society: work, consumption, the family, education, culture. They have been the arguments in negotiations and struggle between social groups. By saturation, I mean that these ideals have not ceased to exist, but the conditions of their application have been radically transformed. Progress towards a society of free consumers, citizens and members of a nation has been a dream that has kept modern capitalism together. Today this dream is the context of everyday reality for most people in western countries. Inequalities do persist, exclusions are frequent but expectations of self-responsibility and participation confront everybody on all sides. The structure and causes of inequalities are no longer the same as they were even half a century ago. Unless we understand the past in which current ideologies and public policy evolved, we are likely to misinterpret the present social world in which we live. Good intentions to alleviate inequalities are likely to be mistaken, too. The unreflective assumption of a conflict between society and the market is one such misunderstanding.

I have felt no need to add to the panoply of horrors and injustices related to lifestyle problems. I have not taken it as my task to convince the public and the authorities once again of the need to do something. Public opinion in all quarters is already filled with agitated opinion about these questions. I am merely offering the reader an understanding of and an explanation for the complexity of the debates.

My deliberately adopted position as a theoretical fence-sitter over policy issues does not mean that the explanation I offer is without practical bearing. I intend to make a sociological intervention into the dominant (dominant because they seem so self-evident) assumptions concerning politics and the regulation of life in consumer capitalism. Ulrich Beck's analysis of the risk society, and the debate that followed it, have in many ways been my inspiration and starting point. However, the diagnoses of post-, trans- or late modernity, including Beck's, have tended to adopt a position of either environmental pessimism, or of political optimism – or both. First, reflexive modernization understood as a generalized spirit of the time may offer social theorists reason for anti-bureaucratic but easy optimism. This book is specifically about the justification of the modern social order and how it translates into contradictory and not always very reflexive politics on lifestyles. Second, sociological critiques of modernity tend to adopt the traditional position of productivism. My starting point is that industrial societies are now a danger to themselves not only by taking over 'nature' and exposing themselves to side-effects beyond human control; they have also succeeded in transforming their *internal* structure in a way that stresses the value of agency in everyday life. Unknown side-effects of production are not our biggest problem; it is the well-known effects of consumption which we are unable to control. The side-effects of production can be restrained, as is demonstrated by several sectors of industry and farming that only a couple of decades ago seemed to be the incurably mad cousins of our well-being. What we cannot control, and what the market as well as public policy seem to be powerless to curb, are our desires and the way they lead us astray in our private relationships with nature. The thesis of this book is that it is not the strength of the desires themselves, nor the strength of 'the industries' to usurp them, which cause the difficulty, but the way that desires are socially produced and regulated. This is where political difficulties start rather than stop, and this is where old political institutions are being put to new uses.

One particular obstacle to understanding the problem of regulation is the myth of modern society as a ready-made product of the Industrial Revolution. This myth includes post-traditionalism, individualism, secularization, differentiation, parliamentary democracy and the growth of scientific knowledge. These are not unreasonable assumptions to characterize our contemporary reality. What is unreasonable in the myth is neglect of the fact which is the object of this study: the very recent *historical reality* in which these characteristics have come into their fullness of being. This book will make historical explorations of the nineteenth and late eighteenth centuries, but the focus is on the last third of the twentieth century, when the arrival of the consumer society occurred in Western Europe – retarded by the Second World War, about one or two decades behind the United States.

Of my references, Daniel Bell's classic *The Cultural Contradictions of Capitalism* has a special place, because it first opened my eyes to the parallelism between the rational and the romantic spirit of capitalism. Robert Castel's and Jacques Donzelot's work on the rise and the metamorphoses of the social question in France have been an indispensable complement to my Nordic and British perspective. The French sociologist Luc Boltanski is frequently mentioned, because his work on the new middle class and his work with Laurent Thévenot and Eve Chiapello on the problem of justification have been a great source of inspiration to my analysis. At a more abstract level, the reader will probably be as surprised as I was in the course of my studies to find such close affinities between the work of Adam Smith and Pierre Bourdieu, not in the fault they have been unjustly accused of – utilitarian thinking – but in their most significant contributions to *anti-utilitarian* social theory. The ground for these affinities is their relationship to the sociological concept of society, Smith only approaching it and Bourdieu making a break with it.

As a diagnosis of the kind represented by this book, the reader might rightly expect a prognosis of the future contours of those processes which I now claim to be saturated. This I am reluctant to venture. Too many externalities may occur before industrial modernization reaches the corners of the world that so far have remained outwith its sphere of influence. Within the internal processes of contemporary affluent capitalism, however, at least the most dismal predictions often put forward do not seem to hold. I see no reason for the optimism of those who see ossified modern institutions opening up to the plasticity of anti-bureaucratic (and extra-parliamentary) action, nor do I go along with the pessimistic paranoia of those who see power and repression everywhere, masked in a rhetoric of agency and freedom. Fears carried over from the old (American) mass society theories of the 1950s and 1960s, of a return to pre-modern totalitarianism, seem to be invalidated by my study. The value of agency in consumer capitalism is so fundamentally anti-authoritarian that any attempt to discipline and homogenize lifestyles in the name of order will be unlikely to succeed even temporarily.

On the contrary, most Westerners would consider the homogenizing lifestyle policies of the past century inadmissible today. We are so accustomed to our individual sovereignty that we in fact tend to forget how normative modern societies have been about the *content* of the good life. We have not lost our moral sense. The main consequence of saturation is that it is different from the morality that guided lifestyle regulation in the process of modernization. Policy deliberations on sexuality and the family, food and alcohol, smoking, drug addictions, gambling, and so on, do not concern the intrinsic value of people's choices. They concern justice: rights to health, security and well-being. We tend to abstract the ethical and aesthetic issues of lifestyle regulation into issues of justice alone.

Our sense of justice stresses the need to protect the innocent rather than reform the guilty. The more innocent the victims – children, foetuses, disabled, animals – the more strongly we feel about the injustice when their rights are violated. The victim's point of view is the flipside of the emphasis of agency in advanced consumer capitalism. Those who do wrong should be punished for their acts; those whose autonomy is threatened should be protected.

The extra years that I spent on my studies to clarify and validate my original argument have not essentially changed my intuitive starting point. Even the title of the book is the same as I had in mind when I decided to write it. I have learned in the process how important it is to see mundane reasoning in the context of social theory, and vice versa. This is reflected in the way that the chapters usually juxtapose theoretical thought with selected results of my studies of mundane reasoning. Chapter 1 presents the summary of the argument and develops a model of basic concepts to analyse the problem of justification. The other chapters, although constructed as a sequence of steps in the argument, can be read in isolation and in a different order. It goes without saying that readers are consciously encouraged to use them as a source of their own reflection and critique, but especially the last two chapters, on the nature of contemporary consumer capitalism and the failure of traditional social theory to grasp it, are pointedly intended to be provocative and polemical.

Acknowledgements

This work would not have taken so long, but nor would it have been as accurate and rich in detail, without my students and colleagues involved in the specific studies I often draw on. All authors of *Broken Spirits: Power and Ideology in Nordic Alcohol Control* (2000) deserve both individual and collective thanks. Katariina Warpenius, Kati Rantala and Mirja Määttä have been particularly helpful as co-authors of articles that I use extensively in this book. My students have been very important, not only offering their own work for discussion and inspiration but also commenting on drafts of the chapters. I am very grateful for comments by Dr Eric Landowski of the C.N.R.S. and Ecole des Sciences Politiques, and by my colleagues at the Department of Sociology at the University of Helsinki, docents Arto Noro and Klaus Mäkelä. The department has generously tolerated the absent-minded professor, and allowed me to spend several months in Paris during each of the four final years of writing. The Bibliothèque National de France with its main library in rue de Tolbiac deserves the warmest thanks not only from this author but also from a huge number of other scholars and students who have used the wonderful collection of over 50 million books and other documents for their research. The Ecole des Hautes Etudes en Sciences Sociales in Paris is to be thanked for hosting the exchange visits. Grants from the Academy of Finland have made them possible. When I started writing this many years ago, Professor Sue Scott invited me to the University of Stirling and Professor Alan Warde to the University of Manchester, to have an opportunity to stay in an English language environment, which helped me realize the dimensions of the challenge of writing an essay in a foreign language. Both gave me valuable comments on the plan and encouraged me to surmount the difficulties, which at the time sometimes seemed more than I could face. My wife Jaana Lähteenmaa has been an excellent support and conversation partner on sociological issues and ideas.

The completion of this project would not have been possible without my research assistants Aino Manninen and Varpu Rantala. They not only helped me out with the daily work in the office thus giving me time to work on 'the book'; Varpu Rantala also read the first complete version, closely and critically, gave me excellent comments, asked challenging questions, helped with translations and filled in sources and references. Finally, I wish to thank the series editor Chris Rojek for his advice, loyalty and patience in letting this project take its time, hopefully for the benefit of the readers.

Publisher's Acknowledgements

Reprinted by permission of the publisher from *Distinction: A Social Critique of the Judgement of Taste* by Pierre Bourdieu, translated by Richard Nice, p.172, Cambridge, Mass.: Harvard University Press, Copyright © 1984 by the President and Fellows of Harvard College and Routledge and Kegan Paul, Ltd.

Durkheim, Émile. (1984 [1893]) *The Division of Labour in Society. De la division du travail social.* Transl. by W.D. Halls. Basingstoke: Macmillan. Reproduced with permission of Palgrave Macmillan.

1

Introduction: the Problem of Justification

Society is not a thing; it is the name of an idea.

(Howard S. Becker)[1]

The threat of culture to itself

The regulation of lifestyles, indeed of life itself, is a burning political and moral issue in contemporary advanced societies. Science and technology have opened unforeseen possibilities for human culture to manipulate, even create natural phenomena. Nature is striking back. The global environment is not in control, but neither are less global concerns. Obesity, addictions, preventable health problems and many other risks depend on cultural practices, yet they lend themselves with great difficulty to conscious efforts of control. Gene technology, brain research, diagnostic techniques and advanced medical technologies are offering improved possibilities to make rational decisions on life and lifestyles, but the consequences of these possibilities are unpredictable and morally complicated. Culture has become a threat, not only to nature external to it, but also to itself.

This threat is the object of many attempts at cultural regulation – by cultural means. The growing ability to make choices weighs down on us as an immense moral responsibility for their consequences. Rational regulation of life practices is everywhere a possibility, and in these matters 'can' tends to translate into 'must'; if we *can* lead a healthier life, which is environmentally sound, then we *should* do so to minimize treatment costs and to maximize the happiness of people around us, and after us, if not of ourselves. Human life has acquired an unforeseen moral loading. Any life is now irrevocably a matter of will: no one can have it or lose it without someone willing. Even in the face of inevitable death, questions arise. How long to treat? At what cost? What if someone had acted differently earlier? There is no absolute health, and the degree of health depends on social definitions of normality. When Jean Baudrillard (1976) said that we have succeeded in 'naturalizing' death, he meant that life and death have ceased to be *supernatural*, beyond human control. Medical technology is now able to postpone death, to cure illness and to prevent diseases to an extent that is beyond our economic and social resources. Choices have to be made; we need principles and practices to help us make decisions on what kinds of life are morally binding and what are not. Technical progress is translated into moral problems, moral problems into judicial problems, judicial problems finally into exercise of power.

Societies are trying to act on themselves, but their achievements are not very impressive. Everywhere today, governments, prevention workers, health promoters, nutritionists, health economists, scientists and sociologists are persuading people to adjust their life practices to the requirements of health, the environment, and safety. A major obstacle stands in their way, however. The regulation of choices requires a moral authority that seems to be missing, and the locus where that authority would have been a few decades ago, the nation–state, seems ever less capable of exercising it today. In industrializing societies, previously, freedom of choice over one's life-course was, for the large majority of people, a distant ideal for the future. Many people hoped that it could be realized by the parliamentary state. Lifestyle movements in the late nineteenth and early twentieth centuries, such as temperance, the youth movement, women's liberation and nationalism, pursued legislative reforms to improve citizens' possibilities to make choices and take responsibility for their lives.

The idea of 'society'

At that time, about one hundred years ago, the principles that guided lifestyle regulation by the state were closely connected to the modern idea of society, as laid down in the works of the classical fathers of sociology: Emile Durkheim, Max Weber, Georg Simmel, Thorstein Veblen and others. 'Society' was something less visible than the state, but not just a collection of isolated individuals either, even though modern industrial society obviously would cause a gradual breakdown of their traditional bondage. Society was a thing in the making. Lifestyle regulation was part of this process. The three projects of this process were progress, the nation, and the ideal of universal individualism. These were the moral yardsticks by which social policy was assessed and justified. In such a society the future was present in the incompleteness of the here and now. Politics of lifestyle could be judged and contested in the name of the common good constituted by these yardsticks, which were used to measure levels and distribution of the accomplishments of modernity in the population.

The idea of society, as developed by the sociological classics, centred on the problem of how to solve the problems and conflicts that arise from divisions in the population, above all according to their class position. The answer was scientific politics to promote the common good. In the social world today, where technological possibilities are greater than the moral capacity of people to choose between them, and where nevertheless the value of agency assigns the responsibility to individuals, the 'common good', has disappeared. The new problem of social co-ordination poses itself in a different way: how does a society that has reached a point of saturation of its modern aspirations deal with the consequences of incompatible lifestyle choices? Homogenization and standardization can no longer be the answer, and the authority of the nation–state is no longer sufficient to administer the choices.

The thesis propounded by this book is that in advanced consumer capitalism, the classical sociological concept of society has become problematic, and the morality that it involved has become difficult to apply. The difficulty results not from the failure of the modern ideals of progress, the nation and the individual, but from their full maturity. It is difficult to see what progress could mean any more; what the nation is in the global world, and in what way universal individualism can be maintained or advanced in mass society. They must be replaced by other principles of justification, and consequently the policies of lifestyle regulation must be matched to these principles. Central among them is the value placed on agency, brought about by the experience of autonomy and intimacy. This value and these experiences are not the outcomes of abstract cultural change, beyond modernity or within it, but expressions of the concrete social circumstances in which people live their everyday lives.

In advanced consumer capitalism, most people have seen their choices multiply. This is most obvious in consumption, but is not limited to the purchase and use of objects and services. Moral questions arise and are resolved every day on what we should eat and drink and wear, on how we should spend our time, how children should be raised, and so on. Similar questions also arise and are resolved on whether people should be allowed to die or be born, often in very delicate situations where the 'quality of life' concerned is in doubt. The dying person may be suffering, or an unborn child may be at high risk of serious birth defects. Somebody must decide.

Choice and the social bond

Even though the notion of the common good has lost its appeal, people must still be persuaded to avoid preventable problems and to prioritize safe and healthy alternatives. The regulation of lifestyles has not turned into an affair of isolated individuals. On the contrary, the extended possibilities of managing illness, treating and preventing diseases and avoiding environmental harm put our lifestyle choices in a new collective context. This is not only because the technologically produced risks are so great; the dilemma is caused by the fact that risks are well known and can be managed, albeit not by individuals, families or informal communities. We depend on the views of experts in most cases: no ordinary individual can determine the risks of even the most regular daily practices. Only experts can tell what kinds of risks are involved in eating ordinary food, and even the most commonly recognized risks such as those related to smoking, are known only through systematic research. We have upsetting images of the suffering caused to animals by industrial farming, and of the environmental damage caused by mass tourism, but only experts can tell whether these images are justified, and the experts differ in their views. Nevertheless, we widely share the understanding that decisions on risks should not be made by experts alone but by the individuals concerned; they should at least give their informed consent to the decisions made by others.

It is exactly this ideal of self-determination and respect of individual life that is today almost impossible to apply in the delicate issues concerning life and its regulation. Individual choice is almost never without consequences for other individuals. Our pleasures incur costs to others: health costs, costs in the form of both immediate and less immediate environmental destruction, and moral costs in seeing innocent others such as children – born or unborn – suffer from the actions of adults. Lifestyle has become a social bond in a new way. It is no longer only a chosen style that indicates and expresses adherence to a group such as social class, and thereby to a position in the social structure. It is a bond that connects individuals in very complex, extensive and intermediated networks of consequences. Yet the state, the local community, neighbours, educators, or even social workers, do not have indisputable moral authority to interfere, and if they do, they have no unchallenged ethical or political rules to follow in doing so. The problem of justification is the issue.

The problem of justification

The problem of justification, to use the expression by Luc Boltanski and Laurent Thévenot (1991), exists in all types of societies, and it is also an integral part of the modern idea of society developed by the sociological classics. Peter Wagner (2001a: 40–53; 2006: 31–2) has pointed out that as the sociological concept of society emerged, the problem of justification acquired a new political dimension. The old concept of the political society of the pre-nineteenth century was replaced by the priority of the social. The state was no longer seen to be the centre of social integration, emblematized by the sovereign ruler. The social – instead of the political – basis of co-operation proposed by the sociological point of view constituted itself at the moment when the notion of the individual, liberated from political and traditional ties, became 'the principal articulation of the social world' (Wagner, 2006). In this way, the political bond becomes an enigma: if members of society do not need political rule to be bonded to each other, what would be the role of the state in modern society?

This question arises if it is assumed that modernity emerged ready-made from the Reformation and the scientific, industrial and democratic American and French Revolutions. It was a founding assumption of sociology that the sum of those transformations was a rupture with earlier modes of social organization by which societies were put on an entirely new footing. The modern society was put firmly in place (Wagner, 2001a: 160). My answer to the question is that in reality, nothing that is usually taken for granted as characteristic of modern society – post-traditionalism, secularization, differentiation, personal biographies, citizenship, parliamentary democracy – concerned more than a small minority of the population in Western countries until after the Second World War. If we include the welfare state in the concept of the nation, as I think is necessary, it was only in its early beginnings in the inter-war period. The universal individual became universally accepted, even as an ideal, only gradually in the course of the twentieth century, and this ideal was applied in very incomplete ways even in the last decades of that period. The 'political' in modern society was a struggle over this incompleteness, attached to the notion of progress in material, technological and cultural terms. This struggle itself *was* the principle of justification, and its transformation now is the outcome of its saturation.

Justification is not only a matter of legitimacy of social reality, with its power differences, inequalities and injustices, in the sense Max Weber used the term. It is also the basis for theoretical understandings of how co-ordination and order are possible in different types of circumstances. As I shall elaborate shortly, it is useful to make a distinction between two types of consciousness, mundane and academic, but it is never possible to understand them in isolation of each other. Justification does not mean consensus or compliance; it makes no sense to oppose conflict theories to theories of integration, because no social formation is ever in a state of complete harmony and stability, and even when conflicts and differences reign, some common ground usually underlies them to make participants understand what the conflicts are about. Justification here means exactly this possibility of mutual communication, even in a situation where interests are not shared and where values attached to interests are different.

Luc Boltanski and Laurent Thévenot (1991) have developed a model for the analysis of justification, which is a useful starting point for the study of the transformation that is the topic of this book. They use the concept of *the cité*, which literally means city, but could also be translated as regime, to distinguish different orders of justification. To simplify a little, the model includes elementary principles to define: (1) what the principles of *the social bond* are that connect people as members of society and of subgroups (the principles of belonging and differentiation); (2) what the meaning of *dignity* and the order of *greatness* (*grandeur*) in each regime of justification are; and (3) how *the common good* can be recognized. Different regimes of justification can be distinguished according to the value of greatness such as closeness to the divine world, domestic hierarchies of domination and subordination, esteem by others or capacity to act as a participant in market exchange. The criteria of the common good and the principles of the social bond are adapted to such regimes.

As to the first element, the social bond, it is commonly agreed that in modern industrial societies of the late nineteenth and early twentieth centuries the nation was the framework of belonging to a society. In contrast, the principles of differentiation that define the internal structure of modern society have been one of the most important disputes in social theory.

Lifestyle is an element of the social bond, but how it is related to 'objective' class structure has been and still is a question of debate. Secondly, the common good has been defined in terms of progress in these principles of greatness since the late eighteenth century. Thirdly, dignity and greatness undoubtedly have been associated with freedom and well-being of the individual, but these involve two sides that may contradict (and they do especially in saturated society): autonomy and intimacy. These three elements of justification constitute the body of my analysis, and here I present the starting points of each.

The social bond

Advanced Western capitalism is based on industrial development, science and technology, the division of labour and the institution of the market. Since Marx, it has been taken for granted that structural modernization is a self-perpetuating process propelled by the capitalist relations of production. This view has not only marginalized the concept of lifestyle in theories of modern society, it has also trivialized the related concept of agency in social theory for many decades.

Most sociologists, not only those of a Marxist persuasion, until the last part of the twentieth century thought that the concept of lifestyle implied, from the outset, an inadmissible voluntarism. This disqualifies lifestyle as an object of structural study of society. Style involves incommensurable values, ideals and moral and aesthetic judgements. According to this view, social structure is based on class divisions and the inequalities they entail. Classes are related to work, employment relations and the market rather than style, however that is determined. Through the class situation, the production system *causally* determines the interests, a sense of belonging, and the ideology of each group. These organize society's members into class action. It would, from this point of view, be more correct to speak of *a way of life*, as determined by its objective conditions, rather than of a style, which refers to choice.

The latter part of the twentieth century marked a sea change in social thought in this respect. The idea of 'society' as a mechanism beyond human will was challenged or declared defunct by many sociologists. For example, Alain Touraine (1973: 35) stressed that it is not enough to place society in history. Sociologists must place historicity – the principle of auto-production – right at the heart of the concept of society. Societies produce and not only reproduce themselves through the actions of conscious and intentional agents.

Human agency, meaning, choice and therefore the taste and lifestyle of ordinary people became central issues in social theorizing. Anthony Giddens stressed in his *Central Problems in Social Theory* in 1979, that people have complex knowledge about the society in which they live, without anybody telling them. Institutions, customs, moral principles, even law and other written rules are known to participants, and they use this knowledge to act consciously. Giddens supposed that the master trend in twentieth-century social thought was towards recognition of the role of agency in the social process. He was certainly right as regards the last third of the twentieth century, as is evident from some of the most influential sociological books of the time,[2] but it should be remembered that the spirit of capitalism, the social constitution of ideas and the mentality of the moderns were already central themes in the works of the sociological classics, Max Weber, Emile Durkheim and Georg Simmel, as well as of many others at the turn of the nineteenth century. The new prominence of meaningful action in social theory was a return to the original problematic of modern social sciences after a rather short detour into false positivism.

When societies are seen as auto-productive systems of meaningful social action, the question arises, first, how do groups and individuals in societies recognize common aims, interests and the will to pursue them together (the principle of differentiation)? Within each of the two theoretical positions, structural determination of class and the social bond as action, there is a tendency to gravitate towards the other (Archer, 1988). Pierre Bourdieu's work illustrates this ambivalence. In his sociology, groups are not causally determined by 'structural factors'. For him, it is the ambivalent concept of the *habitus* in which subjective action turns into objective reality. My thesis is that theoretical ambivalences such as Bourdieu's reflect the real ambivalences of people living in contemporary consumer capitalism, where the meaning of dignity and the order of greatness are attached to the value of agency.

The common good

The second question concerns the justification of inequalities and hierarchies (the principle of the common good). In traditional societies, this is not a problem, but when the modern wage labour society gives rise to the idea of free social mobility and universal individualism, deviations from these ideals cannot be tolerated without a reason. A theory that explains why inequalities can be maintained in modern societies also explains why such societies hold together. Such a theory must be able to show that the individuals who compose the society are 'capable of seeing themselves as equal in some respect more fundamental than all the respects in which they are unequal' (Macpherson, 1977: 274). This book will take up this problem in the light of Adam Smith's social theory, which laid the foundations of modern sociology. It is well known that Smith's answer was progress, but this answer has often been misunderstood as utilitarianism: since everyone stands to benefit from it, we must accept the division of labour and the inequalities that it entails. Smith's real answer was anti-utilitarian and based on what later became a wicked concept for sociology: human nature.[3] The natural propensity of humans to see themselves as if through the eyes of others makes progress a possible and necessary principle of the common good in modern society. We evaluate others according to our moral sentiments, but understand that they, too, evaluate us. When these evaluations are in agreement, relationships of mutual esteem are established. Undisturbed, human potentiality for respectful interaction makes society evolve towards a system of co-operation, which does not need what in earlier social theory had been called the 'political society', i.e. the state, as the centre of social integration. Smith's theory was the first major achievement in modern social thought towards the priority of the social over the individual and over political institutions: towards a *self-policing society*. Its relevance today is obvious when we think of the contemporary predicament of prevention. We must ask, has the self-policing society developed to a point where the very idea of the common good has become problematic and the ethical grounds of regulating lifestyles have lost their binding force?

Dignity and greatness

The principles of dignity and greatness that are specific to modern society, as Adam Smith foresaw it, are based on esteem by and for others, whenever there is confidence that the esteem is justified. The prerequisite for esteem is individuality, which I will in the following discuss in two parts: autonomy and intimacy. Post-, trans- or late modern consciousness tends to take them so much for granted that their real and very recent history is ignored.[4] Without an historical perspective, we cannot understand either why we act as clients and contract partners of society today, or why in the late nineteenth and early twentieth centuries the state had moral authority, which today would be unthinkable. The idea of citizens as autonomous contract-making individuals has not emerged from capitalism of its own accord. It has been the subject of struggles over lifestyle and over distribution of freedoms for two and a half centuries of capitalist development. The struggle for autonomy represented the rationalist orientation in the spirit of ascendant capitalism. The other side of the capitalist subjectivity in the making has been the struggle for intimacy. Individuality involves not only autonomy in the management of one's own biography; it also requires that people have a sense of the self as a distinct and authentic person, separate as body and soul from others, in other words, individuality must be swathed in a sphere of intimacy around the person. The two sides of subjectivity, autonomy and intimacy, have developed in relative harmony until recent times, but today the most burning issue of justification is how to accommodate these two values when intimacy requires the right to authentic and different, whereas autonomy presupposes that everybody is treated in a similar way as a subject of rights and duties.

Saturation

Two major misconceptions block the way to an understanding of how the new consumer capitalism has turned upside down the principles of justification inherited from earlier phases of modernization. The first is an explanation from outside: the dominance of the market over the public interest. This is a widely held view especially in the Nordic countries and in Great Britain, with their strong traditions in the planned economy and the welfare state.

Neo-liberalism, it has repeatedly been argued there, has become dominant in conjunction with the global economy. Global markets and international media networks have inexorably urged nation–states to 'deregulate' the economy, including consumers' choices. The state seems therefore to be unable to represent the public interest in lifestyle issues.

This explanation misunderstands the regime of justification as known during the late nineteenth and early twentieth centuries, and ignores its effects on the regime of justification which we are entering. The market itself is undergoing a change from a standardized and homogenized regime of measurable input to a much more flexible regime of measurable output. It is therefore pertinent to understand how the regime of justification has transformed itself internally, also in areas that have only superficial resemblance to the alleged 'marketization' of politics.

The second misconception is the myth of ready-made individualism. In lifestyle politics that interpretation confuses the new forms of collective action as alternatives to rather than outcomes of the modern regime of justification. I shall show examples of this in later chapters. The forms in which the state now delegates moral authority to citizens and groups result from long and ardent struggles for autonomy and intimacy, not from a nostalgia for community. This book will argue that the contemporary predicament regarding lifestyle regulation is not the result of external forces nor an alternative to individualism gone too far, but the consistent outcome of modernization itself. The transformation of the modern ideals of progress, individualism and the nation should be seen as a process of their qualitative *saturation* rather than either a rupture operated by external forces or as a continuous change.

The idea of saturation comes from Pitirim Sorokin, the Russian émigré sociologist who founded the famous Harvard Department of Sociology (Sztompka, 1993: 151). Sorokin himself hardly used the word, but the metaphor is well justified by his idea of the immanent causation of social change:

> Through this incessant generation of consequences attending each of its changes, a system perceptibly determines the character and course of its future career. The whole series of changes it undergoes throughout its existence is to a large extent *an unfolding of its inherent potentialities.* From an acorn can spring only an oak. (Sorokin, 1974: 696–7, italics in original)

External factors can only accelerate or retard immanent change, they can facilitate or hinder the realization of its potentialities; they may suppress, distort or overdevelop its characteristics and mutilate or destroy its secondary traits. They might even crush the system, but not change its inherent structure. To the extent that the system is able to develop on its own, without interference from outside factors, it is free. But as in physics, there are limits to the processes of internal change beyond which the regularities of normal conditions no longer hold. Thus, water can only be heated to about 100°C; beyond that point it evaporates and is transformed into a gas;

a solution of salt and water can only be enriched as a liquid up to a point beyond which the salt returns to its crystal state, etc.

The principle of immanent causation is essential to an understanding of social change because of the peculiar role of ideas and values involved in the process.[5] Societies are processes of action, and in order to act, in other words, in order to be historical subjects, agents need collective ideals and images of the good life, the good society and the good state. Such ideals do not come from nowhere – they are always products of earlier ideals and actions, and are directed by them. In that process, some of the ideals get saturated: they reach the point where ideals are no longer just dreams but realities, and the images of the good life, the good society and the good state may turn upside down and seem unrecognizable in comparison to the originals.

The saturation argument presented in this book is that the justification of modern industrial societies has centred on three ideals: material and technological progress, the nation–state, and universal individualism. These ideals have now become problematic, not because they failed but because they have succeeded beyond the point of saturation. They still serve as the basis of both justification and criticism, but the form and content of these justifications and criticisms have changed often beyond recognition, and at least their meaning has become ambiguous and disputable.

Critical awareness of the present

Societies are processes of social action; therefore, they depend on cognition. However, institutions or individuals could not survive if they had to think about themselves actively all the time. We would be swamped by an overload of ideas and calculations even in the simplest task of finding food, preparing it for a meal, and eating it, not to mention the complexities of making all this a *social* practice. Cognitive scientists today agree that we are not actively aware even of those acts that we actively plan and execute with our bodies; and we certainly do not know what happens in us when we feel, think and make moral decisions (Dennett, 2004).

Social reality is constructed of very complex ideas and values, which remain in a state of latency most of the time. We are unaware of them, not because they are unconscious or beyond human grasp; on the contrary, we know them so well that we take the social reality for granted – *il va de soi* was one of the favourite expressions of Pierre Bourdieu. Such ideas operate as justifications, as unchallenged elements, self-evident truths that materialize in the regularities of human practices. At the collective level, they form institutions and groups, at the individual level, they organize our positions as parts of the social structure. Thorstein Veblen ([1919] 2002: 1–11) called them 'imponderables' – we do not incessantly deliberate upon them lest our routines become perturbed and our normal life becomes impractical. They become part of us as individuals and as members of social groups, and they become constitutive elements of the objective social reality in which we live.[6]

The imponderable elements of cognition, taken-for-granted things, are articles of make-believe that have become axiomatic by force of settled habit. They serve as justifications of action but also as the basis of criticisms of present reality. Justification and criticism are not contradictory. On the contrary, together they form a common axis of argumentation employed in different directions, criticism pointing out dearth and failure, justification pointing out the values and beliefs against which actions are to be judged. In other words, they constitute the *critical awareness of the present* in each social situation.

For example, the rationalist conception and the romantic conception of the individual constituted the critical awareness of the present throughout the late nineteenth and early twentieth centuries. Both the political right and the political left used them as values in their critique and justification. Sometimes these concepts have been used in concert to defend what is right and proper in human intercourse; at other times, as will be shown in the context of the consumer society, they have been in conflict.

Progress, the typically modern time orientation, has in a similar way been a shared value but used as an argument for contradicting intentions. As Alain Touraine (1978) has remarked, in the aggravated debate on capitalism in the 1970s, the pro-capitalist right argued that capitalism is the best way to secure universalism and to safeguard the democratic nation–state, while the anti-capitalist left accused it of failing on these very same accounts, causing inefficiency, waste, inequality and lack of transparency in power.

At some point the imponderables of society become problematic, however. Enough social development may have taken place to meet the ideals striven for. The point beyond which more is no longer more may have been reached; the pursuit of the ideals grounded in the critical awareness of the present may bring into being outcomes that are the reverse of those intended. At such points, the forms of critical awareness of the present embedded in everyday identities, practices and institutions are no longer sufficient. They will need to be critically reviewed, re-evaluated and revised.

Modern sociology was one form of such critical reassessment when it was formulated in the late nineteenth century. The doctrines inherited from the French and American Revolutions were found wanting: neither the free market nor the state was considered sufficient to meet the ideals of growing prosperity, international peace and social harmony. The concept of 'society' was more fundamental than the market or the state, and indispensable for constituting the social formation based on the industrial division of labour, secularization and anonymity of metropolitan life. The 'social' question was born (Donzelot, 1984; Wagner, 2001a: 7–24).

Religious doctrine, political ideology, philosophical discourse as well as literary and artistic expression may be the platforms where conscious articulations of the social experience perform their act of reform and revision. They too, however, are expert discourses and therefore I call them *consciousness of the pulpit*, in contrast to *mundane consciousness*, or consciousness of everyday life (Giddens, 1979: 248–53). The difference is not to be exaggerated.

Consciousness of the pulpit is not always the more systematic or rational of the two. The distinction is nevertheless important, because the mundane consciousness often takes figurative or imaginary forms, which only systematic research can reveal to be forms of social thought. For this reason also, I prefer sometimes to speak of *social images of reality* instead of social consciousness.[7] To *see* the connection between forms of mundane awareness and the consciousness of the pulpit is the main task of sociology, often necessary to make understandable not only what we see and hear around us in everyday life, but also what we read and hear from the pulpit.

As Luc Boltanski has observed, capitalism has a particularly pronounced need for justification, both in its theory and in its everyday practice, because it is an absurd system in two ways. It offers no motivation for wage earners – especially during the painful nineteenth century of working-class misery – whose efforts and suffering do not benefit them to make possible an easier and more comfortable life outside of work.[8] Why work so hard, why work at all for that matter, if it is so unlikely that one will get to enjoy the fruits of one's own labour? For capitalists, on the other hand, accumulation serves as little purpose. For them, too, growth means struggle for the sake of mere survival; and success involves an ever greater responsibility for the patrimony. As Adam Smith stressed, the purpose of the 'toil and bustle of this world' must be sought not in material results, but in the satisfaction spawned by the social relationships engendered in the acts of production and consumption themselves. Max Weber's thesis of the *Protestant Ethic* ([1920] 2002) is a well-known example of how the motivation to participate comes from *outside of participation itself*; it must constitute an *ethos*, an ethical and an aesthetic experience of everyday life as well as a religious attitude.

The structure of the book

The chapters of this book describe the imponderables that have constituted the critical awareness of the present, and how they have unfolded from the collective unconscious to the centre stage of our critical awareness of the present in the predicament of lifestyle regulation in contemporary consumer capitalism. The next four chapters will present the elements of the model of justification, starting from a discussion of lifestyle as the social bond in Chapter 2. Chapter 3 will present the conception of progress as the common good in the light of Adam Smith's work. Chapter 4 on autonomy and Chapter 5 on intimacy will discuss the principles of dignity and the order of greatness in capitalism.

The following three chapters will present how the elements of justification have appeared in debates on the consumer society, on the welfare state and in preventive social policy. Finally, the last two chapters take stock of the political consequences of saturation and of its implications for social theory.

Before starting the journey, a brief note on the practical nature of this kind of sociological exercise is in order.

A sociological intervention

The predicament of lifestyle regulation raises confusion, anxiety, even despair. Reactions vary from selfish cynicism to vacuous optimism or virtuous prudence. Reconciliation between these positions seems impossible on rational grounds, and even debate is often difficult.

Social science can produce no more conclusive solutions to these dilemmas than any other form of expertise. The task of social science in a situation like this is not only to provide information, even less to serve as a class master, teaching people how to live properly, but in the words of C. Wright Mills (1959a: 5), 'to achieve lucid summations of what is going on in the world and of what may be happening in individuals' own lives'. To see the predicament of lifestyle regulation as the outcome of the huge social change in a very short stretch of modernity – the lifetime of the older generations still among us – is in itself important. In my view, the even more pertinent task of social science is to map the intersection between history and the present in the domain of ideas. What is going on in the world depends on human beings who are guided by ideals and images of reality. In pursuing them they often produce outcomes that nobody wants. This is a law all too well known to any social scientist, but they too often overlook that at each moment in history, people's aspirations are transformations of earlier ideas and depend on them. The current predicament of lifestyle regulation has its roots in the aspirations and ideals of earlier generations, who in the process of industrialization have made consumer capitalism possible.

This book was not written to pronounce judgements on what progress is, what the virtues and faults of individualism are, or what should be done about the nation in the saturated society. The task of general sociology is to analyse the contemporary critical awareness of the present, to understand images of society that are often curiously obscure at the same time as they are also taken for granted or act as a source of enthusiasm.

Notes

1 This is a comment that Howard S. Becker made in the concluding panel at the European Sociological Association conference in Murcia, Spain, in 2003.

2 His own book had the subtitle *Action, Structure and Contradiction in Social Analysis.* Many others have stressed the importance of social action, such as Alain Touraine's *The Self-Production of Society* ([1973] 1977) or *The Return of the Actor* ([1984] 1988), Pierre Bourdieu's *Distinction, or the Social Critique of Taste* ([1979] 1984) or *The Logic of Practice* ([1980] 1990), or Margaret Archer's *Culture and Agency* (1988).

3 In an otherwise excellent summary of Smith's general social theory, Boltanski and Thévenot (1991: 60–82) narrow down its domain to the market economy. It is clear even from their own presentation that Smith's intentions were much wider. It is a different matter that the development of the market implied for Smith progress and civilization, albeit also a certain kind of repression.

4 Peter Wagner (2001b: 4–7; 118–24) makes a similar distinction between 'autonomy' and 'mastery' in his critique of modernism. Modernist social science, according to him, takes as its starting point that people have wills and their actions are guided by them, and that they believe

the world to be intelligible by human reason, and therefore in principle to be controllable by rational means. Modernist social science interprets the modernization process as the progressive application of these convictions, thus conflating 'the imaginary signification of modernity with the reality of life in Western societies'. As a tool for epistemological critique of modernist social science and political theory, the distinction works well. As a tool for diagnosing the problem of justification, it is less satisfactory. It puts romanticism as a practical ideology outside of modernism. In my conceptualization, autonomy contains both the assumptions of will *and* reason. Intimacy refers to the sense of separateness and the sense of authenticity, both emphasized already in Smith's nascent theory of the social. Wagner's presentation is very complex and difficult, which results from its lack of distinction between what I call mundane consciousness and the consciousness of the (sociological and philosophical) pulpits. His treatise is focused on the latter but makes occasional digressions on the former.

5 Pitirim Sorokin was also one of the first advocates of the idea that elements of culture – including law, philosophy, scientific knowledge, art, music and literature – form congruities or wholes, which move and change in similar directions although not exactly simultaneously. Since they are not in one-to-one correspondence with each other in different areas of culture he called them 'congeries' rather than totalities. (Sorokin, [1947] 1974: 151–3, 703) A similar idea of congruence between different cultural forms became dominant in the course of the 'cultural turn' in the 1980s in many sociological orientations.

6 Only the fact that once we have learned a way to act in certain circumstances and habitually reinforce the pattern gives us the possibility to exercise free will. Erkki Kilpinen (2009) has pointed out that although most of human action is habitual and therefore not actively conscious most of the time, it is not mindless routine. On the contrary, we must hide away our conscious thoughts in the cabinet of the habit *because* they are so complex, learned rather than inborn, consciously built rather than hard-wired by nature, lest they overcrowd our cognitive pathways and block any action. Kilpinen prefers to speak of *reflexive habitualities* instead of simply habits of the mind. As they are not deleted and forgotten, just dormant and inactive, they can also be re-activated when the need arises.

7 I call them *images* rather than representations, discourses, explanations or accounts, because, like those who have used similar terminology e.g. Durand's (1960) *imaginary*, Greimas' *figurative* (Greimas and Courtès, 1979: 146–9), or Maffesoli's *imaginal* (1996), I wish to emphasize that in interpreting actions and interactions everyday language employs figures that are not only those of causality, functionality or other forms of the reduced abstract language of science. Images typically involve visual, spatial, temporal and narrative elements, and tend to personify the actions. For example, in lifestyle questions we tend to think of 'us' (in the city, in Finland, as outcomes of our educational process or acquired age) as against 'them' (in the suburbs, in other countries, lacking education or mature adulthood).

8 On the contrary, the rising industry subjected them 'to time, to toil, to weariness, and to the last resort, the death itself.' (Foucault, [1966] 2001: 244). It should be remembered that, for example, paid vacation – free time to allow industrial workers to enjoy the products of their work was first legislated in France as late as in 1936 (Castel, 1995: 340–1), the same year when the International Labour Organization adopted the resolution on the right to paid vacation (Anttila, 2005: 255). In France, the 10-hour day for women and children was legislated in 1900, the 8-hour day in mining was introduced in 1905, and a weekly day of rest was established in 1906 (Nourrisson, 1990: 266).

2

Lifestyle and the Social Bond

> Machines have less problems.
> I'd like to be a machine,
> Wouldn't you?

Andy Warhol
Moderna Museet,
Stockholm, Sweden
10/2–17/3 1968

Social action and the ambivalent concept of society

The latter part of the twentieth century marked a sea change in social thought. Until the last decades of the twentieth century, modern social science had been dominated by the idea that societies exist 'without a subject', i.e. that social evolution occurs as if on its own, without participants having much possibility of influencing it. Individuals and groups do have goals and intentions that may fail or succeed, but for the actual outcome at the societal level, the intentionality of social reality is only an illusion. Societies are like natural evolutionary processes, which can no more be influenced by individual intentions than can geological evolution. Norbert Elias, the great sociologist of modernization, expressed the idea in this way:

> The basic tissue resulting from many single plans and actions of men can give rise to changes and patterns that no individual person has planned or created. From this interdependence of people arises an order *sui generis*, an order more compelling and stronger than the will and reason of the individual people composing it. It is this order which determines the course of historical exchange; it underlies the civilizing process. (Elias, [1939b] 1982: 230, footnote 129)

The theoretical turn challenged the view of society as a mechanism beyond the human will. Human agency, meaning, choice and therefore taste and lifestyle became central issues in social theory. It is no small coincidence that the theoretical turn occurred in the context of two themes: class and taste. These themes belong to the core of the *principle of belonging and differentiation* in our model of justification. To constitute a social bond, the principle of belonging and differentiation requires that differences between those who belong and those who are excluded from society, on the one hand, and between different groups within society, on the other, both exist objectively and are perceived and recognized by participants. This dual requirement opens up the possibility of structural objectivism represented by Elias, and its critique which became prominent in the last decades of the twentieth century.

A landmark event in this critique was the publication of *Distinction: A Social Critique of Judgement of Taste* ([1979] 1984), in which Pierre Bourdieu presented his theory of cultural reproduction of the class structure in France. His theoretical problematic concerned justification, but his empirical material consisted of studies of taste: eating, clothing, photography and other hobbies, including surveys of what kinds of music, films, paintings, cooking or clothing people like.[1] This is why I will use his work as paradigmatic in the analysis of the saturated society.

Class, taste and the subjects of history

The association of the theoretical turn with the problematic of class and taste indicates how closely it was interwoven with the transition in the problematic of justification that was occurring at the same time. In dominant sociological tradition, classes were seen as the constitutive social bonds of social structure and as autochthonous products of the industrial process. According to that tradition, repressed classes may rise from this structure to instigate insurgent action, but their emancipated consciousness is itself a product of the structure. Sociologists revised their habits of theoretical thought when the new middle class was emerging as the dominant group in the social structure, at the same time as when the consumer society was coming of age. These two transformations were intertwined and had combined consequences for the problematic of justification. Lifestyle was no longer inevitably determined by one's position in the industrial process (if it ever was, many would now ask). There was room for choice, and in the words of Anthony Giddens (Beck et al., 1994: 188) for 'biographical decision-making'. As Ulrich Beck ([1986] 1992) observed, class interests in industrial capitalism resulted from class position and lifestyle politics were the outcome of struggles over the distribution of goods, but interests can no longer follow the same pattern when they concern the distribution of risks, as in contemporary consumer capitalism.

In consumer capitalism, the concept of class structure itself becomes unclear. Positions in the industrial process itself are complex and confusing, as ownership is separated from management in big corporations, and when technological intelligence no longer gives unquestioned licence to power. The new middle class has grown in size but has not placed itself in the vanguard of history; it is confused and it confuses all those who have the habit of thinking of class as a structure and of lifestyle as a consequence of that structure rather than as a choice based on judgements of taste.

Struggles over lifestyle today are structured by ethnic, religious or otherwise traditional identities, or they stem from apparently arbitrary moral convictions that seem to have no obvious basis in what might be conceived of as objective social structure. People holding such identities and convictions may have a very strong sense of being part of a community. Few such communities would, however, claim the title of 'emancipating' or revolutionary historical movements in any classical sense of the term; and even if they did, that claim would not be sustainable in the moral and cultural market of contemporary pluralism. The multicultural diversity in contemporary global society does not provide a solution to the dilemma of regulating lifestyles; it accentuates it by challenging any claims of universality for the good life.

The problem of such movements is that in their mundane consciousness they cannot claim to be the product of history, and therefore subjects of progress objectively determined, as the traditional working classes could. In the academic theoretical debate that ensued around the issue of subjective action and objective structure, a curious ambivalence has reigned from the very outset. This is well expressed in the remark by Norbert Elias cited above. When individuals choose their careers, mates, form of family, or moral communities, they obviously exercise their free will rather than follow a rule or are moved by mechanisms of which they are not even aware. In fact, it is a matter of self-esteem for most of us most of the time that our acts follow from our judgement and not the other way round – that for want of a choice we accept as good what is. Nonetheless, it is also obvious to the plain eye, and even more so to the eye of sociologists equipped with statistical research instruments, that judgements and choices form patterns: working-class kids tend to get working-class jobs, as Paul Willis (1978) explained, upper-class persons marry other upper-class persons, highly educated middle-class people like modern concert music, avant-garde theatre and contemporary painting, whereas less educated high income groups like more conventional music, drama and art, as Bourdieu's studies showed. Choices are made under constraints. Low-income groups cannot have expensive hobbies and only educated persons can appreciate hobbies that require sophisticated knowledge of foreign languages or other skills. Wherever there is action, there is structure, too.

The same ambivalence concerns the concept of society as a whole. Societies are moved by historical subjects, individuals as well as groups who act as social movements. As agents in history they always have, as I called it in the first chapter, a critical awareness of the present: a form of consciousness filled with images of how the society in which they live could and should be made different. Such critical awareness of the present is not inevitably progressive, although modern social thought mostly has been. It has envisioned a future much better than the present and the past, and believed that a better society could be achieved with goal-oriented human action. But as we shall see, there are other types of critical awareness of the present, sometimes looking back in time rather than towards the future. Social criticism always involves normative issues related to lifestyles, but in many different ways.

A society where such awareness is completely arbitrary and cut off from historical realities would be a dismal place to live in. Orientation to the future would be difficult, and the very idea of the future would be ambiguous. There would be no motivation to participate in anything but the closest concerns of the individual; the sense of justice would be limited to isolated events of gain and loss. Auspiciously, such a view of society does not correspond to our everyday experience. Societies not only make history; they also have one. People's critical awareness of the present, positive or negative, is structured on the basis of resources from the past, both material and intellectual. Their images of society are organized and do have a structure, even while they are constituted of intentions, aspirations and criticisms.

These ambivalences are articulated in many ways in the theoretical literature on society of the late twentieth century. The major issue concerns the idea of social class and the subjects of history. They appear significantly in Bourdieu's work, which I will use in this chapter to establish a link between them as they appear in the consciousness of the sociological pulpits and as they are ingrained in the everyday experience of people who live under consumer capitalism.

The death of class

The late nineteenth century began a massive democratization of the civilizing process. The pinnacle of this democratization was the period of the 30 'glorious years' (Fourastié, 1979) after the Second World War. The structural factors that made it possible were universal education and inter-class social mobility. In early industrial society, lifestyles and communities were local and tied to the occupational position, but massive social mobility and improved consumption possibilities have turned lifestyle into a voluntary choice. Today, the industrial working class is no longer the largest wage earner group, and the independent peasantry has almost disappeared in terms of numbers, although not in economic and political importance. Wage has become the dominant form of revenue, but as Klaus Eder (1993) has said, the bridge between lifestyle and class position has at once been broken, or at least become very subtle and graded: it is not obvious, from personal characteristics or from manners of behaviour, style of tenure or type of habitat, who is in what position in the system of production. Positions in the division of labour and positions in the division of consumption do not overlap.

Critics of the traditional production-based class concept have argued that the image of the industrial class structure is outdated. Jan Pakulski and Malcolm Waters (1996) have summarized extensive research evidence to argue that the traditional class model might have been more or less valid in the early nineteenth-century industrial capitalism, where property determined the hierarchy of the production process. Owners were engaged in planning and technological innovation, and they were responsible for the management and supervision of the work of the non-owners. Income distribution strongly favoured capitalists and their adjunct staff, and lifestyle differences were clear, partly inherited from the traditional distinction between the aristocracy, the clergy, the bourgeoisie and the poor working classes. By the twentieth century, however, positions in the state bureaucracy and in corporate organizations such as large enterprises, labour unions and political parties, were more important sources of economic rewards and power than the labour process, which had become a complex whole with no clear overlap of ownership and function. In the course of the third quarter of the twentieth century, employees in manual work came to represent a shrinking proportion of those engaged in production, and could not possibly be the only source of the surplus value exploited by capitalists, as the Marxian theory has claimed. Positions in the production process do not even account for inequality in the expected way, the lowest paying jobs being not in industry but in the service sector (the care and service professions). The link between work and property has been broken, whereas the salience of authority relations in organizational contexts, of educational and professional credentials, of occupational divisions, and of the gender division in the labour market has made the old Marxian notion of class obsolete. One argument has been that while occupational position still importantly determines one's life chances, the aggregation of occupations into 'classes' has become arbitrary and without theoretical basis (Grusky and Sørensen, 1998).

Pakulski and Waters emphasized that low occupational position and manual work influence cultural conceptions of the self, group adherence and political affiliation. In that sense 'working class' is still reality, but it does not have political let alone revolutionary relevance. Working-class parties in Europe represent the establishment of relatively affluent and powerful unionized labour, with no great zeal for fundamental reform of the capitalist system. Class is a matter of style and particular interests, not a historical force to change the social system.

Masses and tribes

Two reactions to the death of class suggest themselves. First, mass society theories have argued that if class is no longer structuring the social process, then there is no historicity left in capitalist society, other than elites pursuing their own interests. If class position no longer provides people with group identities, then the struggle for modern lifestyle ideals will also be bereaved of its historical sense. Progress, universal individualism and the nation will be replaced by the immediate concerns of isolated individuals and contingent groups. 'Publics' become isolated members of masses, each trapped by the narrow routines of their everyday life, easy prey to homogenizing and banal mass culture. Lifestyle choices become 'other-directed', as David Riesman, one of the most influential mass society theorists has argued. This view is still rampant in the practical mundane consciousness of many people, as will be discussed in detail in Chapter 9.

The second view emphasizes the structural importance of the highly arbitrary nature of lifestyle. In today's multicultural and pluralistic societies we should have no fear of the calamitous homogeneity of the mass society. Ethnic, religious and linguistic differences offer strong possibilities for identification; group identities flourish around chosen lifestyles, hobbies, consumption, village festivals, community life, holiday tours, cultural events or sports. Michel Maffesoli (1997) has called them tribal associations, referring to the imaginary and non-rational emotional foundation on which they are based. He has argued that in fact even the apparently instrumental, goal-oriented and class-conscious modern social movements of the early twentieth century were driven by the frenzy of emotional togetherness or 'effervescence'. There is no specifically modern social class order, but today's tribal associations accentuate the inexorable expressivity of any social life obscured by the modern illusion of rational interest articulation by objectively determined 'class'.

Maffesoli's choice of words is misleading: tribal communities in the conventional anthropological sense are not self-selected and changeable. Maffesolian neo-tribes are. Whereas class-based cultural communities of modern industrial societies were relatively stable and inter-generational, commitments to contemporary voluntary communities are no longer permanent, and therefore they are also light and segmented. Even when adherence is ascribed rather than individually chosen, such as ethnicity, and emotionally binding such as religious groups, their universality claims for their missions are weak. Robert Bellah et al. (1985: 71–5) have used the concept 'lifestyle enclaves' to highlight the fact that even in the USA, often seen to represent the most extended individualism – or mass society – in Western history, social commitments still bind individuals together, albeit in different ways. Some are committed simply to their families, some to work, others devote their lives to the local community, to the church, or to the protection of animal rights or other charity. Communities are glued together by lifestyles and are therefore the product of taste – active choice that depends on aesthetic and moral judgements and is sensitive to such judgements by others, not necessarily conforming to them but at least being aware of them and their consequences. According to these views, taste and lifestyle should be seen as social divisions that produce and sustain inequities as well as group identities. I call them *taste community theories*, since there are several variants of the approach, all stressing the importance of shared judgements of what is beautiful, good and just.

Community and mission

Advocates of the structural work-related concept of class appeal to empirical arguments. Occupational categories are too many to be used as such as indicators of class. Statistical offices in different countries list thousands of them in labour statistics. But they can be arranged into larger aggregates that describe positions in the labour market. A widely conceptual framework is provided by the CASMIR-scale (Comparative Analysis of Social Mobility in Industrial Societies) developed by John Goldthorpe, Robert Eriksson and their associates (Erikson and Goldthorpe, 1983). The categories of the classification range from (I) owners and top level managers to lower managerial groups down to (VII) unskilled manual and farm workers. Occupants of each aggregate position share similar wage levels, approximately the same number of years spent in educational institutions, and also many characteristics that describe their tasks and position in the work organization. These positions correlate with other indicators of life chances, both subjectively felt and objectively measured. Distributions of the labour force placed in these positions can be compared between countries, and intergenerational mobility between the positions can be measured. The general conclusion is that 'work is still the most significant determinant of the material well-being of the majority of the population' (Crompton, 1998: 20). Let us call this the *labour theory of class*.

There are many variations of the labour theory of class, some stressing the need to use aggregate occupational categories (Goldthorpe and Marshal, 1992; Goldthorpe, 2002), others defending disaggregated methods of using selected concrete occupations as indicators of class positions (Grusky and Sørensen, 1998). From the point of view of lifestyle regulation, however, the major difference to taste community theories in all cases is that the class structure, in which individuals and groups are placed, is given and related to work. As Rosemary Crompton (1998: 208) summarizes the position:

> Although its precise meaning may vary, 'class' remains a concept which links, however imperfectly, social structure with social action, and which can be used as an organizing concept for the investigation of a wide range of issues associated with social inequality and social differentiation.

The difference between the labour theory of class and taste community approaches is not only historical or empirical, so that the labour theory would be valid descriptions of industrial society whereas taste community theories would only hold for consumer capitalism. The difference is theoretical. The two types of theories represent two different modes of understanding society, the labour class theory stressing the structural determination of the social bond independently of human will, whereas the taste community theory places emphasis on judgement and intentions. The labour theory of social class looks at lifestyles in terms of quantities and utilities, and understands agency in terms of rationally motivated interests. Sociologies that lean on the labour theory of class – admittedly, there are several of them, with varying political inclinations – constitute a critical awareness of the present, focusing on measurable differences in resources, and express concerns about justice and distributional issues such as wages, taxation and social rights. Taste community theories understand lifestyle in cultural terms and see social divisions in a multi-dimensional way. The type of critical awareness of the present that they articulate is therefore less exclusively focused on distributional justice and more strongly attached to the sociological mechanisms in which lifestyle and social structures mutually produce each other. However, each of these positions has always tended to gravitate towards the other, and the debate during the past three decades has accentuated the ambivalences in both camps.[2]

The labour theory of class sometimes asserts that it merely purports *to explain* inequalities in causal terms. This is a false impression, however. If this were the only interest of knowledge, a gradational model would suffice and the fixation on work processes would be rather fortuitous: inequalities are generated in many ways, and the labour market is only one of the mechanisms. Since its origins in the work of Marx and the political economists before him, structural qualitative class theory has also been a search for the *historical subject* to change the world in its own interest. Rosemary Crompton's comment above is symptomatic as it relates the work-based notion of class to social action. As John Goldthorpe himself (Goldthorpe and Marshal, 1988) has succinctly observed, attempts at theoretical definitions of class have always been a quest for a subject in history, and also for a mission of intellectuals themselves as advisers and companions to that subject. To act as a historical subject, a group must, first, be recognized and recognize itself as a group, i.e. draw a boundary between those who belong to 'us' and those who are others. Second, they must have a critical awareness of the present, which can be translated into a mission for the public good, i.e. a sense that their claims are *good* and should be recognized as such by others, but also that they are *just*, so that they should be generalized: either imposed on others or others should be persuaded to accept them as their own. In order to recognize themselves as a group, members must have a common code of symbols to represent inclusion and exclusion: their way of behaving, dressing, home-making and consuming serve this function. In other words, a mission without a lifestyle boundary is almost impossible to carry out. Hence the zeal to define the qualitative criteria, or in the words of Luc Boltanski (1982: 91–102), 'the obsession for boundaries', to determine who belongs to the class with a potentially revolutionary consciousness: who are the groups with a potential interest in the mission for social change if this interest be made clear to them? As Bourdieu ([1979] 1984: 53) said, the problem of classification is more dramatic in the social than in other sciences, because it is always part of a political struggle to construct real groups and to mobilize them.

Labour class theory proceeds, then, from the assumption that class formation is based on structures that do not depend on participants' awareness. In contrast, taste community theories proceed from the assumption that the act of classification is itself part of class formation. It need not and cannot be based on hidden interests that could be generalized as the common good once they are rationally recognized. Social scientists who believe that they can classify people by objective criteria are operating under the false premise that they can stay outside the process of class formation. Non-rational or emotional forces are as important in the constitution of modern social movements as they were in the formation of collective identities in pre-modern tribal societies. As Klaus Eder (1993: 33) has pointed out, no modern revolution, strike, political battle or demonstration, however rational its goals may have seemed, has ever been won or lost without song, shouts, marches, emblems, myths, traditions and emotional commotion; and they are as indispensable for social action today as they were in early industrial class struggles or earlier. The social action in itself has primacy over the instrumental goals that are used to justify it.

Curiously, while the labour theory of class explains class formation by reference to structural factors beyond the actors' consciousness, it is nevertheless better fitted than taste community theories to understand how modern consumer capitalism has arisen from the historical action of the working class. The generalization of the wage labour form has given enormous weight to claims that the principle of universality be universally accepted, and to the critical awareness of its violations among the working-class. The liberation of the individual from traditional and particularistic ties has to a large extent been a victory of working-class struggle, and the labour theory of class – despite its structural bias – is useful in explaining this. The weakness of this theory is its insensitivity to the substantive lifestyle ideals, as if the democratization of lifestyle had resulted from just a quantitative struggle for more of the same for everyone, and the principle of historicity would rely on this pursuit alone. The values of the late nineteenth-century and early twentieth-century social movements for temperance, for women's rights, for public education and health care, and the religious revival movements throughout Europe and North America, were often integrated into the labour movements' missions. Progress, nation-building and universal citizenship were not just formal ideals of modernity; they also relished a form of life that suited the individualistic requirements of the wage labour economy.

It is equally curious that taste community theories, with their starting point in meaningful social action, are oriented to explaining how social structures are *in fact reproduced* rather than changed in the cultural process. As I have explained elsewhere (Sulkunen, 1992), this is clearly true of the British cultural studies tradition, which was interested in understanding how the working class reproduces itself.

This emphasis on the reproduction should alone be sufficient to rebuff the accusation that taste community theories are not interested in inequalities and incapable of explaining them. Inequalities are increasing in the contemporary world, and this is very likely to be the landmark characteristic of the contemporary period in world history. Elites are making soaring claims for privileges, building walls around them physically, economically and in educational policy, while growing segments of the world population, even within the rich nations, are falling into poverty and exclusion, and those who do are worse off than ever. These are facts that no reasonable social scientist would deny, and neither did Bourdieu. It is a different matter, however, that the labour theory of class has little power to explain this scourge. Many of the processes of elitism and exclusion follow the orientation of action that Max Weber thought was typical of *Stände*, usually translated as status groups but more precisely it refers to estates, rather than classes. Whereas classes, according to Weber's theory, are groups related to market positions and maintain their differences using the logic of that institution, *Stände* orient their action to tradition and closure of ranks through lifestyle, endogamous marriage and other forms of exclusion. Many of the strategies of the new middle class are in fact closer to Weber's analysis of *Stände* than to Marxist class action (Sulkunen, 1992). The critique of the labour theory of class presented in this book purports to *explain* the new mechanisms of inequality rather than to ignore them from the outset.

The emphasis on reproduction is clearly to be seen in Bourdieu's work, which was concerned with how the cultural, political and economic elites maintain their position in society. Let us now examine in more detail how Bourdieu deals with the structure-action ambivalence for this purpose.

Self-concealing society

To represent lifestyles and group formation as determined by the economy is not to represent them as meaningless, but as having only a very limited scale of meanings that are relevant for the social order, as in the image of the *homo economicus*, obsessed with maximizing utilities and gains. Bourdieu called that image 'an anthropological monster', a caricature of a calculator whose cognition is completely conscious and preferences unambiguous (although they may be contradictory). Given his relentless critique of this image in social science, it is surprising that Bourdieu used economic terms such as capital, investment or interest to analyse cultural practices. This must be understood as a provocation towards the labour theory of class, particularly its Marxist version that was widespread in the 1970s in Western social science and dominant in France. He was irritated by the objectivistic hypocrisy of traditional class analysts, who pretended to remain outside of the class picture they painted, like the position of a viewer in a landscape painting (Bourdieu, [1994] 1998: 53; [1997b] 2000: 33). According to him, intellectuals are part of the class struggle of classification, trying to convert their cultural capital into economic and social gains. The use of the traditional class theoretical terminology was outrageous, particularly as he never even tried explicitly and precisely to justify the analogy. On the other hand, in his studies of the business world, 'investment' of capital always refers to the display of good taste and resources, i.e. consumption, rather than to outlay for production and technology (Bourdieu, 1997a; [2000] 2005). As in the cultural field, the intention was to underline that in the economy, too, success depends on the symbolic social bond of esteem rather than on productivity alone.

The economic terminology might suggest, misleadingly, that Bourdieu's sociology involves underlying assumptions of calculative rationality, although such assumptions were the principal target of his attacks on traditional social science from the start. He endlessly refuted accusations of this apparent contradiction, referring to his concept of the *field*. Every field – literature, art, philosophy, religion, sports, economy, and so on – has its own rules, structures and positions that are specific to it. In the business world, interests and criteria for success are different from those in the artistic, literary or in the academic world. In the artistic field, for example, it is not very relevant to gain much money – on the contrary, an artist whose work is very popular and lucrative might lose esteem and authority among critics and other artists. Differences between fields are reflected in lifestyle through the mechanisms of taste, judgement and comparison. Fields attract similar people; they form the social bond among groups of people who share the same *habitus*, an embodied identity of which individuals may not be completely aware but which they recognize in others and which others recognize in them. *Habitus* 'makes sense', but the sense is not explicit to participants; on the contrary, the secret or the false impression in which it is dressed is necessary for it to function as the social bond.

The theory of the field requires that the traditional concept of interest must be redefined, transformed and widened. Whereas neoclassical economics understood interest to be the starting point of a strategy and a criterion of a calculative logic, in Bourdieu's mind it must be understood as the opposite of what the Stoics called *ataraxia*, the state of not being troubled. A person who is indifferent about the field understands neither the stakes nor the profits of the game. Interest involves a passion for playing itself, not only for the gains and profits from winning. To have an interest is to accept and to understand the rules, structures and positions of the field. Attempts to change the rules indicate that one takes the play seriously, maybe more seriously than those who accept the rules.

Interest is not the starting point and motive of a strategy, and strategy – a plan – is not what guides action. Bourdieu suggested several alternative terms for interest, such as investment, illusion, or libido (Bourdieu and Wacquant, 1992: 116; Bourdieu, [1994] 1998: 149–61). They characterize the different dimensions of the passion to participate in the game. A possible etymology of 'illusion' is that it is derived from the Latin word *ludus*, play. Participation is always to some extent expressive, an activity for its own sake, even when it appears to serve instrumental functions (making money in business; finding the truth in science, etc.). Libido refers to the underlying passion of the game, interest refers to the commitment. Success in the field requires time and energy; it demands dedication.

There are many fields and institutions where the greatest virtue is *dis*interest. Bourdieu followed the classical essay by Marcel Mauss ([1924] 1970), who had argued that calculation is taboo in gift exchange (Bourdieu, 1990a). Gifts involve an irreversible element, a *supplement* that consists of unexpectedness, removed price tags, a secret. The donor must ensure that the recipient is not prompted to interpret the gift as a price for a previous gift, or a response to a request ('Daddy, dear, I need 100 euros for my holiday trip on my birthday'). Gift exchange requires sufficient time to create an uncertainty between the original and the return gift, and it is enveloped in a euphemistic double language to conceal what actually happens: the exchange itself, the equivalence of values, the expectation of a return. The donor should display disinterest; the recipient is obliged to accept the gift to show respect to the donor and expected to reciprocate, often with a more valuable gift, but not necessarily returned directly to the initial donor. In this way networks of the social bond are formed even in very simple societies.

Similar exchange relations are recognizable in contemporary societies where disinterest is the rule, as in the economy of the home, in humanitarian work and in ecclesiastical services, of which Bourdieu ([1994] 1998: 92–126) gives amusing examples. Every time bishops talk about the monetary value of pastoral services they laugh; the verger is not a wage worker but God's servant; the price for coffee or meals at parish gatherings is not a price but a voluntary offering, etc. The double language is indispensable in a special way in an institution 'whose truth is to conceal the truth'. In these institutions different species of capital cannot be converted into each other. Each field constructs an interest that from the point of view of another field appears as disinterested, absurd, unrealistic, even mad. But interest in this non-convertible sense has a function in any human interaction. Even in the business world, which otherwise is dominated by the rules of equivalent exchange, non-reciprocal gift exchange is important. Therefore, to generalize the calculative mode of action from very specific situations to a universal model of social action is to turn the analysis into a terror of cynicism by imputing a motive of self-interest to actions that sincerely are of another kind. (Bourdieu and Wacquant, 1992: 115–40)

Society is formed of practices with different logics of presentation, sometimes calculative and at other times disinterested, but practices constitute structures that misrepresent the source of their hierarchical functioning. Misrepresentation and misrecognition are central concepts in Bourdieu's theory of reproduction. The school, for example, is a system of practices that presents its outcome inequalities as its own product, while in reality its autonomy from the class structure is only an illusion, which misrecognizes academic success as a result of cultivating differential intellectual potentialities rather than of class differentials in cultural capital. Another key example is the field of cultural practices. What presents itself as creative individual action or experience, such as production or consumption of art, is by sociological analysis revealed to be a concealed representation of volume and composition of capital, and therefore a structural fact. Or vice versa, a lifestyle that appears to be rational adaptation to necessity is in fact the symbolic representation of a social relationship, an instance of symbolic power.

The symbolic economy that fills *habitus* with practices, commodities and signs, inevitably gives rise to false impressions. The less the choices are dictated by necessity, the greater the degree of misapprehension:

> While it must be reasserted, against all forms of mechanism, that ordinary experience of the social world is cognition, it is equally important to realize ... that primary cognition is misrecognition, recognition of an order which is also established in the mind. Lifestyles are thus the systematic products of habitus, which, perceived in their mutual relations through the schemes of the habitus, become sign systems that are socially qualified (as 'distinguished', 'vulgar' etc.). The dialectic of conditions and habitus is the basis of an alchemy which trans-forms the distribution of capital, the balance-sheet of a power relation, into a system of perceived differences, distinctive properties, that is, a distribution of symbolic capital, legitimate capital, whose objective truth is misrecognised. (Bourdieu, [1979] 1984: 172)

In artistic fields such as the theatre, where practices present themselves only as manifestations of good taste and not as products by adaptive necessity, the fit of the apparently autonomous spaces of the producers, critics and the public is so perfect that every actor experiences his or her encounters with the objects of their preference as unexpected, as if an 'alchemic reaction of the *habitus* had the capacity to produce miracles of predestination' (ibid.: 234–5). It must be stressed, however, that even the anti-Kantian aesthetics of those who have scarce cultural capital (which is anti-Kantian in the sense that it reduces things of art to things of life, or refuses disinterested artistic contemplation and instead appropriates the functionality and agreeableness of artistic objects) (Gronow, 1997: 83–92) *is a taste*, an inclination to accept and appreciate, although it is a taste for what they are anyway condemned to, *amour fati*, a taste for the necessary (Bourdieu, [1979] 1984: 5, 178–9). Whether the preference is experienced as individual and authentic, as in the 'pure', cultivated taste, or as convivial indulgence in what appears as naturally pleasant, as in the vulgar taste, it is in both cases *a choice* and a *presentation* as well as an instance of adaptation to circumstances. The more perfect the adaptation, the less observable is the miraculous operation of the *habitus*, which becomes, to use Bourdieu's favourite metaphor, like the weight of the water for the fish in the sea.

Society made visible

The social bond in Bourdieu's theories lies in the alchemic operations of the *habitus*, the concealing logic of practices, which evokes fear and outrage when revealed by the sociologist, even when the analysis scrupulously resists the temptation of cynicism. Lovers of modern concert music or of avant-garde theatre do not like to hear that their taste reproduces and accumulates their already generous bursaries of cultural capital and is driven by an interest, not by 'disinterested' and consecrated aesthetic appreciation. Respectively, lovers of 'banal' spiritual or pop music feel that it is beautiful, emotional, etc. and will not be impressed by the idea that their taste is just a necessary adaptation to their scarce economic and cultural capital. Lower middle-class people do not prefer Rafaello to Picasso because there is a norm saying they should. People who possess much cultural capital do not prefer Picasso to Rafaello because this serves a social function for them; they simply like Picasso better than Rafaello. What this preference means and how it has been generated is a matter of *habitus* – it is for the researcher to find out. These preferences are active choices, and yet they are components in the reproduction of symbolic power.

Symbols are not just play; they are indispensable translations of economic and cultural capital into social organization and its hierarchies. The illusion of and interest in authenticity in modernist aesthetics correspond to this translation and serve as its model. Only art which is authentic and original has value. The universalistic illusion detaches the mechanisms of selection, notably the educational system, from the mechanisms of class, and thus makes the distribution of cultural and economic capital appear as the distribution of individual talent, motivation and performance.

The double compromise of *habitus*

The long-standing theoretical significance of Bourdieu's sociology is borne out by his efforts to remove the metaphor of the mechanism from the concept of society by linking practices and structure in the everyday experience of people. But his work also involves a double theoretical compromise, which is particularly evident in the structure of the concept of *habitus*. The first is its 'alchemic' capacity to convert individual choice into structures, which I have discussed above. It leaves room for arbitrary interpretations. The second is an ambivalent choice between, on the one hand, *explaining* practices by external factors such as class, age or gender, and, on the other, *interpreting* them as representations.

It has been said that in anthropology, two traditions existed in parallel. When studying institutional realities, some anthropologists ask what they mean, while others ask what functions they serve (Augé, 1978: 139). The concept of *habitus* is a way of rejecting functionalism. Bourdieu's basic argument against it is that it takes an objectivist point of view, just as the labour theory does in classifying people. There is no functional calculus between the exigencies of survival or social integration and people's practices. They are constantly producing new meanings, and far from being determined by the existing institutions, practices are expressions of interest in the game (Bourdieu, [1980] 1990a: 51–70). On the other hand, Bourdieu (ibid.: 160–2) accuses his teacher, Claude Lévi-Strauss, of seeing practices only as functions of logical integration in his structuralist anthropology. *Habitus* is constantly being formed in daily practices, and while it is a structured system of meanings, it does not follow any formal or 'algebraic' logic. People do not simply reproduce their meaning systems; they also produce and use them in unexpected ways. Actions and thoughts should not be interpreted as 'logics' but in terms of sense (hence the title *Le sens pratique*).[3] The compromise of *habitus* leads to contradictory interpretations: either meanings associated with practices (e.g. consuming high modernist art) organize actual behaviour, or the social functions of practices give structure and meaning to them.[4]

Bourdieu's thinking is structured as a double compromise between these two polarities: between meaning and situation on the one hand, and between structure and agency, on the other (Sulkunen, 1982). Figure 2.1 illustrates the compromise.

The difference between meaning or interpretation and functional adaptation to the situation corresponds to what the French semiotician Eric Landowski (2005) has defined as the opposition between 'programmed' and 'strategic' action. Strategic action is reflected and meaningful (Position 2 in Figure 2.1) whereas 'programmed' action follows automatically from the requirements of the situation, like driving a car or following rules mechanically (Position 4 in Figure 2.1). The other dimension between structure and action corresponds to the opposition between what Landowski calls 'adjusting' and 'accidental regimes' of action. To be precise, Landowski's characterizations describe the spaces between the axes so that strategy is meaningful action

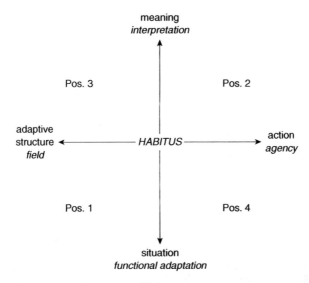

Figure 2.1 *The conceptual structure of habitus*

exercised by individual actors, whereas programmed action is determined causally by the situation, like the reactions of an organism to stimuli, or the functioning of a mechanism operated by an engineer (Position 1 in Figure 2.1). Meaningful but unreflective adjustment to collective meaning-making, such as mass events, is opposed to unreflective individual adaptations to the situation that appear to the observer as accidental, unpredictable and illegible behaviour (Position 3 in Figure 2.1).

Landowski's concepts, like Bourdieu's dimensions of the *habitus*, articulate what Boltanski and Thévenot in their model of justification call the principles of dignity and greatness. For Bourdieu, the struggle to be recognized as a subject of strategic action, i.e. as a subject possessing individual taste, is at the same time a struggle to maintain a high position within the class equipped with cultural capital and esteemed according to that principle of greatness. But even those whose taste makes virtue of necessity and places them objectively in the category of those whose actions are determined by the situation, in Landowski's language, programmed, believe they have taste, i.e. act as agents. Even more so, those who have a good cultural will, but no stock of cultural capital, tend to cherish the illusion of originality even though their real behaviour is adaptive (meaningful but not reflective submission to the taste of the many), rather than strategic. It is typical and symptomatic that Bourdieu himself discusses *habitus* in terms of compromises between the two axes of oppositions. For example:

> I believe that all those who used this old concept [*habitus*] or similar ones before me, from Hegel's *ethos*, to Husserl's *Habitualität*, to Mauss's *hexis*, were inspired (without always knowing it explicitly) by a theoretical intention akin to mine, which is to escape from under the philosophy of the subject without doing away with the agent, as well as from under the philosophy of the structure

without forgetting to take into account the effects it wields upon and through the agent. (Bourdieu and Wacquant, 1992: 121–2. Italics in the original)

Similar passages abound in his work, often constructed around the conjunction neither (structure/situation), nor (subject/meaning). *Habitus* is an internalized and embodied disposition that is neither completely determined by the adaptive requirements of the situation nor completely in control of the agents' intentions. It is neither completely determined by collective culture nor fully open to individual will.

The position of the observer is indicated by which sides of the oppositions are given priority in interpretation. Intellectuals tend to portray themselves as conscious, original subjects in the service of truth, beauty and morality, sacrificing their selfish interests to these higher values. Respectively, their emphasis on structures and causes in understanding other people reflects their tendency to see others' life as an externally determined adaptation to the situation, under-conscious or even under false consciousness. The conceptual compromise of *habitus* is not quite balanced in Bourdieu's own work either: he aims more criticism towards the semiotic and structural ends than the polar opposites of the compromise. This bias reminds us that while it is necessary to see human practices as structured by meaning systems, they also serve various practical functions determined by the objective conditions of existence. And while they are parts of a structure, they are also carried out, produced, and reproduced by intelligent subjects.

From sociology of action to sociology of the actor

I have discussed Bourdieu's work in some detail above, because it reflects the central problem in interpreting and explaining lifestyles and identity in consumer capitalism, not only in the sociological pulpits but in the practical consciousness of everyday life itself. It is because of the synthetic nature of practices, as a situational combination of objective circumstances, subjective action, and intended and unintended meanings (which the actor might only invent afterwards, or meanings that are beyond the actor's control because they are attributed to the practices by others) that the tacit logic of practices is not the logic of the logician. It cannot be represented by a set of rules; it cannot be prescribed by norms, and it cannot be explained as a causal outcome of external or internal circumstances of the acting persons. Margaret Archer (2000: 151–2, 166–7) confuses things completely in her arguments against Bourdieu. She insists that the tacit logic of practice is accessible to the public and logical representation, like maps represent landscape, knitting patterns represent knitting or sheet music represents the acoustic experience. Maps are neither meanings nor explanations of the landscape, knitting patterns do not represent the practices of knitting, and sheet music is only a small part of the cultural practices, institutions, emotions and experiences and cultural capital invested in music.[5]

However, the compromising texture of *habitus* does prompt other kinds of problems. The logic of neither–nor translates all too easily not into both–and (two necessary causes) but into either–or (two alternative sufficient causes), i.e. into circular or ad hoc explanations. Bourdieu was aware of this danger and repeatedly gave reassurance that critics would look in vain to find examples of circular or ad hoc explanations in his researches (Bourdieu and Wacquant, 1992: 129).

Nevertheless, if *habitus* is carelessly translated to mean practice, as it often is, and if the theory is understood as a theory of practices, the risk of circularity is near. This problem disappears if it is understood that the theory aims not to explain action, but to develop a theory of social actors. The theoretical compromise of *habitus* is necessary because it represents ambivalences that constitute *not practices* but *actors as agents*.

Habitus should be understood not as an explanatory model, but as the way in which the ambivalences of autonomous agency itself are reflected. People who experience life as if they were situated in Position 1 in Figure 2.1, being prey to accidental adaptations to their situation, would feel extreme existential uncertainty, not only because their life is unpredictable but also because they have no sense of why they act – or rather react to circumstances as they come. Few people would appreciate their actions being interpreted in this way by others. They will therefore attempt to escape this painful insecurity and therefore imagine for themselves a 'dispatcher' (*destinateur* in semiotic language) who has commissioned them to accomplish a mission associated with values. The image of a dispatcher affords a necessary sense of security derived from the experience that life has a meaning. The dispatcher can be whatever gives meaning to action: a parent, a manager, a god, a class, a nation or why not simply self-interest? Possessing such values, people no longer maintain an image of themselves as acting randomly; they become strategists planning ahead; they can no longer be treated as objects in their interactions, but as partners who must be persuaded to enter into a contract rather than forced to obey orders. They are agents (Position 2). Their life is ordered by modal meanings such as will, competence, obligation and ability. The security thus gained tends to become habitual, even routine, and agents face the risk of fixing the routines to the extent that they fall prey to being programmed by others (Position 3). They become programmers themselves, for whom order or predictability becomes a value in itself, and the slightest deviation from that order becomes an existential risk that threatens their whole form of life. They either lapse into deadly boredom, and tend to rediscover the sense of life through transgression and disorder, or more likely, they 'adjust' (Position 4) to their community and identify with the values of predictability, order and security to the point of becoming maniacs, closing off from the rest of the social world to maintain their own purity, constantly endangered by unexpected hazards and expected dangers (Landowski, 2005: 73–6).

It must be emphasized that from the point of view of sociology of the actor, the oppositions structure/action and meaning/situation, or in the more fitting vocabulary of Landowski, programmed/strategic and adjusted/accidental action, should not be understood as modes of explanation, let alone as behavioural patterns pure and simple, but as *images* of actors expressed in many different ways in mundane consciousness as well as in sociologists' theories. The ambivalences of *habitus* articulate our real ambivalence as social beings also as *interpreted by others*. We are constantly vulnerable to the possibility that whenever we believe we are making autonomous strategic moves in the field, we might be *reputed* to adapt and act as if programmed from the outside, and vice versa, when we believe we are acting in a disinterested way, we might be *perceived* to be orchestrating our own hidden agendas (strategies). The mutual struggle over interpretations is the essence of the social bond in the contemporary world, and this is what makes lifestyle regulation so problematic in the saturated society.

Agency as critical awareness of the present

The ambivalences of the *habitus* are a form of the critical awareness of the present in advanced capitalism. The social bond is more than ever based on lifestyle, not on the structural predestinations of class position in the labour market. Choice is *really* part of everyday life here and now, not a distant dream for the future. Choice is what links us to the communities to which we belong, choice is what determines our biographies, choices that we make tell others about our autonomy, and about our capacity to assume and execute our authenticity. However, choice is a precarious social bond.

We are not only what we choose but also what we are *perceived to be*, and in contemporary society we are principally judged by the standard of being the subjects of our own destinies. From this arises the problem of legitimacy concerning claims for historical agency, or for spearheading the public good. The ambivalences of the *habitus* contaminate any claims by self-selected groups of social reform in that they represent the public good. Greens, feminists, public health advocates, animal rights activists, anti-globalization demonstrators or other groups with their self-representation as defenders of the weak 'others' – the future generations, the 'environment', the battered wives or victims of tobacco and alcohol industries – are always suspected of having hidden agendas of interested adaptation and strategic calculation behind their subjective constructions of disinterest. It is very difficult to make universal validity claims in politics over lifestyle. To escape the indictments of self-interested strategy it is easier to charge citizens themselves with the expectation of agency and let moral responsibility rest on them. The contemporary moral order is an order of suspicion.

The modern idea of progress was a justification of sacrifices and inequalities now because it entailed a promise of less sacrifice and less inequality in the future. The principles of belonging and differentiation put the working class in an underdog position, but it was a position in which a struggle for progress was possible and the value of dignity and greatness in itself. Greater prosperity, longer life, more security and a higher level of at least formal equality and education were hardly questioned as historical goals. The labour theory of class, in its time, was a powerful intellectual tool that was used to justify the claim that the principle of universality must be universally recognized, that everybody should be treated equally as a contract maker in the labour, consumer and political markets. In this way it had a progressive function. Today, promises of progress evoke a vista of new problems, technical, economic, ecological and above all moral. Progress is no justification for sacrifice and no explanation of hierarchies either. The labour theory of class, and much less the labour movement that exploited it, did not account for the fact that similarity of autonomy leads to difference, and finally to indifference. What is happening to our sense of justice, and how is it related to our conception of time and social evolution in these circumstances?

Here we must return to the idea of immanent causality introduced in the first chapter. Instead of appealing to the *deus ex machina* of the market forces or ideological neo-liberalism for an explanation, we must look into the inherent potentialities of consumer capitalism to maintain its social bond.

Notes

1 It is no coincidence that the origin of the famous 'structuration theory' by Anthony Giddens (1984) was his study of classes in Britain. His study purports to show how intentional political action is transformed into unintended class structure. The cultural approach to the study of (the working) class had its predecessors in the work of Raymond Williams (particularly 1961) and Richard Hoggart ([1957] 1981), both in literature rather than sociology, but they became widely known to sociologists through the Centre for Contemporary Cultural Studies in the 1980s. Bourdieu had his predecessors too, notably Paul-Henry Chombart de Lauwe (1977), whose work originally dating from the 1950s was marginalized precisely because it was considered to trivialize the working class as a subject of a way of life rather than as the subject of the historical struggle for progress and emancipation.

2 Ian Hacking ([1999] 2004) has proposed that we replace the opposition between 'objectivism' and 'constructivism' with another pair of concepts that he calls 'indifferent kinds' and 'interactive kinds'. 'Indifferent kinds' are categories such as quarks or electrons that refer to objects, which are not influenced by what we think of them, although they, too, are not 'out there' independently of human knowledge: their existence requires prior theories to construct observable hypotheses as well as appropriate laboratories and instruments for testing them. In contrast, when we are talking about classes, social structure or human nature, our categories sometimes matter a great deal in terms of what the phenomena are like and what we observe. They are therefore interacting with the reality, not only in the world of theorists and commentators but because people react to them and modify their behaviour as a consequence.

3 The argumentation is very similar to Margaret Archer's (1988: 1–21) critique of 'the myth of cultural integration' where she – at that point apparently unaware of Bourdieu's work – refutes commonly held assumptions that cultural meaning systems ('cultural integration') automatically reflect and are in congruence with social structure ('social integration').

4 These interpretations correspond to what Archer (1988: 25–71) calls 'forms of conflation', or temptations to emphasize the meaningful and active aspects of practice at the expense of the structural ones (downwards conflation, from culture down to practices), or the contrary temptation of letting social structure orchestrate the actions of people and take their beliefs for nothing more than outcomes of factors beyond their control (upwards conflation, from social functions up to culture).

5 Archer's critique is of questionable value also because it is based on *The Outline of the Theory of Practice*, Bourdieu's very early ([1972] 1977) attempt to formulate his theory.

3

The Good Order of Nature: Progress and Criticism in Adam Smith's Sociology of Modernity

> For to what purpose is all the toil and bustle of this world? Is it to supply the necessities of nature? The wages of the meanest labourer can supply them ... If we examine his oeconomy with rigour, we should find that he spends a great part of them upon conveniences which may be regarded as super fluidities, and that, upon extraordinary occasions, he can give something even to vanity and distinction.
>
> (Adam Smith, 1790)

Progress towards what?

Are natural lifestyles possible? Is there a natural order of society? To anyone with the slightest familiarity with established sociological theory, even to ask such questions is a sign of scandalous ignorance and lack of ethical sensitivity. The assumption of natural lifestyles would imply the concept of human nature as an axiomatic starting point in evaluating people's lifestyle choices. To assume that there is a natural order of society would imply that there is a way of arranging social relationships which is absolutely correct, independent of the position of the observer. Both assumptions would serve the powerful to legitimate their place.

The young Jean-Paul Sartre ([1948] 1975: 21) represented precisely the sociological air of the times in 1948, when he disparaged the idea of human nature as a bourgeois illusion, a glorification of individuals who were associated by their proximity only, like peas in a can. He anticipated, without knowing it, the sociological constructivism of the later post-war decades as he wrote: 'For us, what people have in common is not human nature but a metaphysical condition ... to be born and to die, to be finite and exist in the world among other people.'[1] Human beings 'manifest' their situation: professional milieu, class, family, sexual orientation, the whole world in which they live. Humans are social constructs, either causally produced by their circumstances, or meaningfully constructed in their social interactions. Social facts should be explained by the social, as the Durkheimian saying goes. This is the essence of Bourdieu's ([1979] 1984) critique of good taste, too, which I discussed in the preceding chapter: it is not naturally given, and its apparent universality only barely disguises cultural power relationships.

But if there is no natural lifestyle, and no natural order of society, what is it that holds societies together? How do we accept and tolerate power and inequalities, if they are social and not natural facts? In the seventeenth and eighteenth centuries, the most prominent social thinkers, Grotius, Pufendorf, Hobbes, Locke and Rousseau, constructed their theories on the idea of a social contract: free citizens must somehow agree that the state and the sovereign are entitled to keep social order and maintain peace (Lesnoff, 1986). Adam Smith was the first who systematically worked out a theory of society in itself, a structure that is self-sufficient and holds together without the support of the state. It is well known that Smith's answer to the question of social integration was progress. But *progress towards what?* It is a common misunderstanding that Smith's answer was based on simple utilitarianism: since everyone benefits from the division of labour, it is in everybody's interest to accept it and the inequalities that result from it. In actual fact, utility is not the answer. Smith was anti-utilitarian, and as he says in the epigraph to this chapter, he thought that material interest alone cannot be the motivation to participate: the mean-est labourer can supply the necessities of nature (Smith, [1790] 1984, *TMS*: I.iii.2.1, 50).[2] We are facing here the question of justification, the principle of common good that drives the social engine forward and at the same time forms the social bond between different lifestyle groups that are differently placed in the system of inequalities and hierarchies.

In most textbooks Adam Smith heralds the myth of the 'economic man', the anthropological monster who is a calculative utility maximizer heedless of other persons' interests and who by his selfish actions nevertheless produces the unintended outcome of greatest happiness for all. In fact, Smith's concept of human nature was much more complex, and therefore his social theory is much more relevant today than the caricature of the textbook version leads us to believe. This chapter looks at Smith's work which in its richness and strik-ing psychological insight describes the potentialities of 'the commercial soci-ety' in a way that is still little understood today; but at the same time it also introduces two forms of criticism of modernity that constitute the nub of even our own critical consciousness of the present, the rationalistic and the roman-tic, which will be the topics of the next two chapters.

Rationalization and difference

In the words of Christopher Lasch (1991: 47), the modern conception of progress was original (compared to ancient Judaic prophetism or to the Christian belief in final redemption), because it was not 'the promise of a sec-ular utopia that would bring history to a happy ending but the promise of steady improvement with no foreseeable ending at all'. In this infinity, the idea is curiously contradictory. From today's perspective it is difficult to understand how extensively and seriously *science was involved* in late nineteenth- and early twentieth-century reform movements such as temperance or eugenics, in both cases in the name of progress, towards a naturally good society. These movements were about to establish scientifically grounded norms of the good life, and to use the modern parliamentary state to legislate and oversee conformity to these norms.

At the same time, it also engendered the idea that the good citizens of the state would exercise their autonomy to act, believe and think as individuals unconstrained by traditional and personal ties. We are expected to be, and we expect ourselves to be modally competent subjects, with a *will* to execute our preferences and to resist excess and unwise practices, with the *competences* to make choices rationally, with a sense of *duty* to avoid harm caused to ourselves and others by our choices, and the *ability* to execute the decisions we make. These are qualities by which we judge ourselves and others against the standard of agency, as self-responsible, autonomous and authentic actors who act neither randomly nor out of emotional identification or adjustment to what others feel, but by strategy and negotiation. Such actors cannot be programmed to abide by an externally imposed order; they must be seduced or manipulated into contracts by persuading them that it is in their own interest to do so.

The victory of the first idea, the science-based good life, was at best temporary, but the victory of the second idea of modal subjects was permanent. To take just one example of the first, it was commonly thought in the early twentieth century that social policy should aim at 'perfecting the human material', as the Swedish social democratic reformers Alva and Gunnar Myrdal (see Chapter 7) formulated the idea in the 1930s. This meant that the hereditary quality of the population should be improved by promoting fertility among prosperous and healthy parents and by reducing it among the poor and wretched. It also implied civilizing public education to teach people good manners that correspond to their natural happiness. This is a view very few people would accept today as the responsibility of the state. For example, Boltanski and Thévenot (1991: 103–7) consider eugenics as a paradigmatic case of a moral order that does not fulfil the fundamental condition of any *cité* of justification, that of respect for human dignity. Instead, today we believe that individuals are the only legitimate experts of their own lives; only fundamentalist moralists claim that their way of life and values are naturally ordained, scientifically grounded and therefore uniquely ethical. Few people would lend their ear to declarations that such values – any values – should be universally respected and applied in the name of progress. Modern sociology outlawed the idea of human nature partly because of the irksome experiences of scientific manipulation of human heredity and racial purity in the 1920s and 1930s.

Chapter 2 aimed to show that even the victory of the second idea, the principle of agency, is unstable. Science and technology offer us in abundance the means to exercise our rational competences. However, if the measure of progress is the rationalization of the world, as Max Weber said, or the guidance of reason rather than custom or irrational belief, then improvement of the human condition leads to conformity. The insecurity caused by lost traditional bonds is replaced by strategy – the plan – which evolves into a programmed society and dull life. Sameness. And little choice!

That tendency, in turn, makes people seek further meaning in irrational action such as heedless risk-taking, violence or collective transgression, and possibly authoritarian reactions. The ambivalences of the *habitus* describe not only the individual risks of being misjudged, but also the ambivalences of modern societies at large. Universal individualism stresses not only similarity but also difference.

As individual difference breeds collective indifference, and as progress requires collective action, how are the modern ideals of progress compatible with individualization in the first place? Does not improvement in the quality of life and the quality of the people lead to homogeneity, and homogeneity to submission, passivity and boredom, end of progress and destruction of the social bond?

Adam Smith found an ingenious solution to this problem, basing it on his understanding of human nature.

Human nature and the social formation

Whereas universal human nature has been an unwelcome concept for modern sociology since its formation at the end of the nineteenth century, eighteenth-century European social thought was still very much centred on the idea. The eighteenth-century belief in progress and universalism was based on two pre-sumptions. First, human nature ceased to be understood as metaphysical and transcendental, as it had been until the eighteenth-century; it became a 'natural' epistemic object of knowledge. Second, human societies gradually became con-strued as objects of empirical science rather than political philosophy. Societies are mechanisms *sui generis*, 'second nature' which cannot be designed and con-trolled by human will and contract. Adam Smith's ([1776] 1976, [1778] 1982, [1790] 1984) work in *The Theory of Moral Sentiments* and in the *Lectures on Jurisprudence* (*LJ*) as well as in *The Wealth of Nations* (*WN*) was seminal in both respects. None of these new ideas was invented by him, but he articulated them in a way that had long-standing influence, and what is more interesting, sound astonishingly fresh in the light of our contemporary debates on lifestyle and their role in the social bond.

According to Michel Foucault (1966: 60–91, 137–76), eighteenth-century sciences were based on the idea of classification and representation. All things were placed in a chart that could be presented as a system of classification according to visible identities and differences, like botanical systems developed by Linnaeus and Adanson. The epistemic function of science was to depict this order, covering minerals, plants, animals, and also humans, naming the classes thus formed and drawing conclusions from the relations of the classified objects. The place of each class in the system constituted its character.

Humans, too, were understood to be part of the divine cosmological order.[3] Human nature was defined by its place in this order, like the char-acters of other species and genres in the world of animals and plants, but it was no longer considered to be necessarily universal. Montesquieu, for example, thought that each form of government – republic, monarchy or despotism – has its own *caractère*, its spirit: republics are based on love of one's country and its government; monarchies depend on honour, and despotism on fear. Human natures are not the same in every condition: the good nature has arranged it so that egalitarian virtues develop in northern harsh conditions where collaboration and peace are necessary for survival, whereas in warmer climates, where life is less exerting, people are lazy and require rule by a solitary prince, either a monarch or a despot. The socio-political order thus depends on climate and the conditions of life, which shape people's beliefs, actions and propensities. Legislators must adjust to the complex fact of the communal spirit (*esprit general* – a concept that anticipated Durkheim's concept *conscience collective*), rather than try in vain to change it (*L'esprit des lois* XIX.i–vi: 556–60).[4]

The metaphysical interest in human nature was thus transformed into an empirical inquiry, notably in the philosophy of David Hume, who wrote in his *Enquiry Concerning the Principles of Morals* that since the foundation of our moral judgements is a 'question of fact, not of abstract science, we can only expect success by following the experimental method, and deducing general maxims from a comparison of particular instances' (Hume, [1751] 1998: 174). Jack Barbalet (1998) has shown that Smith's use of the human nature argument had an empirical origin in the works of his contemporaries and predecessors. As Michel Foucault (1966: 314–53) pointed out in *The Order of Things*, Kant's question *'Was ist der Mensch?'* was no longer rhetorical either, but critical, while also positive and empirical. It entailed the questions about the origin of the human race, its capacity to make judgements about truth, morality and beauty, its awareness of the world and of itself as well as its awareness of what is beyond its awareness: living bodies, unconscious thoughts and feelings, its use of language while the language itself is beyond its control. Not God's revelation in the Bible or inscribed in the book of nature but science authored by humans themselves would tell us what it is to be 'naturally' human (Foucault, 1966: 352). These questions anticipated the end of nineteenth-century human sciences – anthropology, psychoanalysis, sociology, evolutionary theory and economics.

The positive mode of analysing the true human nature organizes normative questions about lifestyle and social order in a new way. The old Aristotelian tradition employed the concept of human nature and the good life in *a discourse of what ought to be*: in normative theorizing about how people should live and how society – understood as a political community – should be organized. When the concept of human nature assumes an empirical content, and as the concept of society at the same time becomes understood as autonomous and independent of the political rule, normative discourse on the good society tends to turn into a *discourse of truth*, asking what societies really are like in their historical existence. Whereas passions and interests were earlier seen as vices and violations of the social order, they gradually came to be seen as a much stronger foundation for it than any direct and explicit ethical rule (Laval, 2006: 108). On the other hand, the critical mode of analysis tends to turn into a *discourse of progress* to reform, first, humans themselves and then the society which they form. Emancipation needs to resort to the positive mode, not only to know how society operates on us but also to prove that the reforming intents are sound and valid. Foucault said that critical and positive modes were by no means alternatives but two poles of the same form of knowledge between which the analysis oscillates. As witnessed by the positivism of Comte and the socialism of Marx, eschatology and positivism are inherently included in each other. In discourse that defines itself both as positive and critical, 'the true human being is at the same time both a promise and a reduction of that promise' (Foucault, 1996: 331). This means that the good life gradually becomes the object of definition for *expert knowledge* with an emancipating function.

Smith: propriety and merit

Sympathy

One reason why Adam Smith's general social theory has been excluded from the canonical lists of *sociological* classics must be that Smith did not yet – quite – see society as a mechanism; his work represents a transitional movement towards such a view. If Bourdieu's, Touraine's or Giddens' critiques of 'structuralism' or class theory were struggling away from the mechanical metaphor, Smith's work was laying its foundations. It is therefore no coincidence that Smith's work has several affinities with these authors, especially with Bourdieu's thought. Smith's theory of the social bond was similar to Bourdieu's in two broad respects: it was based on judgement and comparison, but it was also anti-utilitarian. Although the target of Smith's critique of utilitarianism was different from Bourdieu's, their conclusions were very similar. The calculative model of the economic man that Bourdieu (Bourdieu, [1994] 1998; Bourdieu and Wacquant, 1992) attacked had not yet even been invented in Smith's time. Instead, Smith differed from his friend David Hume, 'the ingenious and agreeable author who first explained why utility pleases' (Smith, 1790, *TMS*: IV.2.3, 188). Hume ([1751] 1998: 176–204) thought that we appreciate benevolent action and respect justice for their usefulness, either for the individual or for society as a whole. Smith did not reject the notion of self-interest or self-love; on the contrary, he thought that a person who does not care for his own needs or follow his own interest neither receives nor deserves the approval of others. For Smith, *all passions*, not only those that derive from the satisfaction of usefulness, are both the source and the object of judgement and comparison of actions and persons, and therefore constitute the elements of the social bond.

Thus, Smith extended the notion of interest in a way that should have pleased Bourdieu, had he paid attention to it, because, for both authors, interest is a much wider concept than self-interest or utility. It covers a wide spectrum of motivations to participate in the game, and approval by others is central among them. In Smith's version of human nature, the driving motives of human action were of three very different kinds: (1) *the social passions* of generosity, humanity, kindness, compassion, mutual friendship and esteem; (2) *the unsocial passions* of hatred and anger; and (3) *the selfish passions* of happiness and sadness or joy and grief. None of these as such forms the basis of social order, or constitutes the virtues on which the social order stands. Only when the unsocial passions are sublimated and transformed into resentment that responds and reasonably corresponds to a wrongdoing, do they turn into moral sentiments and form the basis of the *virtue of justice*. Correspondingly, when selfish passions are regulated by reason and self-control, they develop into self-interest and eventually into the *virtue of prudence*. Excess of these two kinds of passions is a fault. A greedy person who seeks his own success heedless of others does not evoke esteem or affection; a person who expresses uncontrolled hatred and anger arouses fear and aversion. In contrast, no amount of love or kindness – the social passions – hurts anyone (although the world does not deserve it in too great a measure and may expose the excessively kind person to the perfidy and ingratitude of abuse), but, on the other hand, immoderate goodness does not necessarily arouse admiration either.

One should not be confused by Smith's terminology. The social passions of kindness and generosity are no more important for the social bond than selfishness or the unsocial passions, although it might appear so.[5] On the contrary, justice and prudence are necessary virtues for the social order, whereas kindness to others and compassion with them are only ornaments to make it more pleasant and perfect. Gratitude for good works that comes from the sentiment of benevolence cannot be forced, and its absence, or a person's failure to return a received kindness, does not arouse resentment exactly measured to the proper weight of the neglect, although it usually causes spite or even hatred. Being good to others is a matter of will, whereas justice is a matter of duty. For Smith, justice involves reciprocity, and prudence (self-interest) presupposes respect for justice, whereas his analysis accords benevolence only a marginal role in social relationships.

The key to Smith's social theory is his concept 'sympathy'. Its meaning for him was different from our usage (and from common usage in his time, too), for he used it as referring to the human capacity to take into account and orient oneself according to other people's assumed feelings, joy as well as grief:

> How selfish soever man may be supposed, there are evidently some principles in his nature, which interest him in the fortune of others, and render their happiness necessary to him, though he derives nothing from it except the pleasure of having it … That we often derive sorrow from the sorrow of others is a matter of fact too obvious to require any instances to prove it. (Smith, 1790, *TMS*: I.i.I.1.-2, 9)

Since we cannot directly know what others feel, we must enter their situation in our imagination, by conceiving what we ourselves would feel in that situation. Thus sympathy denotes 'our fellow-feeling with any passion whatever' (Smith, 1790, *TMS*: I.i.I.5, 10). On the other hand, sympathy is our capacity to see ourselves through the eyes of others. Both the sympathy that others have with our feelings, and the accord of our sympathy with those of others, give us pleasure and satisfaction. Their joy of my joy enlivens mine, but so too their sorrow with my sorrow gives me comfort. Sympathy has intrinsic value as a social bond, irrespective of the content of the particular emotion that evokes it. Even bad emotions may create a satisfying sense of mutuality, though they are not pleasant in themselves. Therefore, when we judge ourselves, we take the position of the other, the 'spectator', and engage in his/her presumed feelings about us. When generalized to someone other than the actual participants of the interaction, the 'impartial spectator', the basis of generalized moral judgements is created. The impartial spectator is considered to have anticipated G.H. Mead's concept of the 'generalized other' (Singer, 2004: 37) or Cooley's concept of the 'looking-glass self' (Barbalet, 1998: 108). It becomes internalized and is experienced as personal conscience, 'the little man in the breast', who, although subjective, is nevertheless a higher court than the actual judgements of others, because it alone knows our merits, faults, feelings and motives. Human beings naturally desire to be approved by others, but also to be worthy of that approval. Applauded with groundless praise for actions that we have not performed, the little man in the breast humbles the pride, but under the vigilant pressure of unjustified blame it might be too confused and suppressed to reassure us, and then the only consolation can be found in the still higher tribunal of the all-seeing Judge (Smith, 1790, *TMS*: III.2.33, 131).

To attract the sympathy of others, the expression of one's feelings should correspond to what others consider reasonable in the situation, and vice versa, our own ability to enter the situation of the other depends on what we know about it and how we judge it. These do not always meet, and therefore the social bond is never perfect. But if they do, we experience a *sense of propriety* when the 'person primarily concerned' of our sympathy is the agent, and a *sense of merit or demerit* when we enter the feelings of the person acted upon, according to whether or not we feel that the person deserves the praise, criticism or actions of others (Smith, 1790, *TMS*: III.2.33, 74). Many factors enter the sense of propriety or merit concerning actions, feelings and judgements, and the bulk of the *The Theory of Moral Sentiments* consists of an analysis of this complexity.

Since virtues are actual feelings, the laws of morality are objects of empirical study for Smith. His discussions of the moral sentiments are enriched with observations drawn from literature, history, travellers' reports and from his own experience and introspection, on how people perceive propriety and merit (Barbalet, 1998). They lay a foundation for an empirical analysis of the social order, comparable to Bourdieu's social critique of taste. Judgements of propriety and merit, like *habitus*, are objective social facts that account both for the situation and for the mutual interpretations of it, and are adjusted to people's conditions but not determined by them nor reduced to their consciousness.

Hierarchy

Smith's genius is that he recognized the power of factual emotional interest in determining human actions and reactions towards others. No preordained moral authority of the Scriptures needed to be supposed, nor was it appropriate to explain social relationships with human intentions, 'final causes'. The facts of the emotional human constitution, 'the efficient causes' alone, were to be used as explanations of how people act and how they form society in pursuing their interests. However, for Smith, interest does not consist of only being pleased, but also of pleasing, of being approved by others, on the one hand, and of affirming others in their feelings, on the other.[6] Approbation, admiration, joy of one's joy and compassion with one's grief do not follow from a mere desire for them; they must be deserved in the eyes of others by actions that are worthy of them and by emotions that reasonably correspond to the experience that has evoked them. We do not approve of persons who boast of their superior morality without sacrificing anything to apply it, nor do we admire 'intellectuals' who express themselves with clichés and opinions already catalogued as avant-garde, without any real personal investment in learning and originality. Smith's view of the true human nature might be called 'realist ethical relationism': the appropriateness of our feelings and fellow-feelings is also an object of moral judgements in which relatively objective criteria can be applied, not just random or whimsical individual sensations. Competence to make such judgements means the capacity to exercise autonomy in one's pleasures and in lending pleasure to others, i.e. to act as an agent. But it also requires a sense of separateness, feeling one's feelings authentically and trusting the 'little man in the breast' in self-confidence, not immersing oneself in emotional symbiosis with others, however intimately related. And reciprocally, it requires the capacity to recognize and to respect the autonomy and authenticity of others, to be reasonable in one's judgements and to maintain a distance, however unfairly one feels one is being treated, comforting oneself with trust in the fairness of the all-seeing Judge if nothing else.

The influence of the Stoics, especially Marcus Aurelius (Raphael and Macfie, 1984: 5–10), is visible here. Human endeavours do not always come to fruition, and our deepest commitment to justice and righteousness is sometimes misunderstood and received with inappropriate reproach. Nevertheless, we must honestly examine our acts and motivations and if our sincerity allows, trust our own judgement. Smith's view also articulates the core value of modern individualism, that of autonomy, and already contains elements of the second, intimacy. Autonomy entails a minimum degree of equality. Autonomous persons cannot maintain interaction unless they take each others' judgements seriously and mutually respect their feelings. Social structures are not egalitarian, however, and the key issue in modern social theory is how to explain the inexorable fact of inequalities and hierarchies in society that maintains itself in co-operation, without resorting to force.

The Theory of Moral Sentiments contains an explicit theory of the hierarchical and dynamic nature of social structure, directly derived from its realist ethical relationism. The respect we feel before the wealth and success of others is more important than the envy they evoke, for it constitutes the basis for the legitimacy of hierarchy. According to Smith, we are much more easily attracted to feel sympathy with pleasant passions than with grievances, because the latter evoke in the spectator the same unpleasant sentiments as in the person primarily concerned. Therefore, it is also considered appropriate that whenever we experience sorrow, and even much more so, anger, we moderate our expressions of them. It is much more acceptable to exalt the victorious feelings of success and fortune:

> It is because mankind are disposed to sympathize more entirely with our joy than with our sorrow, that we make parade of our riches, and conceal our poverty. Nothing is so mortifying as to be obliged to expose our distress to the view of the public, and to feel, that though our situation is open to the eyes of the mankind, no mortal conceives for us the half of what we suffer. Nay, it is chiefly from this regard to the sentiments of mankind, that we pursue riches and avoid poverty. (Smith, 1790, *TMS*: I.iii.2.1, 50)

For this reason there is an asymmetry between the strength of the social bond from the strong and rich towards the weak and poor, and vice versa. The solidarity of the former with the latter is much less binding than the admiration of the latter for the former (Smith, 1790, *TMS*: I.iii.I.10, 47), so much so that we can wish the fortunate to be immortal and feel that any pain they must suffer is also a great grievance to ourselves (Smith, 1790, *TMS*: I.iii.2.2, 51–2). Smith argues, against Rousseau, that to suppose that kings are the servants of people, to be admired and obeyed or resisted, deposed and punished as the convenience of the public may require, is a doctrine of reason and philosophy, but it is not the doctrine of (human) nature. The loyalty and admiration that the poor and middling classes feel towards their superiors is a fact, as is the kind of propriety by which they must distinguish themselves: probity and prudence, dexterity and industry, generosity and frankness. Men of rank, in contrast, should correspond to the admiration and sympathy of others in their comportment, manners, style and aloofness to gain and to deserve the admiration and trust of others (Smith, 1790, *TMS*: I.iii.2, 50–61).[7]

Human perfection

The civilizing effects of commerce

Smith's optimism concerning the blessings of the division of labour is well known – in fact, too well known, for it dims important aspects of his understanding of both the civilizing and the devastating effects of commercial society, as has been recently stressed in sociological reassessments of his work (Winch, 1978; Muller, 1993; Fleisehacker, 1999; Kangas, 2001). In *The Theory of Moral Sentiments*, Smith answers the question 'What is progress?' in the following way:

> To be observed, to be attended to, to be taken notice of with sympathy, complacency and approbation, are all the advantages which we can propose to derive from it [bettering our condition]. It is the vanity, not the ease or the pleasure, which interests us. But vanity is always founded upon the belief of our being the object of attention and approbation. (*TMS*: I.iii.2.1, 50)

The word vanity in this passage should not be mistaken for the cynicism that had made Bernard Mandeville's ([1723] 1997) *Fable of the Bees* so famous before Smith wrote his major works. On the contrary, vanity here means the positive human taste for pleasing, not only the taste for pleasure, on which the 'social' is based. For this, Smith should be considered one of the founders of sociology rather than of economics, because for him it was the surplus, the social, that was the foundation of economics and its driving force, not vice versa. Like, for example, Samuel Johnson (Laval, 2006: 118), Smith criticized Mandeville for sophism, because he had presented *all* the motives behind people's actions, even the noblest of them, as nothing but signs of their desire for glory at any price, and therefore as hypocritically disguised vices. Since society, however, would be impossible without ambition, interaction and self-interest, with which Smith also goes along, Mandeville can easily arrive at his catch word principle that private vices are public benefits (Smith, 1790, *TMS*: VII,ii.4.12, 313). Smith's work has been interpreted (Hirschmann, 1977; Kangas, 2001: 186–202; Sicard, 2004) as if he were turning Mandeville upside down, from a satire to a serious analysis of beneficial unintended consequences for society from activities that are privately motivated. Progress and well-being of the whole society are a key instance of the theme of *unintended* outcomes of human motivation and interaction that intrigued Smith throughout his work (Muller, 1993: 84–92; Kangas, 2001: 208).

This, however, is not an accurate interpretation and may lead to a misunderstanding not only of Smith's view of progress, but of the immanent progressive potentialities of modern society at large. It is true that for Smith 'the social' cannot be based on intentionality. Individual interests and passions do not need to be of the social type (in Smith's sense of benevolence) in order to yield benefits to society; we do not expect our dinner to depend on the benevolence of the butcher but on his interest (Smith, 1776, *WN*: I.ii.2, 27).[8] Smith often warns that altruistic motives in place of sound and healthy pursuit of self-interest may be ruinous to society (Smith, 1790, *TMS*: VI, ii, 219–37). Prudence – self-interest, regulated by self-command – is sufficient, but it involves propriety and merit, the foundations of justice, not only selfish utilitarian and calculative gain in a narrow sense. Risto Kangas (2001: 137–69, 196–7) has shown that such competences correspond in fact to the disinterested nature of social co-ordination that was emphasized in discourses on manners and good taste. Drawing on the work of Norbert Elias, he has pointed out that co-operation and trustworthiness in the court society require great competence to regulate one's passions rather than using force and fraud.

Smith goes along with a view well established before him that generalized commercial exchange requires a high degree of trustworthiness, confidence in others and physical security. These were thought to be prerequisites for flourishing commerce, the industries and the general well-being of all even by John Locke and several others (Laval, 2006: 236–8). In many passages, Smith argues that the wider the network of commercial exchange partners, the more important such a disinterested attitude is to participants. Progress is a natural consequence of interaction and imagination that allows us to adopt the position of the other as if we were in it ourselves. Acceptance of social hierarchies is an automatic process that requires no force; on the contrary, political intervention was thought to be destructive of the development of character and manners in the court society already long before economic theories of the commercial society. Admiration for superiors and the satisfaction that perfection gives us, associated with our natural respect for propriety and merit, constitute the motives for improvement and civilization, not only the 'invisible hand' of *The Wealth of Nations*, which turns the pursuit of self-interest to the benefit of all.

Smith's critique of Mandeville testifies, therefore, to the great conversion since the sixteenth century in which interest ceased to be the opposite of virtue, and the narrowly understood self-interest was transformed from the lowest of vices to the potentially least hypocritical of the virtues, at least from the point of view of the public good. However, for Smith, the moral sentiments on which virtues were founded were empirical facts, not universal imperatives, and were therefore variable and contextual. Realistically, he applied what we might call the 'principle of moral proximity': we experience feelings most strongly when they are our own; we go along more strongly with the feelings of those who are dear to us than of mere acquaintances or strangers; we have stronger sympathy with our countrymen and the nation than for our neighbours; and only in the last instance do we feel compassion with the rest of the world. In the same way, moral sentiments, including trust, are matters of degree, not algorithms or norms on which calculations and exact plans can be based.

This adds another dimension to the theory of progress: that of human development. For Smith, the potential civilization of humans was not tragic, as 'perfectibility' had been the source of all human misery for Rousseau ([1755] 1998: 61–2). For Rousseau, competition, violence and insatiable desires that result from social ambitions break the original harmony between nature and humans. In traditional and local society the individual competences of autonomy and authenticity are much less needed than in metropolitan society. As Hirschmann (1977: 112) has stressed, the decaying aristocratic court society was replaced by the sociability of vulgar commerce, and this was reflected in Smith's interest in the common man.[9] Commercial relationships not only demand qualities required in impersonal networks of interaction; they also generate such competences by universalizing contract relationships. Even the 'meanest labourer' enters commercial relationships in the labour market and in the market for commodities, and this turns interaction competences into universal virtues. Smith's work thus anticipates the optimism of progress of later sociological modernization theories, notably that of Norbert Elias. From now on, society will be seen as 'tissue resulting from many single plans and actions of men ... From this interdependence of people arises an order *sui generis*, an order more compelling and stronger than the will and reason of the individual people composing it', as Norbert Elias wrote almost two hundred years later (Elias, [1939b] 1982: 230). Society was no longer thought to be a plan, nor a contract; and human nature was no longer a metaphysical principle but an empirical fact and therefore capable of improvement.

We can again see an affinity with Bourdieu's sociological critique of taste. Bourdieu's theory of social integration depends largely on the 'taboo of calculation', most explicitly in the economy of the home (Bourdieu, 1990b) and on the markets for symbolic commodities such as religious services. But even in commodity and labour markets, exchange relations are often disguised in euphemistic gracious double talk that (mis)represents exchange either as gift-giving, sacrifice or as acts of honour, of faith or of benevolence – or of good taste. The 'real' exchanges in which giving is expected to yield a return are shrouded in silence or wrapped in laughter, as when bishops talk about the money value of clerical services (Bourdieu, [1994] 1998). However, whereas, for Smith, such polite distance means mutual recognition between actors in a positive and civilizing sense, for Bourdieu, it is evidence of the hypocrisy of contemporary culture. Human nature for Smith and his contemporaries was an empirical fact; for Bourdieu, human nature hardly exists and what appears universal about it he berates as a stupid illusion, a false impression that barely succeeds in covering up differences in economic, social and cultural capital.

From the good order of nature to the dire order of economy

It is well known that Smith's theory of progress was accompanied by a more dismal view of the effects of the industrial division of labour. A seeming inconsistency has often been identified in Adam Smith's social theory, because *The Theory of Moral Sentiments* is articulated around the concept of sympathy whereas *The Wealth of Nations* centres on the idea of selfishness as the supreme virtue cultivated by the commercial society (Raphael and Macfie, 1984; Kangas, 2001: 217–45; Laval, 2006: 218–27). The problem is rather uninteresting if it is simply a matter of mistaking the concept of sympathy to mean the same as compassion or benevolence, in contrast to self-interest. However, the two books focus on different sets of problems, and that difference is essential. *The Wealth of Nations* opens a new type of critical discourse in modern society, logically as well as historically. It is a treatise on value, divided between wages, profit, rent and taxes. It argues that the quantity of labour determines the wealth generated in the economy. As Michel Foucault (1966: 234) pointed out, this new idea does not contradict the view that Smith received from the Physiocrats about needs and desires as the engine of exchange and interaction. Nor does it mitigate the view discussed above that interaction competences are necessary in the commercial, contract-based society. However, Foucault interprets in his inimitable style that the labour theory of value locates the measure of value in a sphere which is 'heterogeneous' to the sphere of needs: in *The Wealth of Nations*, a commodity is no longer a utility that is exchanged with another commodity representing another utility, and the quantitative calculations that result in the rate of exchange are not, in this theory, based on comparisons between the utilities alone. As Foucault pointed out, commodities ceased to be seen as a system of mutual representations. The equivalence of objects was 'no longer established through other objects and desires, but by a transition to that which is radically heterogeneous to them', namely work. This concerned individual commodities as well as the wealth of a person, even whole national economies. In the new political economy; if there was 'an order regulating the forms of wealth, if this can buy that, if gold is worth twice as much as silver, it is not because men have comparable desires'. Commodities have value 'not because they experience the same hunger in their bodies, or because their hearts are all swayed by the same passions; it is because they are all subject to time, to toil, to weariness, and to the last resort, the death itself' (Foucault, [1966] 2001: 244). According to the new labour theory of value, commodities do not represent the satisfaction of individual desires and wants; from now on, the wealth of whole nations represents the opposite of satisfaction: the amount of time spent at work, and the pain and fatigue that result. The labour theory of value, which Marx also took as the basis of his theory of capitalism, abstracted value from the diversity of social relationships in consumption to the one single variable of time and exhaustion. The fecundity of this work is no longer the function of individual dexterity but of conditions external to it, which are also beyond its representation: of conditions such as the development of industry, the division of labour, the accumulation of capital, the division of productive and unproductive labour, etc. These obey laws that are no longer those of 'human nature'; they are no longer recognized by individuals – or even by governments – as their own, and their operations are no longer responses to the needs and desires of citizens. These laws turn the pain, time and fatigue of work into an absolute limit, and that limit becomes the standard measure of *abstract* wealth (ibid.: 238).

Now we can see more precisely how Smith was able to combine his theory of progress with the idea of human nature. Critics of the market economy such as Karl Polanyi ([1944] 1957: 111–29), have been wrong about Smith in interpreting some of his passages on the universal human 'propensity to truck, barter and exchange one thing for another' (Smith, 1776, *WN* I, II, 1: 25) as an argument that the market economy is an inexorable outcome of the development of human societies, and therefore the misery it inflicts upon the working classes indirectly results from human nature. This was too simplistic a doctrine for an economic historian – and psychologist of human motivation – as competent as Smith. For him, human nature involved sympathy, the capacity of humans to see themselves through the eyes of others and to participate in their feelings. This, and not the propensity to truck and barter, and even less the sole virtue of self-interest (of which Smith prefers to speak as prudence, not as avarice which is a vice), is the natural capacity of humans to build and maintain a society, which by itself cultivates this same potentiality. The growth of industry, trade and commerce as well as the cheapness of goods, i.e. the wealth of nations, is one realization of this potentiality among its other civilizing effects, most importantly peace, social order and justice.

As Polanyi showed, Smith could not yet observe the devastating rural and industrial poverty of the early nineteenth century, which led to the formulation of the iron law of wages, the population law and the law of declining productivity by Townsend, Malthus and Ricardo a few decades later, and which was then incorporated in the critical discourse of exploitation by Marx, Engels and later generations. The economy turned into a mechanism that could usurp nature, in itself passive, drifting and threatening, to produce unforeseen wealth at the same time as it created perpetual and fundamental scarcity.

The self-policing society

The science of policing

It is well known that in Smith's mature social thought, the role of the state in capitalism is limited to three functions. First, it must protect society against violence and invasions by other societies. Second, it must administer justice so that each member of society is protected against oppression, injustice and violation of his rights. And, third, the state must undertake the provision of services and public works that cannot be provided by individuals and operated as profitable business. In the standard caricature of Smith's thought this is often turned into the doctrine of the free market, which should not be disturbed by state interference, because, if let alone, the market by itself translates self-interest to the interest of all. Nothing could be more alien to Smith's own original social theory (Laval, 2006: 229–34). For him, the science of jurisprudence was to advise governments to assure that its laws are founded on right and justifiable principles. Society does not owe its existence to the state, but the state owes society the duty to follow these scientific principles (Smith, 1778, *LJ*: 397, 486).[10]

The idea of a society that functions and develops according to its own laws, and does not need the state to maintain it, was the radical departure that Smith made from the political philosophy that preceded his work, and made him the first eighteenth-century thinker who paved the way for the sociological concept of society, and this later severed itself altogether from the concept of human nature. It did not involve the doctrine that the state should keep its hands off the market; on the contrary, for the first time it presented the reasons why the commercial society does not depend on the state, not even as the administrator and regulator of money, as was commonly believed before (Smith, 1778, *LJ*: 527–41).

The science of jurisprudence, the theory of the general principles of law and government, had four areas of study for Smith: justice, police, revenue and arms. Among these, policing would cover 'plenty, or cheapness of commodities, public security and cleanliness, if the two last were not too minute for a lecture of this kind. Under this head we will consider the opulence of a state' (Smith, 1778, *LJ*: 398). It is confusing that policing covers what we now would call the national economy and crime control – or policing – but not the fiscal regime of states. But this confusion is easily explained when we account for Smith's idea of the self-sufficient society and progress. When modern society progresses and the number of free individuals increases, its social order becomes less dependent on personal control, because 'Nothing tends so much to corrupt mankind as dependency, while independency still increases the honesty of people'. The remains of the feudal manners and dependencies explains that 'in Paris with a large number of police, scarce a night happens without somebody being killed, whereas in the larger city of London this occurs only a few times in a year although the number of police is much smaller' (Smith [1778] 1982, *LJ*: 486). Therefore wealth or 'opulence' and crime are both matters of social order, whereas public revenues belong to a different treatise on the state.

Progress, for Smith, as for the sociological classics a hundred years later, meant an increasing division of labour, freedom to work, and freedom from personal dependencies. As a result, modern society could be expected to become increasingly self-policing and liberated from the tutorial state, as its wealth and abundance grew and its manners became civilized.

Progress and critique

Even though Smith failed to foresee the ravaging effects of capitalism on the industrial and rural proletarians, he did nevertheless recognize the potential intellectual impoverishment of factory workers and the excessive concern for prudence in commercial society, a virtue that hardly arouses the greatest admiration comparable to wisdom and beneficence (Kangas, 2001: 237–9). Smith's theory of progress contains the seeds of its own critique. The progressive scenery shows the possibilities of human perfection, driven by the social qualities of human nature as responsive and interacting with moral awareness. Commercial society both requires such skills and is capable of promoting them. As opulence can become universal, so too can the best qualities of human nature be cultivated.

But Smith also opens a new avenue for social criticism, in which we can easily recognize many features that were later incorporated into modern sociological theory. The pursuit of interest necessarily requires guarantees of justice and a sense of prudence, both being elements of individual autonomy. Excessive predominance of these values may, however, repress those that are the embellishment of social life, and may be summed up under the title of authenticity: the sense of separateness from other individuals, the unique worth of individual life, the respect for human integrity and the appreciation of creative workmanship. When work becomes the equivalent of pain and fatigue instead of an instrument of satisfaction, the constraining effects of prudence turn into the iron laws of capitalist accumulation. The degradation of labour is doubled with the corrupting effects of mass consumption. Smith's work thus anticipated the criticisms of the degradation of work and consumption exemplified by Veblen ([1899] 1961), Mills ([1951] 1956), and in a different way Riesman (1950), as well as the cultural critique of consumer capitalism by Daniel Bell ([1976] 1996), for example.

It appears as if the stable good order of nature was mothering a new and dynamic dire order of society in which a new combination of critical and positive discourses emerges – the critical awareness of the present moves away from the imperfections of human nature to the imperfections of society. Such critique requires a transition from the old conception of political society, where the integrative fabric of society consists of the state, into the modern image of a mechanism without a conscious subject. In Smith's work, this new idea was still in its infancy. For him, virtues, and with them, the social order were empirical facts of human nature. The social was not yet understood as a reality behind our backs or a process without a subject (Marx), or the kind of intangible and intractable collective unconscious into which it developed in the Durkheimian tradition. This was not yet the Sartrean vision of the metaphysical condition of humans between birth and death with a social life in between, determined by a mechanism beyond their control. For Smith, his contemporaries and for several generations of social scientists since then, that idea was used to understand the common good as progress towards a society of autonomous subjects and criticism of the incompleteness of this process.

Since then, the idea of society as mechanism has dominated our sociological *doxa* and become like the weight of the water for the fish, to return to Bourdieu's metaphor. The late twentieth-century theorizing about agency, meaning and culture is an indicator that the weight is becoming too heavy. That *doxa* is now an obstacle rather than a help in solving the problem of justification, particularly as regards the principles of dignity and the order of greatness in the autonomy and intimacy of the individual.

The wisdom that we can learn from Smith is that we should look for the common good in progress, but not in progress of material well-being or 'cheapness of commodities' alone. That would not explain the success of capitalism in the past and would help even less to understand the problem of justification today. In consumer capitalism it can no longer be taken for granted that more is better. What could that even mean, when we know that increases in energy consumption, or millions of kilometres travelled by road, tracks, water or air, or the density and volumes of digitized information flows, to take just a few examples, will have drastic and irreversible consequences on our lifestyles? Less consumption, less ease of physical effort, less easy work, less productivity, less mobility, less information, less complexity, even less and shorter human life are arguably candidates for qualitative improvement.

Smith's analysis of 'the purpose of the toil and bustle of this world' leads us to look for the principles of the common good in the modal competences of human beings in interaction. Of particular significance are the competences needed to make contracts and meet the requirements of trust and justice. The other side of these competences is the experience of the self within its sphere of intimacy. Given the burgeoning necessities of regulating life in our interrelationships, these are the key elements of the problem of justification in the present context.

These are questions to which we turn in the following two chapters.

Notes

1 According to Sartre:

'For us, what people have in common is not human nature but a metaphysical condition: with that we understand the totality of constraints limiting them *a priori*, the necessity to be born and to die, to be finite and to exist in the world among other humans. For the rest, they constitute integral totalities, whose ideas, moods, and actions are secondary dependent structures, whose essential character is to be situated. They differ according to the differences in their situations. Whether a person is a writer or a worker at the conveyor belt, whether a man chooses a woman or a necktie, a person always manifests: his or her profession, family, class, and finally, it is the world which is manifested. ([1948] 1975: 21, my translation)

2 References marked in this way are to Smith's *Theory of Moral Sentiments, (TMS)* edited by D.D. Raphael and A.L. Macfie: Part, chapter, paragraph, page.

3 Smith admired the philosophy of the Stoics, for whom the unity of the cosmological order was important. Even events which seem adverse from a single individual's point of view are good for the totality, and thus ethical rationality requires us to humbly accept pain (Raphael and Macfie, 1984). From this perspective, too, utilitarianism is an impossible attitude for Smith.

4 Montesquieu ([1748] 1951). The reference cited here is to the 1951 edition: Book, chapter, pages. Because of this argumentation, the young Durkheim ([1893] 1984) recognized Montesquieu as one of the first sociological analysts of society (Kangas, 2001: 167).

5 Here Smith differed from his teacher Francis Hutcheson and many others who thought that the social order is based on the virtue of benevolence.

6 The French semiotician Eric Landowski (2004: 250–6) makes a similar distinction between *goût de plaisir*, taste for pleasure, and *goût de plaire*, taste for pleasing.

7 This distinction could have been inspired by Montesquieu's work in which it has quite considerable weight in the comparison between the spirit of monarchies and the spirit of democracies. It could anticipate Veblen's opposition between producers and predators, or between the instinct of workmanship and pecuniary emulation.

8 Smith ([1776] 1976). References marked in this way are to Book, chapter, paragraph, page.

9 Hirschmann actually argues that Smith's work put an end to 'earlier speculations' about the civilizing effects of commerce (the *doux commerce* thesis), because Smith relied so heavily on the unintended effects of self-interest: 'There seems to be no place here for the richer concept of human nature in which men are driven by, and often torn between, diverse passions of which "avarice" was only one' (Hirschmann, 1977: 108). I do not find the interpretation well founded. As explained above, Smith's concept of sympathy covered *all moral sentiments and virtues*, not only self-interest in the narrow sense.

10 References marked in this way are to Smith's *Lectures on Jurisprudence*, edited by R.L. Meek, D.D. Raphael and P.G. Stein (Smith, [1778] 1982). Only page numbers are relevant in this case.

4

Autonomy: the Contracting Individual

At the same time as real forces essential to socialism grow, also the technical means of realizing socialism will advance. The nation will occupy more and more economic functions, which is the prelude pregnant of socialism. The great urban industrial communities will increasingly enter the centre of the problem of property and the domain of collective administration of hygiene, housing, lighting, education, nutrition and democracy.[1]

(Jean Jaurès, 1934)

The contracting society and politics of partnership

The contemporary mode of governance appears to be pervaded with contracts. The market – the contract of purchase – has taken over functions that since Smith's time have been taken for granted as the responsibility of the state: protection against external enemies, the maintenance of legal order and justice, and the provision of non-marketable facilities (infrastructure) and services. Energy, health, education, social services, part of the administration itself, even social control and security functions, are either privatized altogether (including private security forces, prisons, even armies[2]) or produced by public companies competing in the market. Contract as a mode of governance is particularly important in the regulation of life practices that involve moral choice, such as health promotion or drug prevention. Partnerships and contracts have also become the favoured mode of relationships between public officials and private citizens. Contracts between parents and the school or day-care institutions are a recent application of this mode of governance to solve problems of child rearing and discipline in education (Vincent and Tomlinson, 1997: 361).

About 30 years ago, public management reforms were launched as a matter of rolling back the state on relatively straightforward neo-liberalistic grounds. Saving public expenditure was the immediate target. The ultimate objective was to lower taxation. Since then more subtle objectives have been declared. Experts of public management (e.g. Trosa, 1999) stress that 'contractualism' is also a reaction to internal pressures within the administration: it aims to replace the paternalistic idea of an imposing state with partnerships with users who are expected to know best what they need. To a large extent this has been a reaction to the post-war 'statism', plans and regulations imposed by the state. Combined with strong trade union institutions, the state's role has been seen as blocking the way to technological innovation and the requirements of a more flexible labour market (Boltanski and Chiapello, 2005).

New contractualism is often interpreted as an ideological reaction to the welfare state, and as a return to the liberalism of the free market society (Barry, 1996). However, this simple explanation overlooks the fact that the contractual social bond is a much older phenomenon than the market relationship even though its contemporary form is quite recent. The contract is an image of society in a much more intricate way than conventional market contracts. Especially in the contemporary rhetoric of lifestyle regulation, citizens are seen as partners rather than as subjects of state control or as the state's clients or customers.

This chapter will take a historical look at the genesis of the contracting individual. Autonomy of the individual is an indispensable prerequisite of the contract relationship, and in that capacity it is one aspect of the 'principle of dignity and greatness' in the justification of modern society. It will be argued, however, that until this principle acquired its current position as an unchallenged value, it was an object of struggle and a theme of conflicts for about one hundred years. Furthermore, the capitalist state has been a central instrument in bringing this idea to maturity. The great social movements of the nineteenth and early twentieth centuries played an important role in this history.

The right to work and the right to live

Robert Castel (1995) has shown how difficult it was politically to make the transformation from a monarchical state to a state that was capable of addressing 'the social question'. The social question could only arise when it was realized that submission and co-ordination of individual citizens by the state must be replaced, not by the free market, but by an ethos of mutual rights and obligations. Charles-Louis de Secondat de Montesquieu was the great eighteenth-century social thinker who first formulated the principle of mutual rights and obligations between the state and the individual. Individuals in any form of government are responsible for their upkeep, but on the other hand the state also has a duty to provide the means of subsistence to citizens who are unable to do so for themselves.[3] The French revolutionaries amended this obligation of society towards the individual with a corresponding duty of individuals not only towards the society but towards themselves: to seek and accept work or other means for their upkeep.[4]

This duty to care for oneself, and the right to choose how to achieve that, was not taken for granted at that time. Adam Smith in Scotland and his contemporary and slightly younger intellectual companions in the French Revolution were not defending the right to work against nothing. According to them, behind the scourge of penury lay the devastating system of corporations that strictly categorized, under the auspices of the absolutist state, the kind of work that each person was entitled to, leaving a large and growing part of the non-agricultural population on the margins of the labour market. To eradicate this wretchedness, the first labour law after the French Revolution stipulated:

[T]here are no longer corporations in the State; there are no longer other than the interest of particular individuals, and the general interest. It is not allowed to anybody to institute on citizens an intermediary interest, to separate them from public interest in the spirit of a corporation. It is obligatory to apply the principle that it is a matter of a convention between individuals to fix the duties of each worker, and it is then up to the worker to adhere to the convention he has made with him who is his employer. (quoted in Castel, 1995: 190)*5

It was long expected that free bargaining and equal political participation in the form of universal suffrage would be sufficient to establish a government that was capable of meeting its duties towards the citizens while forcing them to meet theirs. Today it is well known that in early liberalism, the system of free and vagrant labour protected only by a minimal state was disastrous for the populations without property in all countries where the 'freedom' to work was established. The idea of capitalism as a system of contracts between free individuals was an illusion from the outset. The working class remained attached to their local community, to the family, as well as to economic, judicial and political dependencies on their employers, and not only in agriculture but also in small industries.[6] The position of domestic servants was especially in breach of their rights as citizens. As E.P. Thompson ([1963] 1980: 231, 233–88) has emphasized, in the 1830s, domestic servants were still the second largest group in the active population after agricultural workers in England. Their personal ties to their masters made the actual reality quite distant from the idea of a free work contract.

The absence of the other side of the freedom – institutions guaranteeing security to the invalids, orphans, old people and the rest of the deserving poor – maintained the territorial bounds that had hindered capitalist development at the beginning of the Industrial Revolution. Later, during the course of industrialization, labour unions and the Fordist type or paternalistic social responsibility of employers constituted entirely new social networks and ties, so that for more than a whole century the contractual and individualistic cell-form of the wage labour system was wrung beyond recognition (Castel, 1995: 213–32). The ideological cornerstones of capitalist contract society had been laid, however; it just took a long series of battles, intrusions and efforts at self-education before the principle of autonomy became translated into an awareness plain to every observer and based in the everyday experience of the major part of the population.

Emulation, imposition, emancipation

Émile Durkheim ([1893] 1984) thought that individuals are products of modern society, serving their own interests and thereby contributing to the organic solidarity through the division of labour. But how does 'society' achieve all this? What revolutionary liberals in both France and England[7] were unable to foresee – and what the wide range of taste community theories have

---

*Castel, Robert (1995) *Les métamorphoses de la question sociale. Une cronique du salariat*. Paris: Fayard. Librarie Arthéme Fayard, 1995.

continued to ignore – is the all-important role that the state has had in adapting 'human nature' to the new kinds of authority relationships and self-control required by capitalist culture.

Most theorists of modernization, including Norbert Elias and Pierre Bourdieu, whose work has been discussed in earlier chapters, have thought that the civilizing process flows down through emulation and imitation from above, from the educated and prosperous to the poor and ignorant. According to this view, competition, for esteem trickles down the ostentatious patterns of consumption, and lifestyles are embodied in the physical appearance of the persons concerned, in their way of shaping and bearing their bodies. For Elias ([1939a] 1978), the hierarchical nature of the civilization process was at the heart of the transformation of the court society into modern individualism, and, for Bourdieu, the hidden structures of symbolic capital also imply – surprisingly – not only conflict and symbolic violence but also integration, in much the same way as for Smith.

Theories of social integration that stress the diffusion of lifestyles and values from the elites to the masses underestimate the role of the state even more than early liberal social thought in one respect. The liberals of the industrial Enlightenment such as Smith or Turgot and their ideological followers in England (Thompson, 1980: 101–103; Polanyi, [1944] 1957: 93–129) well understood that even if the capitalist state might be minimal in economic terms, it needs to be a *centralized* one to serve competitive accumulation.[8] The social support systems that had tied the propertyless workforce to their native territory, such as the parochial general hospitals and ateliers in France, or the workhouses in England, needed to be administered, funded and maintained not by local but by national governments. The famous Speenhamland Act of England, adopted in 1795 to adjust wages to local price levels with a parish tax, was the last major social policy effort designed with the understanding that 'society' consists of *local* social relationships. From then on, it gradually came to be taken for granted that local social responsibilities must be replaced by a centralized government to meet society's debt to the 'deserving poor'. The 'social question' that gradually gained autonomy vis-à-vis the question of political participation, was still a territorial one, but now the territorial basis of 'the social' was the nation, not the local community, as it was the nation and not the local parish that had an economy with a population, labour force, land, natural resources and the total stock of capital. Political relationships of authority were also to be de-localized and de-personalized: as the 1789 declaration says, 'all sovereignty comes from the Nation'. This was still very far removed from the mundane consciousness in the early decades of the nineteenth century, and it was far removed also from the constitutional reality of political institutions. It was only in the latter part of the nineteenth and first half of the twentieth century, in the context of constructing national 'people's states' with universal suffrage, whether monarchic or republican in form, that Western capitalist societies began formally to resemble the political ideal of communities of individual citizens.[9] The centralized national state, with a universalist and legalist *Rechtstaat* ideology, was especially important in the newly established small nation states such as the Nordic countries, to obtain the support of the rural population to safeguard its equal rights in courts (Slagstad, 1998).

Even in the labour market itself, the contractual relationship became established only in the course of the decades after the Second World War, when the rights of association were fully extended to the labour market partners. It was only recently that collective bargaining and the right to strike were established in international labour law and in national constitutions (Sulkunen, O., 2000: 163–251).

The expansion of the industrial and then post-industrial institutions of wage labour makes every employee a contract partner in the labour market, and consequently also a contract partner in the market for commodities and services. The institution of the market is individualistic and has a universalizing impact on the *habitus* of the participants. The individualistic virtue of the autonomy of the bourgeoisie has gradually become a generalized ideal of the poor as well. These virtues of the elites have no doubt been emulated by the wage labour classes but it would be wrong to believe that they were taught to them against their own will. The process has also involved *emancipation* of lifestyles by popular movements and through self-education, and finally it has been *imposed* by law and by force.

Nowhere have these tensions been more dramatic than in the alcohol question, deeply embedded in the economic and political intricacies in the evolution of Western democracies, and a seismic ground for the moral issues that arose between private freedom and public regulation in this process.

Self-control: reforming the self and the other

Temperance, Puritanism and progress

The temperance movements of North American and Western European countries were prime examples of the modern project, for two reasons. First, these movements had an impact that was far wider than the social and moral issues associated with the problems related to drunkenness as such. Second, they were an integral part of turn-of-the-century progressivism in almost all Western countries. For them, progress meant a 'reform' of both of the two facets of modern subjectivity: the self and the society that conditions the self. The progressive intention was both to make life better and to create in persons who led that life a character that was fit for autonomy. Therefore, the notion of progress rested on a general understanding of what the universally good life is, good not only for the individuals and their families but for society as a whole. The vehicle of progress was thought to be the state, not only as a shield against the ruthless laws of the market, but also as an instrument in the production of the modern individual itself.

How was it possible that the same movements that stand for universal individual freedom of will also relied so heavily on the capitalist state to achieve that freedom? The temperance movements aimed to create 'the good man who is able, through his character to win the victory of Will over Impulses' (Gusfield, 1963: 31), but they also believed that this could be achieved by using the state and the law to impose this character on the popular classes. They demanded restrictions on availability, in some cases, even the abolition of alcohol altogether, thus eliminating the very possibility to exercise free will.

We are dealing here with the problem that was at the heart of Max Weber's ([1920] 2002) analysis of Protestant self-discipline and Michel Foucault's analysis of sexuality in late nineteenth- and early twentieth-century modernity. If the Protestant ethic stressed the virtues of frugality and self-determination, how could it also promote legal regulation rather than individual action to attain its ideals (Weber)? If, on the other hand, the modern social order stresses discipline and control, how is it understandable that contemporary morality turns into discourse about caring for the Self rather than about subjugation to legal constraints (Foucault)? And how have free will and legal control co-existed, only now becoming contradictory alternatives?

In *Cultural Contradictions in Capitalism* (1976), Daniel Bell argued that the coming of the capitalist consumer society that began as early as in the 1920s signalled already at that time the demise of the Weberian ideal type of inner-worldly or mundane asceticism. The spirit of 'modernism' (Bell uses this word to mean mundane hedonism) took over the puritan heritage as soon as the mass consumption society began to flourish. Mass-producing industrial capitalism runs smoothly 'only if the machinery of gratification and instant demand is well oiled, usually with cosmetic fragrance' (ibid.: 283). Puritanism and its values, adjusted to the needs of production and accumulation, are functional only in the very early phases of industrialization, whereas the consumer society requires a culture of acquisitiveness and hedonism.

The temperance movement won a transient victory in Prohibition, which in the American tradition represented, so Bell argues, fear of change. Although the temperance movement had its source in the puritan 'doctrines of industry, thrift, discipline and sobriety', the creation of the Anti-Saloon League in 1896 was a defensive reaction of rural small-town America against the cultural threats posed by the immigrant Catholic population, the debilitating effects of urban life and the corruption of public sociability (ibid.: 64).

This is indeed how the once flourishing temperance movements now look in North America and Europe. They are rural, mostly followed by old people and animated by tradition rather than by progressive spirit.[10] The idea that hedonistic 'modernism', the opposing twin brother of the Protestant ethic of capitalism, with its values of instant gratification, pleasure and egoistic individualism, has gained the upper hand in consumer capitalism, seems like a fitting description of the legitimacy crisis of public lifestyle regulation today.

On the other hand, it is too simple to associate temperance with moral or cultural conservatism. The anti-alcohol and other lifestyle movements (charity, settlement, missionary, youth, sports, family, etc.) and of course the labour movement of the early twentieth century were reactions, certainly, but more to the misery and moral confusion caused by the change that *already had* occurred in the industrializing societies than to anticipated modernization. In their own way, each of these movements advocated a vision of progress that involved a new and better form of life. The centre of that new life was the individual, and the communities that individuals constituted were, first, classes and then increasingly nations.

Reforming the Self ...

The temperance movements that spread across Western Europe and North America in the late nineteenth century[11] were an ideal type case of the inner-worldly asceticism that Weber thought was functional in generating the spirit of capitalism.[12] The useless pleasures of intoxication and spending money and time on alcohol, and the immorality associated with drinking, especially in public drinking places, was the antipode of the accumulative ethos of entrepreneurial life.

Religion and individual perfectionism went hand in hand. The first major efforts to reform American drinking habits in the early nineteenth century were led by the Calvinist ministry of New England. To be saved was evidenced through a change in personal life. The man of spiritual conviction could be known by his habits (Gusfield, 1963: 41, 45). In Britain, too, the earliest temperance pursuits were born among the Calvinistic Protestants. In Wales, the mid-nineteenth-century temperance movement was influenced by Welsh non-conformist theology that required followers of Christ to be noble examples of self-denying abstinence from all excesses, in business and in pleasure. In eating, drinking, dressing and all things pertaining merely to this life, they should be 'moderate and reserved' so that they give proof of their heavenly citizenship (Lambert, 1983: 117–19).

Max Weber stressed the Calvinists' duty to rationalize the whole of life in the name of salvation. According to the doctrine of predestination, rational asceticism and good works were not seen as a means of attaining salvation, but as an indispensable sign of election among the few loved by God: 'The Calvinist, as it is sometimes put, himself creates his own salvation, or as would be more correct, the conviction of it.' The most difficult challenge to bringing all of life to heed reason was the power of emotions: 'The most urgent task was the destruction of spontaneous, impulsive enjoyment; the most important means was to bring order into the conduct of its adherents' (Weber, [1920] 2002: 115, 119).

... and the Other

Weber's analysis has been criticized for its one-sided emphasis on the rising bourgeoisie at the expense of the far more important popular classes, for its historical mistakes, and for its neglect of consumption, and also for its indifference to the all-important issue of power (Turner, 1992). Here a few points need to be made about power and the production of the capitalist subject. Most progressive movements were not content to reform their own ranks but wanted to impose their moral views on the rest of society as well, by legal and sometimes by coercive means.[13] As Foucault (1987) said about the discourse on sexuality, the modern temperance discourse not only advocated the repression of bad behaviour: it *produced* it as a category – or a set of categories – of power over others. As the temperance movements developed into a 'moral crusade' (Gusfield, 1963; Lambert, 1983: 252) they started a struggle for prohibition[14] – denying the right either to produce, to sell or to consume alcohol – for everybody and often especially for 'others'.

All prohibitionist temperance movements were anchored in three different social classes: the entrepreneurial middle class, the new nationalist middle class and the working class. Whatever their class background, and whatever the corresponding motives and interests that they pursued, the temperance groups were out for political and not just for personal reform. The entrepreneurial classes in Western European societies found it quite easy to amalgamate teetotalism into their own religious doctrines and their everyday practices as businessmen and industrialists. However, they were not necessarily thinking about themselves at all when they campaigned against the café, the public house or the saloon. Their interest was to discipline the rising working class for whom public drinking places were seen to be venues of political agitation and shelters of 'pre-modern' attitudes toward factory hours (Harrison, 1971: 62; Dingle, 1980: 18; Lambert, 1983; Rosenzweig, 1983: 95; Magnusson, 1985; Brennan, 1989: 269–310; Barrows, 1991). E.P. Thompson (1980: 307–8) has shown how the worldly asceticism of English Methodism in the counter-revolutionary decades 1790–1830, was particularly suited to discipline the working class in conditions where 'the factory system demands a transformation of human nature, the "working paroxysms" of the artisan or outworker must be methodized until the man is adapted to the discipline of the machine'. In a similar way the temperance missionaries in North America and Europe half a century later were quite useful in the accelerating process of capitalist accumulation, not only in supporting factory discipline and alleviating the miseries caused by drinking males to their families, but also in diverting attention from the 'social question' – salaries, housing, health, education and working conditions – to the need for self-control. This sort of 'false consciousness', imposed by the bourgeoisie on the working class, came to be the major argument why first the English labour movement, and later many other European socialists withdrew from the temperance cause.

In France, the rise of the anti-alcohol movement was closely connected to political events throughout the nineteenth century. The first legislation to regulate public drinking places was introduced in 1851 by Napoleon III in the name of moral order; it was renewed and given an explicitly disciplinary, even repressive, hue after the Commune in 1871, notoriously labelled as the riot of drunkards. Thus the French anti-alcohol movement acquired a bourgeois if not royalist imprint, which to this day has undermined its attempts to approach the popular classes (Nourrisson, 1990: 204–9, 255–69).

But the cultural issues of late nineteenth- and early twentieth-century Europe and North America were not a matter of interest to the aristocratic and bourgeois political elites alone. The rising nationalist middle classes – teachers, journalists, the clergy and civil servants – had their own stake in the cultural struggle. They depended on the support and loyalty of 'the people', whom they romanticized as the natural source of national identity and pride (Gellner, 1983: 62). As the reality of the lower classes hardly matched the idealized image, zealous reform attempts followed. Nationalist middle-class temperance policy was a key strategy in combating misery and immorality, especially with respect to family life. This was particularly important for women, who were largely responsible for the new reform movements in all parts of the Western world. In France, bourgeois reformers combined anti-alcohol propaganda with other life-improving initiatives, such as miniature garden-houses for the working class, but it was the nationalist cause that mobilized the top political, military and cultural elites to promote working-class temperance in the years following the Franco-Prussian war (1870–1871) and before the Great War at the beginning of the twentieth century.[15]

Furthermore, the 'dangerous classes' – industrial workers and the agricultural proletariat in different types and degrees of serfdom to capitalists and large landowners – were in a situation where inner-worldly asceticism acquired for them a meaning very different from that in entrepreneurial culture: not accumulation, but survival. The fight against the alcohol capitalists was an early form of class consciousness and organized political activity, including street demonstrations and parliamentary action, as soon as political platforms were opened to them (Rosenzweig, 1983; Roberts, 1984; Gutzke, 1989). Some of these activities were called 'drinking strikes', anticipating industrial strikes and collective action that later became important in labour organizations: meetings, picket lines and mass mobilization (Sulkunen, I., 1986).

It is remarkable how easily the temperance movements united in their efforts to discipline the 'other', even though they represented conflicting class interests and cultures. There were two reasons for this. One was the changing political institutions of the modern state, the other was the notion of the good life that was thought to be the content of progress and that was surprisingly similar in different temperance groups, independent of their doctrinal background, social class and even national traditions.

Will, duty and moral superiority

Max Weber ([1920] 2002) stressed that in contrast to earlier forms of Christian asceticism, the Protestant ethic demanded the rationalization of the whole of a person's life under the power of reason. This is why inner-worldly asceticism is often thought to represent the Rationalist aspect of modern individualism (Campbell, 1987: 105, 219). Temperance reformers made the modern distinction, so important to Enlightenment thinkers earlier, between will and desire, or interest and passion, as Montesquieu and Steward had called the distinction (Hirschman, 1977). As Harry Levine (1978) has argued, the disciplined will was seen as a reasonable regulator of the natural desires, while alcohol was seen as a poison that destroyed, not only challenged, one's will, the most valued underpinning of human dignity and safeguard of social order. This distinction made it possible for the early American temperance movement to define alcohol abuse as the result of *defective will*, no longer of *defective desires* such as drunkenness, as in colonial pre-temperance morality. The will had to be trained to master lower passions – hence, civilization required education and monitoring (Valverde, 1998). The Enlightenment idea, so important to Adam Smith, of the good order of nature that was to be sought rationally, was widely used in temperance rhetoric. As the influential American temperance intellectual, Reverend David Dorchester wrote:

> To infer that man's original susceptibility to stimulation is prima-facie evidence that the wise Creator intended that his physical nature should be kept under the dominion of powerful intoxicants, and that their free indulgence is in the legitimate line of his being ... are conclusions palpably fallacious and ruinous. The world has seen too much of the destructive effects of such indulgences to believe that they come within the scope of the wise Creator's plans. The true philosopher discriminates between acquired desires and appetites, or vitiated, perverse, and inordinate impulses, and those which are normal, necessary, and beneficial. (1884: 2)

In most European temperance movements, too, the idea of free will was associated with the rise of total abstinence rather than moderation. For teetotallers in Britain in the 1830s, the idea that man must trust his reason in not drinking excessively was foreign. Impulse renunciation and the control of desire and spontaneity could best be served only by total sobriety, which ensured self-command (Harrison, 1971: 115; Lambert, 1983: 66–7).[16]

At the turn of the century, there were few competing discourses and they were notoriously unsuccessful. The obvious alternative was medicalization, but even in France where medical doctors were quick to gain authority over the problem, alcoholism never developed into a clear-cut clinical category. The stumbling block was precisely the issue of free will that was defective in this particular 'monomania', but could not be properly analysed as a medical condition (Valverde, 1998: 43–68). In England, the Society for the Study of Inebriety was, in its early phase, even more determined that alcoholism was a physical disease and that the Society would be strictly committed to a scientific rather than a social reformist stand in the matter. Compromises had to be made, however, and increasingly the issues of character and preventive policy were integrated into the Society's programme (Berridge, 1990: 991–1003).

The political focus for the temperance mainstream was character reform, but not in isolation from major social questions. In the Protestant ethic, above the individual rational will, there was, according to Weber, a sense of duty. To be industrious in business and assiduous in work was a calling, a duty to obey the will of God, and the same duty applied to the pleasures of life as well as to the efficient use of time. The highest duty of all was confidence in being chosen among the elect; and rational, will-controlled life was the indispensable proof of this faith. The higher order that ordains the rationalization of life justifies contempt and hatred towards those who disregard their duty and thus demonstrate that they are the enemy of God (Weber, [1920] 2002: 122).

Since the good Protestant was among the elect, he or she was entitled to feel moral superiority, but the pious also had a duty to institute the will of God in the secular world through law. Therefore American and later European prohibitionists were not inconsistent, when they insisted that the state should impose a total interdiction on drinking, while they also thought that the problem was the diseased individual will incapable of self-control. For them, alcohol was the agent that destroyed the will, and thus the rational willpower of individuals to control their desires and impulses could not alone be trusted. Instead, it needed to be supported and guaranteed by prohibitive legislation and control mechanisms.

The self and the citizen

Thus, among the Protestant temperance movements, the mission of liberating the whole society from the curse of alcohol posed no major doctrinal problems. Their version of prohibitionism followed directly from their religious background. However, the same combination of the two ideals, free rational will and legally decreed alcohol-free society, was also characteristic of other temperance movements, whose contact with the Calvinist doctrinal tradition was less obvious or even hostile. Working-class temperance movements in Britain (Harrison, 1971: 28, 367), Sweden (Ambjörnsson, 1988; Johansson, 1992) and Finland (Sulkunen, I., 1986) were based on the ideals of working-class respectability and self-reliance, while they also aimed at legislating out the non-respectable, both among their own ranks and in society at large.[17]

The prohibitionist argument, which required extended state intervention, was based on the modern (in the current, wide sense) idea of constructing the inner selfhood by external means. Temperance was not only about not consuming alcohol, nor only about eliminating the profit motive from its production and sale, but also about the formation of character in a free society. For example, the United Kingdom Alliance, founded in 1853, refused to see any conflict between individual liberty and state intervention. The Alliance reformers working in mid-Victorian slums realized that government actually had to *create* the rational citizen who makes his economic decisions after mature consideration of his long-term self-interest. The care which prohibitionists wanted government to bestow on its citizens did not involve direct provision for their welfare: the aim was to give indirect aid by cultivating citizens' initiative, rationality and providence (Harrison, 1971: 205–7).

In temperance discourse, the modern individual, developing in nascent industrial culture, was therefore divided into two parts: the *inner self* or *authenticity* and the *external citizen*, or *autonomy*. The enlightened nation–state committed to moral and social progress, was thought to be the external instrument for constructing the inner self of citizens, capable of self-control and competent to act as sovereign members of society. This was believed to be possible on the condition that legislation had its roots in the will of the citizens, and that this will was formed in the political process within the democratic institutions of the nascent nation–state.

The rise of parliamentary politics: 'Reform everything!'

The rise of temperance activity was not only a matter of enthroning reason to rule everyday life, but was also a showcase of the new parliamentary democracy. Since the French Revolution, a strong conviction had emerged among republicans everywhere that universal suffrage and parliamentary legislation would as such be sufficient to eliminate injustices and suffering. In France, this view was represented by the Abbot Sieyès, one of the key authors of the Declaration of Human Rights, and by many members of the important Committee on Pauperism under the Convention (Castel, 1995: 204–6). In England, partisans of this view included republicans such as Thomas Paine himself, the poet Wordsworth, journalists like Carlyle, Hetherington, Holyoake and others (Thompson, 1980: 103). If liberty and equality were assured by parliamentary democracy, fraternity would follow by itself, and no social policy, i.e. interventionist state, would be necessary. Only the revolutions of 1848 made it clear that even democratic states need to be allotted more than minimal functions in order to attain dignity of human life for all – the 'social question' was born. The influence of Marxist socialism, despite its perpetual ambivalence about the state as an instrument of class oppression and as a necessary institution in the scientific management of society, cannot be overestimated in this respect, even in movements where it was not recognized as the source of the idea (Donzelot, 1984: 34–9).

The temperance movement was strongly influenced by this republicanism and by the rise of the social question. All prohibitions in the USA, in Britain, Norway, Sweden, New Zealand and Finland were voted in, down or out either in parliaments recently elected in general elections or in a referendum. Moreover, the women's suffrage movement was closely linked to temperance groups in the USA (Gusfield, 1963; Rose, 1997) and in Britain (Harrison, 1971; Dingle, 1980). Rural middle-class progressives in America considered prohibition an effective measure against big business and political corruption (Timberlake, 1963: 121–4). According to Dingle (1980: 13–4), the relatively short prohibitionist phase – from about 1850 to 1875 – of the British temperance movement differed from earlier activities not so much in ideological argumentation as in political methods. The belief in eliminating demand through the individual pledge of abstinence eroded when the British Parliament became an open forum that could be used to outlaw supply.

The association of prohibitionist movements with parliamentary politics explains in part why the duality of its argumentation did not appear contradictory, when on the one hand it cherished the value of individual freedom to exercise self-control, and on the other sought a total solution through legislation that left little room for individual self-determination. For about a century, the republican tradition in Europe understood the universal suffrage in terms of Rousseau's general will: once the election assures the consent of citizens to parliament, the law represents the will of the people and compliance becomes everyone's duty. For the success-ful temperance movements, sobriety was only one element in a new total way of life steered by rationality and self-control. Its function was to ensure progress, merging the public and the private good. To end forever the practice of imbibing liquor would serve the interest not only of the individual self, but also of society as a whole, and therefore this goal deserved to be written in the law (Gusfield, 1963: 56). Thus, the mission of temperance was far wider than just the control of addictive alcohol use. It was based on belief that the abolition of drink from society would cor-rect all evils, even those brought about by industrial poverty, political cor-ruption and irresponsible citizenship.

Exemplary in this respect was the most important movement in American temperance history, the Women's Christian Temperance Union (WCTU), which joined forces in 1898 with the Anti-Saloon League (founded in 1895) to pursue prohibitionist policies (Rose, 1997: 29). Their ideal was an abstemious and hard-working lifestyle. That ideal is today associated with right-wing traditionalism, and, in fact, this is what the WCTU came to represent even in the lifetime of the Volstead Act. But before the end of the nineteenth century they were not tradi-tionalists at all. They were allies of all the major reform movements to support woman's suffrage (adopted, incidentally, in 1920, the same year when the national prohibition came into force), dress reform, cremation, vegetarianism, Christian Socialism, the Populist Party and the labour movement. Frances Willard, the legendary WCTU leader, once declared: 'We believe in a living wage; in an eight-hour day; in courts of concilia-tion and arbitration in justice as opposed to greed and gain; in "Peace on Earth and Good-Will to Men!"' (quoted in Gusfield, 1963: 76).[18] Willard's conclusion was her slogan: 'Reform everything!' The Prohibition Party, founded in 1869, advocated a federal income tax, women's suffrage, the regulation of railroad rates, the direct election of United States senators, free schools, and an inflationary monetary policy. These were the same issues that animated the agrarian populism of the late nineteenth cen-tury (Gusfield, 1963: 94–6).

In the Nordic countries the progressivism of temperance movements led them to collaborate closely with the nationalistic people parties, the peas-ant parties and the labour movement (Sulkunen, I., 1986; Johansson, 1992; Fuglum, 1995; Slagstad, 1998; Warpenius and Sutton, 2000). For all these groups, adherence to sobriety imposed by the state was the key to real emancipation, a belief particularly expressed in the temperance rhetoric close to that of the labour movement.

The conscientious character

Recognition

If freedom from slavery to King Alcohol was viewed as emancipation in working-class culture, the theme of emancipation was even more important in the culture of republicanism, to which the temperance fight was closely connected. Nineteenth-century reformism was more than a claim for formal political and legal rights for the working class and for women. It aimed at liberating individuals from personal dependencies on their masters, lords, corporations, employers, or local communities, and in the extreme case on their families. The ideal was inherited from French Revolutionaries, but the actual everyday experience of the vast majority of industrial populations, well into the middle of the twentieth century, remained worlds apart from the utopia of free, individual citizens earning a living either as entrepreneurs or wage earners. However, in the course of the nineteenth and early twentieth centuries, the utopia stayed alive, conquered space and gradually developed into tradition in the practices of social and political movements, stubbornly defying even extreme forms of political repression in restorations, counter-revolutions or in times of war.

Experience of personal independence in everyday consciousness means two kinds of things: first, it must correspond to a sense of equality. Being independent is being equal, having a say, setting oneself up as an agent who is interacting with others on terms that *are known*, not imposed in an arbitrary manner. The terms of interaction may be extremely unequal, as was the case in nineteenth-century capitalism, but claims of engaging in it as a person, both in a legal and in a moral sense, can still be respected to meet the requirements of *recognition*. Egalitarianism implies rules that define the limits of what can be agreed about and stipulate the procedures that must be followed to make valid agreements. Constitutions are indispensable to the republican tradition: rules that declare how far one can go in limiting the freedom of the parties in a contract, and how the legal framework of those contracts must be built. But it also requires a character and a certain form of comportment towards the other, and these were cultivated in the modern social movements through their practices of self-education.

The Jacobinist tradition and the conscientious character

Republicans did not everywhere apply drastic legal measures such as prohibitions to cultivate human nature to qualify as an agent of contract. Lifestyle issues in general weighed much less in 'the social question' in France than in the Anglo-Saxon world and other Western European countries. In so far as they did carry weight, it was the political right that set up the ideal of responsible family life as an alternative to state-organized social protection. For example, when the 'social economists', represented by Charles Gide, introduced the Bismarckian social insurance in late nineteenth-century France, conservatives such as Frederick Le Play opposed it. They were in favour of pre-modern paternalistic responsibilities of the family, of the local community, of workers themselves – and of employers. The social economists presented their programme, again in the republican tradition, to liberate individuals from paternalistic and traditional dependencies and humiliation (Donzelot, 1984: 148–50). According to Donzelot's analysis, the very 'social question' arose after 1848 from the contradiction between the political sovereignty and the *de facto* misery of the classes without property and status.[19]

Until Durkheim's criticism of the social contract theory, the social question oscillated between two alternative roles of the state: all or nothing. If the individual is seen to be the instrument of progress and the sovereign source of the government's authority, the state's role must either be a minimal one (to guarantee only the right to property and to exchange); or, if society *really* meets its duty to guarantee work or alternatively subsistence, the state must become a massive employer and in the end destroy capitalism at its core – the exchange between capital and labour power. In the words of Marx, the workers revolution in June 1848 not only returned to France its republic; it gave it socialism, because

> [B]ehind the right to work there stands the power over capital, behind the power over capital the appropriation of the means of production, their subjection to the organized working class, therefore, the abolition of wage labour, of capital and of their mutual relationships. (Marx, [1850] 2003: 63)

Durkheim's idea of solidarity made, for the first time, a distinction between the *electoral legitimacy* of governments and the interests that their *policies de facto* represent. Now it became possible to evaluate policies from the point of view of their effects on the type of solidarity, and the individual could be seen, in the words of the radical socialist Léon Bourgeois, not as the instrument but as the *objective* of progress (towards greater organic solidarity) in a society based on a high degree of division of labour (Donzelot, 1984: 86–120).

The republican dilemma – the political sovereignty of individuals and the economic and social inequality that follow from capitalism – was central in French social thought as well as in French social policy even in the period from the turn of the century until the establishment of the welfare state institutions. When other nations in the West were building their welfare infrastructure in the 1930s, the French socialists still believed in the ability of the republic to correct the injustices inflicted by capitalism and to maintain the dignity of peace and solidarity. For example, Jean Jaurès, the great socialist orator, pacifist and key member of the Socialist International, had very little to say about lifestyle other than that democratic socialism, contrary to what critics say, would by itself enliven rather than repress 'the force of instincts, the warmth of blood, the appetite for life ... disciplined and harmonized by a high and widespread culture' (Jaurès, 1934: 352–3).

Socialist agitation in other countries, although more centred on concrete and substantial issues of lifestyle and civilization, also highly valued the symbols of republican egalitarianism, especially in their early phase. E.P. Thompson describes how English Jacobins cherished their egalitarian values in their practices of association, calling themselves Citizen so-and-so, whatever their background and status, sharing responsibilities and duties in the organization, rotating chairmanship of committees, and emphasizing in every other way that every man was 'capable of reason and of a growth in his abilities, and that deference and distinctions of status were an offence to human dignity' (Thompson, 1980: 201). Fifteen years later, the friendly societies of craftsmen and workers, the predecessors of trade unions in Britain, continued and cultivated the egalitarian etiquette, while at the same time cherishing collectivist values, mutual help as well as temperance (ibid.: 460–7).

Egalitarianism is a way of showing universal respect and recognition of another person as a separate and equal partner in a struggle for a common cause. Self-education was felt to be everyone's duty, and in no way an alternative to (lay) formal schooling. Mutual recognition of human dignity naturally implies also responsibility and fraternity towards other equals. Ronny Ambjörnsson, the Swedish cultural historian, has identified a term that the Swedish temperance socialists used to describe their ideals of enlightened modern working-class life: *skötsamhet*, best translated as conscientiousness (Ambjörnsson, 1988). It combines the cultured virtues of the enlightened *Bildungsbürger* with his self-control. It contains the same elements as its British working-class equivalent 'respectability': cleanliness, orderliness, temperance and self-respect, even a sense of superiority (Lockwood, 1958). But the Swedish word (*sköta* = care for) also implies reliability and a sense of responsibility for others, even for society at large, as well as a sense of duty towards one's own responsibilities. Unregulated sexuality, gambling and immediate satisfaction also implied unregulated and conflict-ridden social relationships, whereas individual abstinence represented a wider belief in progress and civilization, through '*bildning*', self-imposed development of the working class towards full sovereignty as political citizens and dignity as human individuals.

Associational life was concerned with the fight against ignorance and poverty. Reading and debating were important practices with which to cultivate a more dignified future life, preparing participants not only to see their individual lot in a societal perspective but also to take a wider responsibility in parliamentary politics. The parliamentary culture was symbolized in rituals and organization of the temperance lodges and union shops. Whatever the problem, committees were always elected to 'clear' the issue. Committees reported to the general assembly of the local groups, and local groups sent elected representatives to national and even international temperance organizations like the International Organization of Good Templars, the strongest temperance group close to the Nordic labour movement.

Ambjörnsson underscores the importance of the new literary culture that was formed in the course of the associational activities early in the century. A new way of reading emerged, similar to what Richard Hoggart ([1957] 1981) describes in his classic study, *The Uses of Literacy*, of British working-class culture in the early twentieth century. The new way of reading was different from the traditional popular and church school reading, which reflected Protestant beliefs in the God-given worldly hierarchy, including memorizing parts of the Bible, the Catechism and other doctrines of the Church. This was replaced by a reading that corresponded to the Lutheran principle of the equality of all humans before God. The new way of reading was personal and at once collective and democratic, based on the Evangelical culture that had spread to the Nordic countries with revival movements in the late eighteenth and early nineteenth centuries. Its purpose was to question and debate, not to memorize and absorb the doctrines given from above. Growth of individual personality through shared literary experience and discussion became even more important in the later temperance lodges and study circles of the union shops. Discussion served to develop a fuller understanding of what was read, in order to 'bury the words in one's inner self'. Reading materials consisted of cultural history, travel books and literary works.[20] This reflects how the romantic part of the individualization process was coupled with the rational ethos of self-control. I return to this part in the next chapter on Romanticism. Discussion topics included questions such as 'Has human culture progressed?', or 'Which is more destructive to cultural progress: war or drunkenness?' The romantic yearning for the strange and distant was reflected in lectures prepared by participants on imagined journeys to Stockholm and southern Sweden, along with topics that stressed rational control of the self, such as 'The importance of personal hygiene' and 'The morality of marriage' (Ambjörnsson, 1988: 123).

The new respect for individual dignity and autonomy implied a changing form of democratic relationships in reading practices and discussion circles. It was proposed, for example, that the old custom of standing up while speaking would be discontinued, so that the one who speaks should not rise above the others. Personal integrity could not be sacrificed to the eventual hierarchies that emerged in the collective learning process.

The plight of paternalism

The metamorphosis of progress to conservatism

Temperance movements gradually lost their progressive and utopian role to other movements. In fact, many of them were transitional organizations that channelled religious and moral energies into political parties (Harrison, 1971: 31). In the process, the temperance mission faded and its influence in society ebbed. By the end of the century, the British prohibition movement had become one of the conservative elements (Dingle, 1980: 222–5; Schiman, 1988) that we today associate with the term 'Victorian'. Victorian conservatism argued that social ills could be explained in terms of individual character weaknesses. After 1890, most British socialists considered the temperance movement to be diverting the working class away from its proper interests rather than serving them (Harrison, 1971: 397–403).

American temperance movements, too, increasingly adopted a defensive position in national policies. Following Richard Hofstadter (1955), Gusfield (1963) concludes that, moving from an assimilative to a coercive doctrine of reform, prohibitionism became a theory of conspiracy. It was believed that evil men in the East Coast cities were manipulating currency, tariffs and national policy to their own advantage. The temperance movement identified itself with an underdog position to defend people's right to self-government and justice. The polarization evoked ideas of a plebeian dictatorship of the majority in much the same way as in the socialist revolution in Russia. The nationalism embedded in the temperance argument turned inward and became identified with political conservatism. As in Britain earlier, prohibition became an isolated issue, and its extrication from wider political concerns was inevitable, although its core values of the home, the nation and individual citizenship were still the same as before.

Although almost all national prohibitions in Christian countries ended by the mid-1930s,[21] and most temperance movements lost their vigour, the climax of state intervention into lifestyle was still to come, in the course of and immediately after the Second World War. This was the start of the build-up phase of modern welfare states, which is discussed in detail later. The tension between the three forces to civilize the masses – imposition, emulation and emancipation – continued not only in the alcohol issue but also in the control of other aspects of lifestyle, notably sexuality. One way to alleviate this tension was to focus on the population rather than on individuals or on particular groups, at least in argumentation if not in methods. Solutions to the population question – insufficient growth and degeneration – that was common in all Western countries since the late nineteenth century, were sought in the guise of the national interest, but some of the techniques that were used, such as incarceration, involuntary abortion or involuntary sterilization, went beyond what we now would consider acceptable for the recognition of individual dignity and autonomy.

In alcohol control, the tensions were even more in relief in countries where there had been no attempt at prohibition, but where the working-class parties retained some influence over moral control. In Belgium, for example, the Vandervelde legislation from 1936–37, named after its author Émile Vandervelde, one of the leaders of the Second Socialist International, stipulated that strong alcohol could neither be served in cafés nor sold in quantities less than 2 litres, to protect the working class from alcoholism. In England and Scotland, the opening hours of pubs were regulated to support the factory discipline, and in Sweden, monthly purchasing allowances were introduced that varied according to class, gender and marital status.[22] In all these cases the justification was, first, the national interest, and second, the protection of the working class, usually with its own consent if not on its own initiative, but the paternalistic interpretation of these controls surfaced easily and overshadowed the liberating and civilizing intentions that were incorporated in them.

The point is illustrated by an anecdote from Social-Democratic Sweden. The 'October Revolution' in 1955 that replaced the rationing system with a personal purchasing permit, began the era of 'free spirits', but the civilizing policy objectives remained in place and even hardened. *Systembolaget*, the state alcohol retail monopoly, was responsible for ensuring that liquor was not sold to persons who were known to have alcohol problems or who had been caught for 'breaking the alcohol law' (mainly illegal distilling or selling alcohol on the black market). By 1962, the number of blacklisted people had climbed to almost 20,000. It was not possible to control every purchase. Nor was it acceptable to allow the shop clerks to select arbitrarily those to be checked, since the clerks might have discriminated against the working class, against women or against the small ethnic minorities (mostly Sami or Gypsies) in favour of middle-class males. Therefore randomization was entrusted to an objective electronic device that was developed for this particular purpose. A red lamp on the device was lit up randomly on top of the cash register at each purchase, and if the lamp was lit, the clerk – then called *tjänsteman* (civil servant) – took the customer's ID card and checked it against the blacklist (Ragnarsson, 1993: 62–4). The red lamp machine symbolized the problematic balance between paternalistic control and the neutrality of the *Rechtstaat*, where all citizens are treated fairly and equally, disregarding gender, race and social class.

The two fictions of contract

I have discussed the history of the social question and the temperance movement as an important example of its extension to the regulation of lifestyle to show that the contemporary contractualism or politics of partnership is not just a fashionable form of talk from the pulpits of public management experts. Nor is it simply the result of the extension of market relationships to the area that used to be discussed in terms of social control. It is a historical outcome of capitalist subjectivity that has developed since the days when commercial relationships first started to reach large masses of the population, created the work contract and gradually required that individuals exercise autonomy as political citizens and consumers. An early outline of the contracting citizen was provided in Adam Smith's writing about the progressive and civilizing effects of the commercial society as well as in Montesquieu's and Steward's idea that self-interest exercises discipline passion, which was so important for the early temperance reformers. This process accelerated in the post-war expansion of the welfare state, as will be explained in more detail below.

The form of the social contract in lifestyle regulation today is a fiction as much as it was in its pre-sociological meaning. Hobbes, Locke, Pufendorf or Rousseau never thought that the social contract would *really* entail a juridical pact to be adjudicated by an established court. In the pre-sociological form, the fiction was used to emphasize the secular rather than divine origins of the power of sovereigns, and by that token define its limits and the responsibilities of kings towards their subjects. The fiction of the contract in contemporary individualistic societies underscores the reverse meaning of the term subject, that of agency, of individuals as citizens, as wage labourers and as consumers. It took many decades even for the wage labour relationship to become dominant in the capitalist economy; it required imposition, emulation and struggles for emancipation before universal suffrage was established and before the large majority of working people had sufficient means and enough time to experience themselves as choice-making contract partners in politics and consumption.

The period of social history that I have looked at in this chapter through the temperance movements epitomized a kind of watershed between these two fictions of the social contract. The waters that flow backwards in history orient themselves to the cataracts of the early nineteenth-century revolutions, particularly those of 1848, that reacted to the contradiction between republican ideals of free and equal citizens, on the one hand, and the *de facto* dependencies that structured the lives of the proletariat on the other. They continue further down to the optimism of Adam Smith and classical economic liberalism that believed in the enormous capacity of human self-interest to fuel the engine of progress if unhampered by inauspicious interventions by the state. And they flow quietly to the long tradition of beliefs, advocated by Montesquieu and Steward that by themselves human passions cancel each other out and civilization follows by itself. The waters that flow forward, towards our present, spring from the dream-wells of self-controlling and separate individuals, they pass by the universalism of the *Rechtstaat*, by the realization of the debt that society owes to its needy members through the institutions of the welfare state, and join the parallel positivist currents of scientific management of society at the post-war juncture of the Big Plans. They are now blended with other kinds of individualism, properly called Romantic, to which we come in the next chapter. Autonomy implies another kind of order, of psychological and physical rather than juridical nature, namely a sense of separateness vis-à-vis others and vis-à-vis the physical environment. Such a sense is necessary to construct a sphere of intimacy, which delineates the individual's own protected sphere: the bodily functions that should be hidden and respected as such. This is exactly the Eliasian sense of civilization, sanctioned by the sentiments of honour and shame, dignity and impropriety.

But between these two long flows there was the uneven highland of beliefs in progress and prosperity through the power of the newborn parliamentary state, of which the period of temperance ideology was one part. As we have seen, repression was often the form in which this ideology was imposed by the state; emulation could also be sometimes state-imposed as in Nordic alcohol policy after the brief period of prohibition in Norway and Finland. Neither of these forms of paternalism could have borne fruit without the sense of self-improvement that the labour movement perpetuated among its ranks, for example, in the words of Émile Vandervelde[23] from 1910:

> We want men who have sensitivity to their misery to make it disappear; we want men who are not asleep but awake; men who have a clear intelligence and a firm will. We fight alcohol not only because of the ravages it causes but also because it poses an obstacle to the emancipation of a class who, for us, holds the future in its flanks! (Vandervelde, 1910: 49–50)

Notes

1 Jaurés, Jean (1934): Etudes socialistes. *œuvres de Jean Jaurès. Textes rassemblés, présentés et anotés par Max Bonnafous.* Volume II: 354–9. My translation.

2 The *Guardian*, week 31 in 2007.

3 According to Montesquieu:

> Public provisions are a sacred debt. Society owns subsistence to its unfortunate citizens, either providing them work or ensuring the means of existence to those whose condition does not allow them to work. (Montesquieu: *De l'Esprit des Lois*, XXIII, xxix)

4 'The alms given to a naked man in the street do not fulfil the obligations of the state, which owes to every citizen a certain subsistence, a proper nourishment, convenient clothing, and a kind of life not incompatible with health' (Montesquieu [1748] 1989: XXIII, xix). This principle was inscribed in the Constitution of 1793. The duty of society towards its citizens, supervised by the state, is also inscribed in the Declaration of Human Rights, which states that the right to be born and to live 'free and equal' is basic and inviolable. The same prerogative was reinforced in the Constitution of 1848, and again in the Constitution of the Fifth Republic in 1946; and various formulations of the same principle are to be found in the constitutions of many European constitutions and legislations even today.

5 The right to seek work, by the way, is still inscribed in the proposed European Constitution of 2005: 'Any citizen of the Union has the liberty to seek employment, to work, to settle or to provide services in any Member State.' This is rather close to what Turgot wrote more than two hundred years earlier: 'What the State owes to its every member is the destruction of the obstacles that might perturb their industry or interfere with their right to enjoy the products of its results' (A.R.H. Turgot: *Edit portant suppression des jurandées et communautés de commerce, arts et métiers,*; quoted in Castel, 1995: 176)

6 Around 1848 three-quarters of the French population lived in the countryside. Out of a working population of 4.4 million, only 670,000 worked in industrial establishments employing more than 10 workers, and half of them were women and children. The independent male labour force consisted of well below 10 per cent of the working population (Castel, 1995: 225–6; Rioux, 1971: 170).

7 Notably Thomas Paine, the author of the famous republican pamphlet *Human Rights* ([1791] 2003) and a central figure in the movement for constitutional reform in England before the Napoleonic Wars, believed that only a minimal degree of state control is necessary to 'police' society (Thompson, 1980: 83–118).

8 The Declaration of Human Rights stated that: 'The principle of all sovereignty resides in the nation. No body nor individual may exercise any authority which does not proceed directly from the nation.' (Article 3)

9 The first universal male suffrage in parliamentary elections was established only in 1877 in France, and later in other European countries. France was also the last democracy to adopt women's universal suffrage – this was as late as 1945.

10 By the end of the nineteenth century in the USA, the main supporters of temperance movements were fundamentalists and conservatives, and the age of the members rose during the early decades of the twentieth century (Gusfield, 1955; 1957). In the Nordic countries, temperance movements declined after the 1910s (Johansson, 2000; Sulkunen, I., 1986) but they maintained their political influence even though the number of members decreased sharply again after the Second World War. Due to urbanization, people lost their connections with former temperance organizations and thus the movement became mostly rural. The older generations were significantly over-represented and the movements failed to recruit from new generations (Warpenius and Sutton, 2000).

11 Harry Levine (1992) makes a distinction between two temperance cultures at the turn of the nineteenth and twentieth centuries: English-speaking (Britain, the USA, Canada, Australia and New Zealand) and Nordic (Iceland, Norway, Sweden and Finland). Two features explain the strong position of temperance movements in both areas: a specific heavy drinking habit (use of spirits) and Protestantism.

12 Weber himself did not use temperance ideology to illustrate the social effects of secular self-control, but his analysis of the Protestant ethic applies perfectly to the anti-alcohol rhetoric of the time.

13 In certain religious temperance movements the ascetic principle did imply an inwardly oriented concept of reform. Lambert (1983: 115, 117), for example, observes that in Welsh Calvinism this theory

> resulted in an attitude which took obedience to the will of God as implying complete satisfaction with, and acceptance of, things as they were. In practice religion became an apologia for social inequalities instead of a criticism with a new standard of values to impose upon the life of men.

However, in Protestant temperance movements, this was the exception rather than the rule.

14 Prohibition was a serious political option in all the temperance cultures that Levine (1992) analysed: in Britain, the USA, Canada, Australia and New Zealand and in Nordic countries: Iceland, Norway, Sweden and Finland. Sweden never had prohibition but instituted other forms of rigorous availability controls. The Norwegian prohibition (1916–27) remained partial, excluding wine and beer (Fuglum, 1995). In Switzerland, Austria and Germany (partial) prohibitions were proposed, but they never gained wide political support (Roberts, 1984; Eisenbach-Stangl, 1991; Spode, 1993).

15 At the outbreak of the First World War, the President of the Republic, Henri Poincaré, the philosopher, Henri Bergson, the radical socialist, Léon Bourgeois and several generals were among those who joined the national temperance league LNCA (Ligue National Contre l'Alcoolisme) in the interest of national defence (Nourrisson, 1990: 287–93).

16 The doctrine of teetotalism was imported to the Nordic countries a couple of decades later with the same content: total abstinence is best because drink destroys, not only challenges the free will of individuals (Eriksen, 1996; Sulkunen, I., 1986).

17 The connection between the working-class question and the alcohol question was decisive in terms of the actual establishment of alcohol political regimes. In those countries where the working-class movement and temperance movement maintained strong interconnections, prohibition had the strongest support. The working-class question was supposed to be solved via the control of alcohol use. In Britain (Harrison, 1971; Dingle, 1980) and Germany (Roberts, 1984; Spode, 1993), labour movements rejected this line of reasoning and criticized it as being too individualistic; in Finland (Sulkunen, I., 1986), Norway (Fuglum, 1995: 51–4), Sweden (Ambjörnsson, 1988), Scotland (Paton, 1977; Smout, [1986] 1997: 146–7), Belgium and Holland (Roberts, 1984: 90–2), temperance reform was regarded as a major tool to achieve social reform agitated for by labour movements. Differing religious orientations and positions of class struggles gave contexts in which the alcohol question was interpreted, but despite national differences alcohol was defined as a severe social problem in all industrialized modern countries during the late nineteenth century.

18 Many Protestant followers were progressives who believed that the Kingdom of God was coming on earth as a result of human efforts to spread religious liberty and democracy. Advances in science, technology and culture as manifested in a broad range of economic, political and social reforms were regarded as evidence of the second advent of Christ (Timberlake, 1963: 36).

19 In fact, this theme persists as a red thread throughout Bourdieu's work on the invisible mechanisms of symbolic violence within publicly professed universalism and egalitarianism.

20 It is not insignificant that the literary tastes preferred the (national) romantic works of Lenngren, Tegnér, Runeberg, Rydberg, Topelius and Lagerlöf (Ambjörnsson, 1988: 250). See also Arvidson (1985).

21 The last to be abolished was prohibition on beer in Iceland in 1978.

22 The rationing system, developed by Dr Ivan Bratt, was voted in the referendum of 1922 where prohibition lost by 49 to 51 per cent. It was replaced with a personal purchasing licence with no pre-defined monthly ration in 1955 (Bruun, 1985).

23 My translation. Vandervelde (e.g. 1910) was by no means an unhesitating *étatist*; on the contrary he was strongly against state ownership of industries if it was only for fiscal purposes. On the moral education of the working class, his position was firm: the state must mobilize its authority for the improvement of human nature.

5

Intimacy: the Romantic Self

Historians taught us long ago that the King was never left alone. But in fact, until the end of the seventeenth century, nobody was ever left alone. The density of social life made isolation virtually impossible, and people who managed to shut themselves up in a room for some time were regarded as exceptional characters: relations between peers, relations between people of the same class but dependent on one another, relations between masters and servants – these everyday relations never left a man by himself.

(Philippe Ariès, 1962)

A sense of history

'Us' and 'them'

In my research on attitudes to alcohol control among members of the new middle class – journalists, businessmen and businesswomen, stockbrokers, physicians, nurses, engineers, etc. – I have often found this opinion: controls are necessary for people who do not yet have a sophisticated drinking culture – the working class, the uncivilized, the poor. They make no distinction between what they drink, as long as they get drunk. Relaxed sales regulations or lower prices of alcohol would lead them to more violence and to ruin their health. For us, in contrast, controls don't matter, since we control ourselves. Such regulations have historically been stipulated by the political class (and indomitable temperance frets lurking behind it) and they stand in the way of developing more civilized manners; the attraction of the forbidden fruit destroys the sense of self-control (Sulkunen, 1992: 112–29).

Similar comments are also quite common in the literature on 'recreational drug use' associated with new synthetic drugs in the club culture in the 1990s in many Western countries. Clubbers themselves, and often the sociologists studying them, have constructed two categories of drug users. In the first category are those who know how to handle drugs, know the effects and are selective about the substances, limit their use to specific club scenes, and are competent to integrate their drug use with normal working life, often in jobs that require advanced technical skills such as ICT engineers. Using these drugs requires skill, too, and knowledge about them can only be obtained from other like-minded users. These substances, often called dance drugs, are mostly taken in the form of pills that have no taste or smell. Users represent themselves as the avant-garde of 'postmodern' scientific and technological culture, which is not constrained by conventional moralities. Being illegal and underground, its hedonism is contrasted with the *ennui* of the many, but also with those who belong to the second category of drug users. They just get drugged with anything available, inject, are not aware of the risks and ruin their lives (Decorte, 2001; Parker et al., 2001).[1] Controls are necessary for the second category, but for the first category of users external controls are a waste of time, even detrimental to their capacity to cultivate an avant-garde drug culture.

The use of intoxicating substances is a special case, since intoxicants have the dual functions of the *pharmacon*: they are the product of culture (animals seldom seek intoxication) while they also are poison. Therefore their use always raises the question of control, knowledge, possession or dispossession of culture. Intoxication is a symbol of adulthood in most cultures, and, vice versa, loss of the right to get intoxicated is a reduction of adult sovereignty over one's body and soul. But it should be observed that these categorizations are not about intoxication itself, they are about the logic of control and the social bond determining that logic. They involve a time dimension: 'we' the avant-garde, 'them' the reargard; and they involve a separation of the instance of control from both 'us' and 'them', as a faceless third who offends us by making no distinction between our competence and the incompetence of others. These self-images represent them as agents of their lives who appreciate voluntary communion with other like-minded individuals but are prickly about uninvited interference by outsiders.

These dual images of subjects of control have a counterpart in the images of governance that will be analysed later as the *ethic of not taking a stand*. This mode of governance constructs part of its subjects as competent to regulate their own lives, the other part as non-subjects. The competent ones are irritated by interference because they have the identity of reflective consumers in the search for authentic pleasure, sometimes beyond the limits of conventional life of the masses. These images and the corresponding mode of governance are part of the phenotype of subjectivity produced by mature consumer capitalism.

These classifications highlight agency as the principle of dignity and greatness, to refer again to our model of justification. Like the order of subjectivity that arose from the elementary work contract and gradually turned individuals into autonomous contract makers with and clients of the state, also this second aspect of agency has undergone a long process of historical transformations and has now reached a point of saturation. But the self-images of this type of competence appear to be the opposite of the autonomous order of subjectivity in three ways. First, they have a time orientation towards the past from which they seek to liberate the modern individual, not towards the future like the progressive individualism of the nineteenth century. They are images of *bon vivants* today rather than of prudent savers for tomorrow. Second, the universalism of the order of subjectivity pursued by the modern mass movements has been replaced by the dualistic division between competent subjects and those who do not qualify as subjects of their own life. Third, the progressive movements for autonomy formed collective goal-oriented organizations, whereas the mundane *avant-gardists* today do support group identification but do not claim the status of spearhead in the convoy to generalize their values in the name of a better future.

Are these two orders of subjectivity contradictory, one in the service of prudent accumulation, the other sacrificing the virtue of prudence to the vice of prodigality, made necessary by the excessive capacity of capitalism to produce commodities and services? This chapter will show that these orders of subjectivity are a double outcome of modernization that has matured into consumer capitalism, and are not limited to issues of regulating the use of intoxicants. The image of the avant-garde competent consumer stems from a sense of intimacy, an experience of one's self as an authentic person, separate from others, who rightly claims the right to be left alone. It is an inadvertent but necessary sensibility in, and even outcome of, mature consumer capitalism. The apparent contrast between ebullient ideals of autonomy, based on rational self-control, and bohemian images of avant-garde consumerism is misleading. The figure of the rational contracting citizen, and the other figure of hedonistic post-modern consumer, are not only compatible; they are the progeny of common forebears of modern individualism. The first parent is the rationalist spirit of capitalism struggling for individual autonomy, as discussed in the previous chapter. The second, to be discussed in this chapter, is the Romantic sense of the self. These two dispositions, autonomy and intimacy, are separate and may occasionally be in conflict as we shall see shortly, but nevertheless they result from the same double trajectory from collective traditionalism to contractual individualism, intertwined and like two criss-crossing striated beams of light.

Orders of time

The remarks on 'us' and 'them' quoted above reflect three levels of time-bound reality. The first is a *universal* distinction, not historically specific at all. 'We', as a group, are different from and superior to some others because we have the modal qualifications required of subjects, of being sovereign agents of our actions. We know how to enjoy the pleasures of drinking, and we have the necessary will to keep our desires under control. Others act as if they were 'programmed' by the system or by their habitual desires; or they may react 'accidentally' without any motivation; or they simply adjust their behaviour to what others do and desire. The French semiotician Eric Landowski (2005: 16–39) has suggested that the three images of action as 'programmed', 'accidental' or 'adjusted' represent action as devoid of meaning, and therefore as absence of agency. Only when action does not occur randomly, but is not fixed by conformity or programmed by habit or external circumstance either, does it bear the mark of meaningful behaviour. This does not necessarily mean that it is the result of free will. Other modalities may be involved, such as *fulfilling one's duty*, having exceptional *competences* (as in the self-images of recreational drug users), or *being able to overcome* obstacles that seem insurmountable.

The distinction between action resulting from the exercise of agency, and action that is devoid of meaning, is as old as culture itself. As soon as human beings realize that they can influence themselves and their environment, and that they have a choice, they become aware of their feelings and of their capacity to collect and assess information to support their decisions. Humans are conscious of themselves as cultural actors, oriented by their modal existence in contrast to the environment, considered as having none of the modal qualities of willing, obligation, ability or knowledge. This distinction is extended to categories of other humans: 'them' in contrast to 'us'.

Second, the consciousness of us and them – let us call it awareness of alterity – always has a *context* in time and space. When humans classify themselves as distinct from others, they define what it is to be like them. To say 'we' is to recognize a social bond. To say 'them' is to consolidate that bond by identifying the qualities that define the group we belong to.[2] Usually the distinction places the 'other' in the class of non-modal beings: those who neither can nor know how to act as subjects, who have no sense of duty to fulfil or to resist, and who have no free will to direct their own conduct.

Sometimes the positive and negative poles are reversed: *we have a problem* as representatives of an inferior culture compared to others that are more civilized (in the alcohol question often figured as the French and the Italians). For example, a small-town businessman and two journalists remarked in a group interview:[3]

> *Hannu, manager (M)*:   You should think about the culture and about the kind of people, Finnish people have become used to obeying and observe a strong central government under Swedish rule, then under Russia they picked up Russian habits like drinking. Finnish people don't seem to have the manners and even if you should give them responsibility you can't and then, of course, think about young people ...

> *Maria, journalist (F)*:   The experience we have is that ... restrictions ... they do not solve the problem anyway

> *Susanna, journalist (F)*:   It makes it into a forbidden fruit, and we all know how tempting that can be.

We come across this distinction between 'us' and 'the others' everywhere in everyday talk about identities. As Clifford Geertz (1973: 448) wrote, these are 'the stories we tell about ourselves to ourselves', and they have a similar structure in all cultures. That structure articulates the distance of agents who have modal competence to (imaginary) actors who are not thought to be in possession of such qualities. However, the context is not always the same; stories of 'us' cannot all be identical but reflect the values we recognize as constitutive of our group.

But, third, people's awareness of alterity also represents *a sense of history*. The awareness of alterity that contrasts with the value of dignity and greatness attached to the authenticity of agency, is structured by an image of time flowing from a murky authoritarian past towards a society of free and equal self-controlling consumers and citizens, who no longer need the paternalistic state to escort them to civilization. It is a glance from the present standpoint backward to the marshy highland of state-centred moral reform, represented among other things by the temperance movements in the past. Although the structure of the contrast is similar, and probably universal, at least in contemporary Western European societies, it also transmits a vision of social change. Consider this example:

> This is an age-old discourse. Is Britain uniquely uncouth in our filthy drinking habits, or do our peculiarly restrictive laws cause the desperate drink-to-get-drunk-quick mentality? Why, oh why can't we be more like Italians? Take away the urgency and the mystery, and maybe we could all tipple a little nip in the coffee without making a fetish of alcohol. After all, why are we – and our Viking neighbours to the North – such drunken sots compared to the Mediterraneans? (Polly Toynbee, *The Guardian*, 21 January 2005)

England has a much richer drinking heritage than the Nordic countries, where alcohol has been excluded from the everyday life of the vast majority of the population for at least one hundred years. Nevertheless, the British journalist paints a very similar image of 'us drunken sots' as her colleagues in the Nordic countries frequently do. Here the positions between 'us' and 'them' are – or rather seem to be – the reverse of the typical case where it is the others who have no modal qualities. But the appearance is misleading, because the journalist is using the first person plural only as a second-level stylistic device in order not to offend the readers by criticizing them, while at the first level of signification she in fact represents herself as one of the (few) who do have the competence to make a distinction between cultivated manners and drinking-to-get-drunk.[4] The image constructs a sense of history that could properly be expected to belong to the past but, to the annoyance of the journalist, still seems to persist among many Brits.

This sense of history is articulated in the manner in which the context is described. But it is essential to realize that it does *not come from* the context; it rather *flows back on to it* from the experience of the self and the society in which it is enveloped. The story of the context is not uniquely historical but has rhetorical functions. For example, the contrast between the Mediterranean cultural heritage and 'our' dismal authoritarian past, which has dispossessed us of our potential for self-control and harmless pleasure, constructs a pending narrative[5] about our culture – a story of evolution that is interrupted at the moment of its recital, to be continued, maybe, if the addressees join the narrator and the good forces of history, to bring forth the paradise of harmless civilized pleasure.

The intractable new middle class

Who are 'we' in these ornate stories? The sense of superiority and inferiority is attached to a two-layered group-sense, that of a nation (which is inferior to more civilized nations in the alcohol stories above) and a group within the nation (which is superior to other groups). It is very difficult to define either of these associations. Nation is a vague and heterogeneous notion in contemporary multicultural world, but the superior group-sense within the nation is even more intangible in this imaginary history. The 'etc.' I attached above to the list of new middle class professions represented among those we interviewed is extremely important. In our research we wanted to interview what we thought would be a relatively easily distinguishable category, comparable to that of the 'cadres' in French social statistics, extending from the lowest managerial level to high positions in business, civil service and the academic professions. We had earlier conducted a study of the working class and their understandings of alcohol and alcohol control (Sulkunen et al., 1997), and we wanted to make a comparison.

But we were left astounded by the actual reality of the new middle class. When we asked, they could not decide what it is that makes them feel to be among their kin. We listed and presented to them what they had indicated as significant qualities of their companions: college education, profession, family background, income, property, or employment status. Whatever criteria they had used, even employment, some among their closest friends would always end up in the wrong category (some of them were unemployed at the time). 'Them', the others, on the other hand, were described not by socio-economic properties but in figurative terms, such as 'those who live out there beyond the Ringway' around the city of Helsinki, 'welfare scroungers', 'poor people' or 'cap-heads'. The dimension of superiority was as intractable in the low end of 'them' as it was in the high end of 'us'. Even their opinions, political or otherwise, did not mark the difference. Some among them were politically conservative, some supported the left; some were ardent environmentalists, others did not care; several males were traditional in their views on gender but some women were outspokenly 'feminists'. Still, they repeatedly emphasized that the most important factor that keeps them together, as distinct from other groups, is that they are 'like-minded'.

We have here a sample of the social reality that sociologists have discussed in terms of the intractable class structure in middle-class or consumer capitalism. The traditional industrial working classes, employed in material production or in transport, are reduced to less than a third of the economically active population (Therborn, 1995: 76). They still retain some of the features of class culture and class-based way of life, although misery is now exceptional among them. Fifty years ago, David Lockwood could, in his classic study of *The Black-Coated Worker* (1958), defend the view that office workers had a distinct class consciousness, which was based on the actual reality of their life experience. They were *in fact* placed in more favourable positions than industrial workers. Today, office workers belong to many different categories, and even though these groups still distance themselves from manual workers, they hardly have a consciousness of themselves as a class. The main part of the population belongs to groups who have little in common except that they are *not* industrial or agricultural workers or *not* part of the old elites. They are sales clerks, educators, administrators, employed in health care or in the provision of social services, or they are in office work of various kinds at different levels: secretaries, marketing personnel, shop floor managers or company executives; students, researchers, designers, journalists.

These people are in the middle in two ways, vertically and horizontally. All of them work in a world of hierarchies which are at least theoretically fluid both upwards and downwards. Positions within these hierarchies may be determined by the level of diplomas, by experience or by performance, but also quite often by personal qualities. Whatever the grounds for advancement, and whatever the personal motivation to achieve it, the prospect of a career is always present. Much of one's value is measured by 'success', in terms of income, the size of organizational budgets one handles, or the number of subordinates one has.

Being in the middle, better than someone else, or better than one was before, but not yet what one could be in the future: a sense of hierarchy is the overriding sensibility of new middle-class people. However, their positions in the hierarchies of the workplace are not determined by what they actually do for work. Both position and work itself in new middle-class occupations can be quite abstract. It is not easy to determine when an administrator has done his job well or achieved something; when businessmen plan and carry out commercial campaigns, merits are often distributed according to who was in which position rather than on the basis of who did what. Yet position itself is often a vague measure of career success. Boundaries between positions are never unequivocal; even the strictest public bureaucracies have informal hierarchies which appear as personal power and influence that bear on, among other things, one's own and others' career prospects.

But the new middle-class groups are in the middle horizontally as well. They are surrounded on all sides by other middle-class groups. Being in the middle often means uncertainty or status panic, as C. Wright Mills ([1951] 1956: 239–58) said. Whether one wants it or not, expectations are inevitably organized around the notion of social comparison or social ascension, but what this means is not certain. Work and position are two distinct dimensions in new middle-class – mostly female – occupations, and work is often the lesser in importance. A traditional working man is proud to see what his hands produce; he feels he has advanced if he gets to produce longer series and use bigger, more complicated machines and instruments. A middle-class office worker is proud if she gets paid more than someone else, perhaps if she has more subordinates, and certainly if she is on good terms with management who decide on promotions.

Elitism from below

Against this structural background, it is not surprising that the imaginary view of history that we so often encounter in discourses on moral issues does not appear to be a story about the evolution of a class or a group. Unlike the progressive discourses of nineteenth-century reformists, the new middle-class culture seems to be a more diffuse discursive disposition that pulses in contemporary society almost randomly; an attitude almost anyone can assume and employ to organize the social world and one's place in it.

The dimension of superiority in the distinction between 'us', who are at an advanced stage in the progress of civilization, and 'them' who lag behind, appears, at first sight, to be the perfect opposite to the classic distinction between the working-class 'us and them' described by Richard Hoggart ([1957] 1981: 72–3): '"They" are the people at the top, the high-ups, the people who give you your dole, call you up, tell you to go to war, fine you, talk posh, treat y' like muck.' No, on the contrary, middle-class morality is ciphered in a self-hagiographic *avant-gardism* towards 'them', down below and in the *reargard*. But not quite. Our middle-class interviewees pronounced a similar feeling of being *subjected to* rather than *subjects of* power ('... take a firm look up there, at the bosses!') when they were talking about the inauspicious consequences of alcohol control policies, claiming that they feel patronized as if they were offered 'a dummy in the mouth' instead of being treated like responsible adults. The superiority that they felt with respect to less competent folks did not translate into any feeling of being able to participate in the exercise of power and influence in society. It was elitism from below.

We are dealing here with a certain kind of critical awareness of the present. But what kind of mundane consciousness is it part of, and what consciousness of the pulpit is it related to?

The Romantic ethic

The hubris of intimacy

The new middle-class is intractable – it cannot be identified as one social 'class' or group but not others – but it is also fragile. It is rather like a mentality or a disposition. People who have it are very sensitive about symbolic violations of their hubris. What does their hubris consist of? It goes without saying that the quotations at the beginning of this chapter refer to autonomy, an identity of individuals who control their desires, and manage the risks by themselves. The new middle-class mentality is the outcome of at least two hundred years of evolution that has liberated the contracting individual from authoritarian bonds, but the humiliating experience of 'being told to' – or even worse, being told *not to* – prowls everywhere, and gets translated into a fancied past where people were not treated as mature adults, like us, but bossed around like children, or into images of those incompetent others who need to be controlled lest they let their savage desires destroy them and spoil the life of those around them.

Autonomy is necessary in modern society to manage one's individual biography and to articulate one's interests. However, exercise of autonomy also presupposes distinctness: awareness of oneself as a unique person separate from others, and it needs to be driven by authenticity: consciousness of the self, of what one wants and desires. Distinctness and authenticity construct a sphere of intimacy around the individual. One's own experience is protected against the experiences of others, and they seem to stem from the inner self rather than from the outside, even when they are reactions to outside influences, such as the presence of a loved person. Like autonomy, the sense of intimacy has a real as well as the imaginary history described above. As Philippe Ariès (1962: 398) says in the epigraph to this chapter, these are modern inventions. Colin Campbell, in his landmark study, *The Romantic Ethic and the Spirit of Modern Consumerism* (1987), has shown that these two real histories, that of autonomy and that of intimacy, are in fact cotemporaneous. As the capitalist spirit became oriented towards competition and accumulation, assiduity in work and frugality in consumption, another Protestant ethic developed. Whereas the first ethos was helpful in turning work into a calling, the second was important in motivating consumption and in handling one's emotions. Campbell (ibid.: 61) argued that it is the ethic of Romanticism and passion, a preoccupation with authentic pleasure, 'a self-illusory hedonism ... characterized by a longing to experience in reality those pleasures created and enjoyed in imagination, a longing which results in the ceaseless consumption of novelty ... and a continuous dissatisfaction with real life'.

Romanticism as a style, philosophy or an epoch is notoriously difficult to define. Art historians conventionally date the 'Romantic period' in Europe to around the decades before and after the French Revolution. A reaction to the rationalism of the eighteenth-century Enlightenment, Romanticism was opposed to unifying systems of ideas, and therefore it has been said that the attempt to define it is in itself unromantic (Lovejoy, 1955). On the other hand, although not a philosophical doctrine, Romanticism as a world-view in a more elusive sense has been described as a 'shift in consciousness' which cracked the backbone of European Enlightenment (Furst, 1969: 27). It admires creative chaos and eschews order and discipline. It is attracted by the strange and curious, including distant cultures as exemplified by the late eighteenth-century Orientalism. It is oriented towards the unfamiliar rather than the matters of fact of everyday life; it is fond of melancholy rather than optimism, and it is more given to anxiety than to serenity.

Sociologically the Romantic ethos nevertheless has a clear function in consumer capitalism. Campbell argues that although modern hedonism was necessary for the rise of the consumer society, it is not aimed at material welfare alone. On the contrary, it is non-material and mental because it is personalized; like romantic love, it depends on imagination, a constantly renewable desire that can never be brought to final satisfaction. While only reality can provide satisfaction, both illusions and delusions can supply pleasure (Campbell, 1987: 205).

Like the instillation in everyday consciousness of the autonomic, self-disciplining morality, the sensibilities of individual distinctness and authenticity also matured in the intellectual labours of social movements. On the surface, the evolutionary histories of autonomy and intimacy are contrasting.

Whereas the first took form in the great projects of mass mobilization, the protoplasm of modern political institutions, the Romantic ethos has been voiced by limited circles of intellectuals. One could even argue that most Romantic intellectual groups have not been movements at all in the narrow sense of the term, with a life history from birth to mobilization, to organization and finally to institutionalization (Eyerman and Jamison, 1991). They have been transient communities, leaving their mark on history as intellectual products of individuals, not as institutions. Their interests have been those of intellectuals everywhere: moral issues encompassing the meaning of life rather than legislation on everyday life. Their mundane concerns have been global rather than local or national. In contrast to ascetic modernism, the Romantic liberation of the self has involved sexual emancipation as well as drinking and drugs.

Some of these intellectual groups have been literally expatriates, like the American 'Lost Generation' authors and intellectuals in Paris in the Prohibition era; some, like the Existentialists in post-war France, have been marginalized in their own countries before they were raised to celebrity and veneration. Similar intellectual movements emerged in all Western European and North American countries throughout the inter-war period. These movements have had a long-term impact on the post-war youth cultures that culminated in the moral revolution of 1968 and the critiques of capitalism that ensued. I shall come back to these two examples in a later section.

Distinctness: the hygienic drive

Let us go back to the people we interviewed about drinking, believing that we could identify social groups properly called the new middle class. If they had so much difficulty defining their superiority in class terms or socio-economic qualities, how was it grounded? Why are 'we' better than 'they out there, in the suburbs beyond the Ringway'? The hierarchic dimension appears in their remarks about the kinds of pubs 'they' go to and how 'they' behave there. But alas, on objective criteria there seems to be little difference! The features that are highly valued in their own milieu but somehow degraded elsewhere are the same, if taken literally. If their pubs are small, they are cosy, informal and comfortable, others are smoky holes, noisy, messy and cramped. Whereas they call their own space an arena of communication and small talk, they think that others are filled with fathomless hubbub. The distinguishing principle is the image of cultured *order* that they have of themselves as compared to people who are either too young to have culture at all or too immersed in culturally acquired pleasures such as smoking and drinking so that they are dirty or polluted. Cigarette smoke is mixed with breathing air, sounds of talking and music turn into noise that obstructs communication, contacts between people are disorderly, involuntary or quarrelsome, and therefore polluted and avoidable. And of course, drinking, which for our middle-class interviewees served the functions of pleasure and sociability, was represented as excessive and mindless drunkenness among the 'cap-heads'. Pollution, dirt and unruly sociability evoke fear and disgust; hygiene, cleanliness and well-behaving interaction represent culture and civilization. Cigarette smoke, like fighting, is an involuntary physical contact and all the more abhorring as it is mediated by excrement, exhalation of air that has already been used.

The contrast between cleanliness and disorder is as old as human culture. As Claude Lévi-Strauss (1964: 56–91; 1968: 391–411, 412–22) has shown in his immense anthropological work, categorizations between legitimate and illegitimate sexual partners, between edible food and poison, between appropriate methods of preparing and consuming food, differ between cultures, but everywhere mixing these classes through contact, contagion or violation of interdictions arouses repulsion and fear, which is represented in timeless myths. The imaginary stories articulate human awareness of the distinction between nature and culture (Sulkunen, 1990). Purity is a central element in the civilization process analysed by Norbert Elias as discussed earlier, and, for Mary Douglas (1966), impurity is an object of fundamental fear of mixing vital cultural categories. Sanitation has had a special place in the modern sense of civilization since the nineteenth century, and it also constitutes an important ingredient in the sense of fancied history that forms the identity of new middle-class people today.

As industrial urban populations began to grow in the nineteenth century, sanitary conditions became a problem. Lack of clean water, drainage, air, light, decent housing and inappropriate nutrition caused pandemics such as the cholera that killed 20,000 Parisians in 1832. Huge armies were victims of epidemics for the same reason. For example, thousands of Napoleon's soldiers died of typhus near Moscow during one single week in September 1812 (Vigarello, 1985: 191).

According to Bruno Latour (1988), before Louis Pasteur's scientific discovery of the microbe, hygienists[6] had a weak strategy because they were looking for the enemy on all fronts, working conditions as well as the urban habitat. Nothing could be ignored. Pasteur's discoveries were an immediate success, because they provided laboratory proof of the idea of *contagion*, which until then had remained an unreliable intuition, obscured by what was called 'random morbidity'. Infectious diseases were transmitted from person to person, yes, but often without direct apparent contact, and on the other hand physical contact was not a sufficient cause either. All seemed to depend on 'variation in virulence' or 'contagion environment' that could never be completely controlled – therefore *all* precautions had to be taken. Pasteur's discoveries made visible the unseen parasites whose purulent presence everywhere made weird connections between people and things. The morbid populations of microbes were, as Latour (1988: 40) remarks, like Freud's unconscious, 'invisible, rejected, terribly dangerous forces that must be listened to if civilization was not to collapse. Like the psychoanalysts, the Pasteurians set themselves up as exclusive interpreters of populations to which no one else had access.'

The hygienists, informed by the new microbiology, were an active and noisy sub-profession in social medicine, but the implications of their work extended far beyond the concrete practices of sanitation. It was the social bond in modern wage labour society that was being transformed, and hygiene was part of that transformation. If the microbiologists had not discovered microbes and demonstrated the mechanisms of contagion in the laboratories, they would have been invented by moralists and social reformers. Contagion means not just pernicious transmission, it is contact that must be controlled, categorized, identified and negotiated lest it smears everything.

Let us take an example by Vigarello (1985: 105) about the Marquise de Chatelet's bath in 1746, originally told by her male valet, S.-G. Longchamp. While the lady was in the tub, naked, he maintained the temperature of the bath, adding hot water, watching attentively over her comfort. No sense of prudery was present, the lady not even bothering to obscure the surface of the water. The distance between them was too great to arouse any sense of embarrassment about the contact through eyes and the medium of water. Compare this with another of Vigarello's bath stories. The Countess de Pange describes the prudence with necessary ablutions, touching the body parts 'that are least exposed to air' with eyes closed, using water from shallow basins but never immersing in a bath, a practice that was considered heathen if not culpable. When the doctor prescribed the daughter of the family a warm bath to contain a fever in 1900, the tub had to be borrowed. But then a new problem arose: should the poor girl be undressed? Impossible. So she was bathed in her night gown (ibid.: 190).

Among the nobility and the bourgeoisie, the 'Victorian' decorum was an obstacle that the hygienists had to fight to convince them of the protective effects of water still at the turn of the century. For the working classes the problems lay in poverty, but as soon as their circumstances allowed, hygiene entered in unproblematic complicity with their sense of decency. With the democratization of the civilizing process, the sensibility of being clean, orderly and separated from both filth and from other persons also became part of working-class normality. The historian Ronny Ambjörnsson (1988: 225) describes how a visitor to a Swedish working-class home in a small sawmill town in the 1930s would be struck by its perfect order and tidiness. No dishes to wash around, books placed in their shelves, the newspaper in its rack. Everything would be clean and polished, the fireplace glimmering white, the family portraits on the dusted bureau in rows with the marriage photograph at the end. Even the clock would sound like it was made to tick peace and *hemtrevnad*, cozyness of the family homestead. The garden around the small house was usually a small wonder of organized gracefulness: flourishing flowerbeds in straight lines, lilacs and grass mats, before whose well-clipped rim the last standing dandelion had to give up the fight.

The sense of order and sanitary appropriateness in working-class homes no doubt reflects the success of hygienists; no doubt it also has been swayed by the pruderies of the bourgeoisie. But Richard Hoggart ([1957] 1981: 78) must have been right in stressing that it also is a way of maintaining self-respect in a situation where recognition by others, 'them', as a person is constantly at risk and threatened:

> At the centre there is a resolution to hold on to that of which one can be rightly proud; in a world which puts so many stumbling blocks in the way, to hold on at least to be able to say 'ah've got me self-respect': although it can be said meanly, it makes up for a lot.

Contrary to what many writers on the working class think, those who aim at cleanliness and thrift are not imitating the lower middle class, as in some ways traitors of their own class, anxious to head off from it. For Hoggart, this effort

> arises more from a concern not to drop down, not to succumb to the environment rather than from an anxiety to go up; and among those who altogether ignore these criteria, the uninhibited, generous, and carefree spirits are outnumbered by the slovenly and shiftless whose homes and habits reflect their inner lack of grip.

Authenticity

If distinctness of the person has been a relatively easy ideal to be combined with rationalist values of self-control, the Romantic value of authenticity has caused frivolous conflicts over lifestyle as the state-centred positive utopia gained ground in advanced industrial societies in the early twentieth century and culminated in the two decades after the Second World War. The inner experience of the self was no longer automatically compatible with what the social engineers of welfare societies regarded as the march to prosperity and civilization.

Not surprisingly, the body has been the focus of these debates, because the body is the site where the social and the natural meet and challenge each other's licence over human pleasure. Sexuality and intoxication in particular were at stake: pleasures that produce consequences for society beyond the individuals immediately concerned: the population question and the social order, especially the order of the nuclear family, and this is the gist of the frictions that we see in the attempts to regulate lifestyles today in the name of health and justice.

I take up two examples of intellectual groups that have been influential in the production of the ethos of authenticity, the American 'Lost Generation' and the post-war Existentialists. Robin Room (1984) has shown that the generation of authors born between 1888 and 1900 played an important role in the cultural shift against the increasingly state-supported moral conservatism of Prohibitionist America. Many of these writers, including Sinclair Lewis, Robert Benchley, Dorothy Parker, E.E. Cummings, F. Scott Fizgerald,

Hart Crane, Ernest Hemingway and Thomas Wolfe, spent time in Paris in the inter-war period, constituting a critical expatriate community of intellectuals that later developed into the romantic stereotype of 'Americans in Paris', celebrated in films, popular novels and music. The contrast between cosmopolitan Paris and the temperance culture of rural conservative America was especially pronounced in attitudes towards alcohol, France being then by far the most drinking country in the world. Paris, however, was not only an alternative cultural milieu in terms of everyday life and alcohol. *Fin-de-siècle* literary circles associated alcohol and drugs with the imaginary and the irrational in French symbolism and expressionism (Room, 1984).

Paris was also the scene of the other celebrated – and ignominious – culture of intellectuals in the twentieth century: Sartre and the 'Existentialists' in the 1940s. Tiina Arppe (1998) has shown that before it became a fashion and diffused among the respectable middle class, the press presented the Existentialists dancing in nocturnal jazz clubs and drunken promiscuous parties with their untidy appearance as a threat to social order. But the underground image was also a self-conscious revolt against the bourgeois moral order. The critique continued the Bohemian tradition of the accursed, lonely cultural hero. Intoxication, even in a context where alcohol was liberally used in everyday life by most people, was a way of setting oneself outside of the requirements of everyday responsibilities and routines; and this externality was symbolized by the use of non-French products like American whiskey and cigarettes, as well as non-alcoholic intoxicants, especially amphetamine (ibid.).

Sartre and de Beauvoir were moderns in two ways. First, the Bohemian myth of intellectuals had its origin in the Victorian cult of uniqueness. Second, although apparently outside the orbits of respectable academic life, the Existentialist community was an integral part of the surrounding bourgeois society: its mirror image. It aroused horror and disgust, but also fascination. Like other Bohemian communities elsewhere, it was an expression of the conflict at the heart of modern bourgeois culture itself – the rational discipline and self-control versus the realization of the true authentic desires of the self.

The Sartrean experience of authenticity developed into the Romantic image of the heroic intellectuals' calling, known from many intellectual cults even in popular culture. Even if painful, marginality is the sacral fate of the intellectuals, part of their function as the medium of redemption like Christ's death on the cross. Being excluded and 'hated by others ... reveals my objectivity', as Sartre declared (de Beauvoir, 1963: 164).[7] Impetuous use of alcohol and narcotics was part of the self-sacrifice that befalls the fate of the genius. Asked in a late interview about the risks involved in his lifestyle, Sartre said that it was more important for him to write something significant and meaningful than to be in good health. Success, fame and power are at most a very partial counter-present in the gift-exchange between the genius and his society. Sartrean Romanticism about marginality and the celebration of the self was, in its very essence 'highly ascetic, even Christian' (Arppe, 1998: 425–34).

The fascination and overindulgence in drink among the Lost Generation and the Sartrean tribal community were two examples, one literally and the other symbolically outside their societies, of a tradition of Romantic intellectuals sacrificing themselves and seeking authenticity with the use of alcohol and drugs that had been in existence since British Romanticism one hundred years earlier (Taylor, 1999). The same semi-sacral image of drug-taking artists repeated itself in the Beatnik generation (Margolis, 2002), and later in underground rock music (Martin, 1981). From its intellectual origins the search for authenticity spread out to youth cultures throughout the Western world in the 1960s as 'part of a radical turbulence of bourgeois consciousness that widened the dominant world-view as a response to the ideological flexibility required by modern capitalism' (Mäkelä, 1976: 68; Sulkunen, 2000: 76–7). Permissive attitudes towards sexuality, alcohol and drugs were essential elements in that turbulence. The Romantic values of authenticity clashed with the ascetic values of autonomy inherited from the Puritanism of the Protestant ethic.

The Romantic ethos and the state

Whereas the ideal of self-control was relatively easy to incorporate into the politics of emancipation through the state, as demonstrated by the history of the temperance movements, the Romantic ideals of distinctness and especially authenticity have been difficult to turn into political action. Ambivalence about the state is even today a central part of the crisis in life-regulation politics, and a great deal of this ambivalence is built into the structures of the Romantic ethos itself. On the one hand, the penchant towards the imaginary has inherently progressive potentials. On the other hand, Romantic individualism has often found allies among the politically conservative on the grounds of its suspicion of the notion of the public good. Sexuality, even more than intoxication, has constituted a mine-field in national politics of lifestyle because it directly involves legal regulations of social relationships in the family, and besides that, bears on national interests in the population question.

In the first half of the twentieth century, a Romantic type of republicanism had an influence especially in lifestyle politics, first in the American 'transcendentalism' of the late nineteenth century, represented by Henry Thoreau and Ralph Waldo Emerson, and later in the 1960s when the youth movement adopted them as their intellectual heroes. Although Thoreau was Rousseauian in his critique of civilization, he never accepted the idea of the general will, and certainly not as articulated by parliaments and the law. His republicanism was for a minimalist state.

The debate around D. H. Lawrence in the 1930s is a good case, particularly as it unfolded outside of the British, rather singularly anti-sexual context. For him, the object of emancipation in politics was to obey the law of the self:

> A man's self is a law unto itself, not unto himself, mind you ... The living self has one purpose only: to come into its own fullness of being ... But this coming into

full, spontaneous being is the most difficult thing of all ... The only thing man has to trust to in coming to himself is his desire and his impulse. But both desire and impulse tend to fall into mechanical automatism: to fall from spontaneous reality into dead or material reality ... All education must tend against this fall; and all our efforts in all our life must be to preserve the soul free and spontaneous ... the life activity must never be degraded into a fixed activity. (Lawrence, [1910] 1990: 91–2)

As Raymond Williams has emphasized, this is the context in which Lawrence's explorations of the sexual experience must be placed, to avoid that 'misunderstanding from which he so scandalously suffered' (Williams, 1961: 212). Sexuality was for him only the climax of human energy imperilled by 'our civilization', i.e. the bourgeois form of life. Property lies at the root of the systemic destruction of human dignity; industrialization aggravates the effect and the utilitarian (and nationalist) state's repression gives it the final touch. Democracy for Lawrence should not imply uniformity, and it contradicts any attempt 'to determine the being of any other man, or of any other woman' (Lawrence, [1910] 1990: 208). Community and human contact are, of course, the pride and dignity of citizens, but not equality in lifestyle. The legitimate function of the state is to provide security and to ensure a decent level of material satisfaction, but the rest should be left to the individuals. Thus Lawrence clearly antedates the resource theory of welfare that became the cornerstone of Nordic welfare state policies in the 1970s.

Lawrence represented the type of intellectual that Ron Eyerman (1994: 99–104) calls the dissenting tradition. He belonged neither to the Bloomsbury Group that included J. Maynard Keynes as well as Leonard and Virginia Woolf, nor the Fabian Society with George Bernard Shaw and Sydney and Beatrice Webb, although he was a working-class intellectual. He was never associated with any movement, but his influence was, perhaps for that reason, great in countries where intellectuals maintained a historical distance from the state. Among the Nordic countries, this was the case in Denmark and Norway. In Sweden and Finland, the ideals of civilization and progress through rational planning incorporated the intellectuals into the state and the labour movement, and consequently there was less room for Lawrencean individualism outside literary circles until the crisis of the last third of the twentieth century (Longum, 1997; Nielsen, 1997).

The democratization of intimacy

Tactful distance

The new middle-class sense of history is composed of the Romantic sensibilities discussed above. It distances itself from the past, but it is also its product in its concern for intimacy and in its suspicion towards the state. The sense of imaginary history that is so pronounced among the new middle class is not a sense of emancipation forfeited; it is a passion for agency, which is largely a passion for experiencing oneself as a person.

The people we interviewed on their attitudes towards drinking were proud of their cultivated manners as opposed to those who have not 'yet' reached their level, or those who have been carried away by their desire and become alcoholics, putrefied with over-done culture. It is essential that the Romantic sensibility, although it stresses authenticity and the inner experience of the person, is disposed to display these in public, not to close them away in the private soul sealed off from the regard of others. This is what creates the tension between originality and public avant-gardism of Romantic intellectuals, and the same tension appeared within the sense of intimacy of our bar visitors. They articulated this superiority as tact in relationships between people. Tact had to do with distinctness. They disliked bars where regulars are too snobbish to engage in conversations with strangers, and valued their own favourite pubs because there they 'always had someone to talk to':

Markus, dentist (M):   No, that's definitely one of the good things about [our bar] that is. It's just not in the reputation of being a pick-up place. You can really go in all by yourself and go over to the bar and talk to anyone you please and no one's going to have any ideas. (Sulkunen, 1992: 100)

On the other hand they considered other places disgusting for almost the same reason: .

Liisa, writer (F):   X is quite a desperate place really, lonely people trying to find company, to communicate, they all crowd into the pub and so there they are packed like smoked herring. Then after your sixth beer if you haven't been able to make contact with your neighbour who's usually of the opposite sex, he'll usually spill something so he'll have had it for that night, he'll have to leave or he'll be chucked out. (Sulkunen, 1992: 101)

Places where you cannot meet people – either because they are uninteresting or because they are too snobby and exclusive – are bad, whereas their own bars can also serve as resorts for silent lonely reading or meditation. The value, either positive or negative, is not in having company or being alone as such; it is the distinctness of the persons and the voluntary choice that either joins them or keeps them apart – the modality of willing in the semiotic sense. Tact is a matter of self-control but also a skill gained through training, education and practice.[8] Both solitude and sociability can be valued depending on whether they result from choice and display a cultural competence of discreteness, and they are abhorred when imposed by others, particularly when approaches by others are disgraceful and intrusive.

Tact is the essence of intimacy in modern human relationships in general. Anthony Giddens has used the term 'pure relationship' to describe what we normally call romantic love, and argued that it is only possible to the degree that both parties have autonomy to 'deliberate, judge, choose and act upon different possible courses of action' (Giddens 1992: 58, 185). Autonomy is indispensable for pure relationships not only for the obvious reason that they depend on choice, a willing continuation of the tie, but also for the same reason that inter-personal hygiene is important. Hygiene means more than just separation from virulent matter and control of the flow of invisible microbes between bodies. Touching becomes dangerous and always involves a risk that *cannot be seen*, it is there, in the other but I cannot control it. There can be no innocent touch; touching implies involvement between two individuals as whole persons inside as well as outside. Therefore the rules of touching must be made explicit and unambiguous as to what kind of personal relationships are inferred. Intimacy should be symmetrical, like the dangerous touch, but it should also be private and confined to a sphere where further contagion is impossible. Being the object of another person's sexual desires without intimacy is degrading because it denies the recognition of me as a person; but also to be interested in another person in that way is degrading because it is denying oneself the recognition of personhood, giving one part of me away to uncontrolled, raw desire.

Bars are public spaces where the conditions of intimacy have always been risky, and therefore they also have been objects of moral concern and social control. Potential sexual encounters make them perfect scenes for displaying and observing the principles of intimacy, and our discussions with the regulars were most instructive in this respect. Again, what could be objectively described as exactly the same event, can be looked at from completely antithetical points of view: from the point of view of the subject it might be called making new friends, meeting new people, or flirting elegantly. It is honourable to make advances. However, from the object's perspective such events may be viewed as derogatory and described in terms such as picking up, intrusion, disturbance, and egregious advances by stinking drunks.[9] Nobody wants to be picked up; yet all like to say they do it, at least faintly, taking a look, starting a conversation. The whole confusion about a pick-up relates to the very delicate matter of who is the agent of the occasion, and whether the other is recognized as a person.

Claude Lévi-Strauss has shown (1964: 74–91, 152; 1965) how cultural images represented in myths universally have this strange but intuitively understandable reflexive structure. In myths about food, for example, nature is represented as the raw material from which food is processed and elaborated through cultural classification and techniques of preparation. On the other hand, food may return to nature by rotting, getting spoiled or dirty, or because it has already been used for food (excrement). We regularly observe similar distinctions in representations of transgressing experiences such as intoxication.

In our interview discussions on picking up, the social space is represented by two categories of physical space. The spatial category *My Bar* in the city business district represents the cultural apex around which adult individuality revolves: volition and social skills in the interaction with

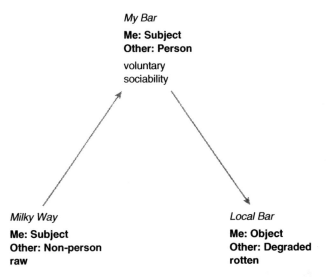

Figure 5.1 *Intimacy in an interview study on bars*

other people. It was contrasted with other places such as a dancing hall restaurant *Milky Way*, situated in a working-class or lower middle-class neighbourhood, where the speaker, the 'me', felt that he or she is the object of involuntary contacts, the 'other'. *Milky Way* was to *My Bar* what nature is to culture: the 'others' who go there are understood as non-persons, incompetent objects of physical desire who do not belong to 'us'. Another contrast to *My Bar* was represented by images of local bars in low income suburbs, frequented by old alcoholics, criminals and other down-and-outs. This contrast represents pollution or death. 'Me', the speaker if he or she went there, would again be reduced to an object, but the 'other' would also be degraded. Sociability in low-class locales is corrupted and decayed, since the imagery associated with it refers to mixing the two entities of culture and pure, uncultivated nature into something that is culture driven too far, exaggerated and dominated by asinine desires and instincts and therefore degraded and rotten: noisy, vulgar, drunken, smoky, dirty; a place for monsters to pick up each other.

The figurative, concrete expressions in this discourse refer to the context: *My Bar*, *Milky Way*, and *Local Bar*; but its structure refers to the universal distinction between culture and nature, and to the fancied history of evolution between the two. The 'other' is depicted either as raw, for example, a child or a savage who has not yet learned what it means to be intoxicated in a civilized way – and who has not attained the status required for engaging in it. Alternatively, the 'other' can be described as rotten, such as a dirty, stinking and irresponsible alcoholic, who has engaged in too much of the cultural practice of drinking but lost hold of the imagery and rituals that distinguish the experience from the mere visceral fact of being drunk.

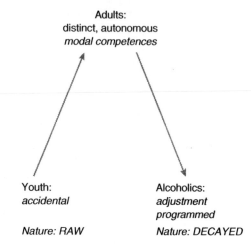

CULTURE: elaborated

Adults:
distinct, autonomous
modal competences

Youth:
accidental

Alcoholics:
*adjustment
programmed*

Nature: RAW

Nature: DECAYED

Figure 5.2   *Culture, nature and modal competences*

In an abstract form, Figure 5.1 can be redrawn as in Figure 5.2. *My Bar* stands for distinctness and autonomy between sovereign adult persons (our interviewees liked to use the expression 'we are adult persons' to justify their self-granted licence to indulge in drinking and talking in the bar). It is a product of culture, as cooked or otherwise elaborated food is the result of culture's operations on raw nature. The raw, immature sociability symbolized by *Milky Way* represents such uncultivated, immature or youthful human relationships. But culture's products, like adulthood, always risk decaying back to nature through over-processing, being used or neglected, and this may also take place in human interaction, as among alcoholics in the low class locals.

In the semiotic terminology I used in Chapter 2, referring to the French semiotician Eric Landowski, the 'raw' part represents action that is simply accidental; it is not regulated by modally competent subjects who are agents of their own actions. The mouldy boorishness of the local lower-class tavern stands for action that is programmed to take its course as if by custom or tradition, or simply adjusted to go along with what others experience and expect. No modal competences are attributed to their clients. Intimacy, as it develops in perfect complicity with hygiene, is control over the self through maintaining boundaries between the self and others, between the self and nature, and between different segments of the self. This regulation is only possible because 'we', the subjects, have modal qualities such as will-power to exercise choice and self-control, cultural qualifications to recognize what is in good taste and abilities to exercise taste allotted to us by our socialization to good manners. In middle-class consciousness the pinnacle of the fancied sense of history is selfhood which is both autonomous and intimate, surrounded by

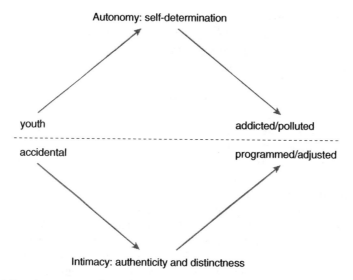

Figure 5.3 *Autonomy and intimacy*

others who respect that sovereignty and expect similar respect in return. As our interviewees said, they 'are like-minded'.

Recognition and respect

The yearning for intimacy is also a yearning for supremacy, like the fret about autonomy and distinctness. But it is an abstract and figurative superiority, a sense of sovereignty that seeks itself and its opposite in fancied images as in Figure 5.1. Although found to appear as the value of the shadowy margins of society, intimacy is in fact also an indispensable sentiment of modern subjectivity as agency, our capacity of experiencing ourselves and others as competent persons. It is a mirror image of autonomy, its 'underground' form, as in Figure 5.3.

The experience of intimacy requires mutual recognition and respect. If I feel that somebody is using me as an object or as an instrument of his or her interests, my experience of intimacy is violated; but equally, if I feel that I am, myself, relating to the other as an instrument of my interests without his or her participation, I experience a reduction of recognition in that relationship. There is no recognition *a priori*, it must be achieved in the course of the interaction itself, and therefore it is so vulnerable. Respect must be gained and it can be – and often is – lost.

Symbolic violations of intimacy are hard to bear but also difficult to avoid. This is why social pedagogy, parents' training programmes and interactive therapies focus on making a difference between oneself and the other, on listening more than on speaking. The difficulty is amplified because intimacy is no longer something that we can either find within ourselves, as if through self-exploration alone, or that would be given to us with our social roles, but it must be created and expressed for others to see. Charles Taylor (1992: Chapter VI) has made a very important observation in pointing out a parallel between the modern conception of personal authenticity and the Romantic conception of artistic production. Romantic art is conceived as *creation* rather than as *mimesis* or representation. Since the early nineteenth century, artists have been seen as heroes who have visions about the great issues of human existence and the ability to create cultural values. In the same way, authenticity in contemporary individualistic culture is not something that represents the inner reality which is already there, it *creates it* from whatever elements are available; and since what is available is very much the same for everyone, it is the *display* of one's preferences and pleasures rather than the preferences and pleasures themselves that create identity. In such culture, intimacy is public; in contrast, its regulation is confined to be a matter of the private free will rather than a matter of law or the public control apparatus. Transgression of the ordinary generates profits in terms of the appearance of authenticity, but at the same time it bears all the costs of marginality. These costs constitute the assets in the gift exchange between the self-sacrificing genius and society. It is not a coincidence that the Lost Generation and the Sartrean intellectuals were idols and models for the youth generations of the 1960s, by preparing the way for the cult of authenticity in the consumer society.

The consumer revolution

World-wide uprisings of students in 1968 and the political activism that ensued marked a turning point in the individualistic development in consumer capitalism. They were part of a revolution in the politics on lifestyle, 'a revolt against the father', in Gerard Mendel's (1968) words. It was a revolt against the father in the literal sense because it was generational. It was a revolt against the father in the metaphorical sense, because it went against all forms of paternalistic structures of domination. And it was a revolt against the father also in the second metaphorical sense that the young generation actually was claiming the right to autonomy and intimacy, which the young had been taught to respect by their parent generations.

The revolt took the form of 'liberalism', or I would rather say tolerance, in cultural policy, sexual policy, alcohol policy, even in drug policy, in a wave of reforms that were brought to completion by the mid-1980s. These included abortion laws (allowing abortion on non-medical grounds), sex education and contraception (Therborn, 2004), permissive policies on homosexuality, liberalized drinking laws in the Nordic countries, the UK and in many North American, New Zealand and Australian jurisdictions (Babor et al., 2003), a gradual onset of harm-reductionist drug policies (Tammi, 2007) and other measures increasing consumers' right to choose and to display their choices. With the new consumer society there was a lot to choose from. The Romantic spirit of capitalism was there, ready to welcome and consolidate the change. But as all other forms of consciousness, also the Romantic ethos functions not only as justification but also as critique. This duality will be the topic of the next chapter.

The saturated logic of justification

Now I have discussed all three elements of our model of justification, originally proposed by Luc Boltanski and Laurence Thévenot (1991): (1) the principles of belonging and differentiation that constitute the social bond; (2) the principle of the common good understood as progress; and (3) the principles of dignity and greatness as they appear in the sense of agency in its two aspects of authenticity and intimacy. Thus far, I have taken the reader through a historical journey, to show how difficult and complex the evolution of these principles of justification has been, and to stress how recently the universal acceptance of those principles has been achieved in many cases. Even when accepted, the application of these principles has not nearly always led to unanimity and consensus; on the contrary, they have been a matter of struggle and conflicts, although so many people now take them for granted, as they have been taken for granted in much of the literature on late, post- or trans-modernity. (It must be added in parenthesis that such principles could not serve as the grounds for justification unless they were, to some extent, taken for granted.)

Dictated by the nature of my endeavour, the presentation has been sketchy and selective. Many details, specifications and detours could be added and tricky questions asked. However, my task has been to show that the principles of justification, however hard-laboured in the past, have served the development of capitalism to the point of saturation, where the principles themselves have become ambivalent. All ambivalences point in the same direction. The issues of equality and class as both structure and action, as treated in Bourdieu's work, are ambivalences about agency. The issue of progress, far from concerning only the human capacity to control nature, has been about building the basis of cooperative human interaction within society. Constructing the contracting and self-controlling individual, with claims and rights to intimacy, has been the objective and the result of legal development, of modern political institutions, and of hard work in schools, associations and self-educating groups.

Today these principles no longer work as grounds of justification in the same way as they have before, because they have become saturated. Since we cannot observe the process of saturation *in abstracto*, and by only looking at the past, we next move to the three great domains of lifestyle regulation, in which the saturation has appeared more concretely, namely the coming of the new consumer society, the evolution of the welfare state, and finally, preventive social policy in which the encounters of the state and citizens take place on a face-to-face basis. In each of these domains, all three principles of justification have served as grounds for criticism as well as legitimation, both in the consciousness of the pulpit and in the mundane consciousness of everyday life, and I shall use analyses of all these to demonstrate my point.

Notes

1 This classification has been identified among drug users in countries as different as Great Britain, the USA, the Nordic countries, Estonia (Lalander and Salasuo, 2005) or Australia (Fitzgerald, 2002). Sometimes the sense of superiority among drug users is contrasted with the boorishness of normal everyday life and turned into 'sub-cultural capital' (Thornton, 1996), often with tragic consequences as among heroin addicts in a small Swedish town studied by Philip Lalander (2003).

2 This is why Bourdieu ([1979] 1984: 467) could say that classification also classifies the classifiers.

3 This was a group interview study of attitudes towards alcohol policy among influential people in *Lahti*, a town of about 70,000 inhabitants in Finland (Sulkunen, 1997a: 270).

4 In semiotic theory, these discursive operations are called de-clutching (*debrayage*)and re-clutching (*embrayage*). In the first, the author detaches herself from the world she is describing; in the second, she re-establishes a position for herself among those who appear in the description (the Brits) (Sulkunen and Törrönen, 1997b).

5 *The pending narrative* is a semiotic structure often employed in persuasive texts. It sets the stage and distributes the roles in the story, so that the author and the reader are on the same side, opposing the malefactor who is external to the text. But the narrative is not brought to an end, the struggle must continue, and the common destiny of the author and the reader depends on their determination (Sulkunen and Törrönen, 1997b).

6 Hygienists were the nineteenth-century predecessors of the professions now called public health and health promotion. Even then not only medically trained persons but also charities, churches, settlement workers and other working-class reformers attempted to improve the sanitary conditions in cities. The first Chair of Hygiene was established in the year II (of Robespierre' calendar) in the Medical Faculty of Paris (Vigarello, 1985: 182–4).

7 He was expressing in this way a deep-rooted conviction among French intellectuals about the blessing – and the curse – of being in the margins, ever since Flaubert. Pierre Bourdieu (Bourdieu and Wacquant, 1992; Bourdieu, [1980] 1990a), as well as Alain Touraine (1978), although in many ways so different, identify themselves as marginal intellectuals among sociologists, in distinction to those who are 'engaged'. Bourdieu explicitly considered the 'compulsive engagement' to be the inherent contradiction, even dishonesty, in Sartre's portrait of himself as an autonomous intellectual.

8 In semiotic theory, four kinds of modalities can be distinguished: willing, competence (knowing how to do or be), duty and ability. Willing and competence are inherent capacities of the person; ability involves a helper who provides the means to perform a task, and duty involves somebody (a dispenser) who has set a task or a goal for the action. Therefore, the first two modal dimensions are called 'endotactic' and the two latter are 'exotactic' (Sulkunen and Törrönen, 1997a). Modalities are used to express values such as subjectivity based on free will, as in the example above. Treating other persons as if they had no modal qualities is tactless.

9 The same sense of distinctness is expressed by avant-garde drug consumers when they compare their club scenes with ordinary pubs:

> As a girl I just know that when you're out at the pub, there's always some bastard trying to grab you and you're like, hey, that's my body, what are you doing? When you go to techno parties, there's none of that. You can talk to a guy and know he's not after something, because at techno parties you don't pick up people. But when you're out at the pub, every damn chick is looking down upon you, hey, who do you think you are? And the guys think you're just a damn object that everyone can grab hold of. (A Swedish techno clubber, Sjö, 2005: 36)

6

The New Consumer Society
and Its Critics

We consume advertising when we eat and drink, we nourish ourselves
with them. We must denounce things in order to allow people to enjoy
them. Things that are not what they pretend to be are institutions – objective
non-spirit (*objektiver Ungeist*). Also the concept of *Charaktermaske* has
melted into air: behind masks there are no faces any longer.

(Hans-Jürgen Krahl, 1971)

The arrival of the consumer revolution

The consumer society has been one of the three most important topics in discourses of justification in modern capitalism, both in mundane consciousness
and in the consciousness of the pulpits. The other two, to be discussed in the
next two chapters, have been the welfare state and life-regulation policy. The
three principles of justification that I have analyzed – those of belonging and
differentiation, those concerning the definition of the common good, and
those defining dignity and greatness – have been part of these discourses, each
employed in critical as well as affirmative uses. I begin the examination of the
saturation of these principles with the topic of the consumer society, because
in some ways it forms the foundation of the points I shall be making of the
other two.

In everyday language the term 'consumer society' is used with admiring
as well as disparaging overtones, referring to affluence and well-being but
also to waste, bad taste and useless pleasures. In theoretical social science
the concept has mostly suffered a bad reputation. As a vision of advanced
capitalism it has an air of ideological complacency. It depicts consumers as
people with common uniform interests rather than as conflicting classes.
It hints at general affluence and suggests that consumption is the most
important content of life and support of group-sense, but does not account
for inequalities and other determinants of social structure, notably production and the labour market. On the other hand, consumer society has
been the object of moral, economic and political condemnation for giving
priority to material values at the expense of spiritual, cultural, social and
environmental interests. In particular, the Romantic spirit of capitalism
functions as an affirmation of the consumer society but also as its critique.
While offering unforeseen possibilities of meeting insatiable desires by the

largest number of consumers ever, it also turns consumption into uniform and standardized mass culture, with little possibility of really authentic choice.

It is nevertheless a fact that alongside wars, revolutions, inequalities, racial and political repression, poverty and despotism, the twentieth century produced in advanced Western countries a phenomenal growth in consumption possibilities that has no parallel in human history, not relatively speaking and certainly not in absolute terms. The earlier consumer booms of the sixteenth and eighteenth centuries in England (Mukerji, 1983; McKendrick et al., 1982) and still in the nineteenth century Europe (Williams, 1982) were limited to small elites, but the development of the new consumer society in the twentieth century was a phenomenon of the masses and encompassed the structural foundations of industrial society. In retrospect, this change was so drastic that it has been given dramatic names, such as the European golden era (Therborn, 1995), the golden years of capitalism (Hobsbawm, 1995), the glorious thirty years (Fourastié, 1979) or even the second French revolution (Mendras, 1988). It changed the make-up and technology of everyday life. It reconfigured social structures as well as people's way of thinking about themselves and about their relationships with others. It brought to ordinary people a quantity and diversity of goods, pleasures and uses of time that either had never existed before or had been accessible only to the very privileged. Luxury was democratized and became part of everyday life. The pleasures of consumption and sensuality became publicly presentable, in everyday life as well as in the media and in marketing, whereas they had earlier been excluded from public discourses and left to the private sphere. The Weberian values of industrial society – frugality, industriousness and achievement orientation – were replaced by post-industrial or postmodern values that stress pleasure for its own sake and cherish its public presentation. These values spurn any attempts to exercise public control over private consumption. The Romantic ethos of capitalism seems to have gotten the upper hand.

However, the consumer society brought with it a double problem. First, consumption itself is risky. The threat of want has been replaced by threat of excess in food, drink, drugs, tobacco, amusement, shopping, gaming and other pastimes. Consumer items contain substances that make perfidious contacts between people, but unlike microbes they have effects that cannot be known to the user. They are also baffling to the producer. The second part of the problem is the sovereign consumer itself, the topic of this chapter. Consumers are autonomous contractors on the market but they are vulnerable in their sense of autonomy and intimacy. Any risks involved in consumption, but also any attempts to minimize the risks by public interference, are suspected of being interpreted as a symbolic violation of that fragile sovereignty. But why is this sovereignty so fragile, threatened not only by any attempts to constrain the consumers' choice for the purposes of protection, but also by the very marketing techniques and product differentiation that make choice possible?

The imperative of choice

The consumer society has put ordinary life into a quandary that in previous generations had to be faced by very few people: choice. The shift from self-provision to the cash economy introduced a new element of choice for millions of Europeans in the post-war decades. Increasingly, choice has penetrated our lifestyle as a whole. The French sociologist of food practices, Claude Fischler (1990), described the perpetuity of choice of food with the term *gastro-anomie*. The British sociologist Alan Warde (1994) has stated respectively that the modern consumer, facing the endless necessity of choice and no guidance from clear norms or traditions, is in the situation of Durkheim's anomic suicide candidate amidst the anxieties of uncertainty.

The obligation to choose imposes itself not only in the area of consumption here and now: lifestyles chosen today have enduring consequences for the life-cycle of the person and the family in the future. Educational careers have become longer and more complex, demanding unremitting reflection and decisions. Sexuality became radically separated from procreation with the introduction of the contraceptive pill in the 1960s. The institution of the private family has started to adopt new forms, also adding to the imposed freedom to seek satisfaction in the 'fullness of life', to use the words of D.H. Lawrence. New dimensions of choice have opened up as medical technologies have continually improved and new life-regulating technologies such as genetic testing have developed since the 1980s. Personal life has become a project that needs planning, decisions, and resources to make those decisions, but there is even less certainty than before about the outcome of the expectations. The degree of contingency has increased.

Astounding mass consumption

Although in retrospect the change has been dramatic, bewilderment and disbelief continued for a long time about whether any improvement in 'living standards' actually was taking place. As Eric Hobsbawm (1995: 257–68) has pointed out, the change was vertiginous seen backwards from the present, and, even in the life course of one single generation, the improvements in nutrition, comfort and the conduct of everyday life were concrete and noticeable during the third quarter of the century. However, in day-to-day life the change took place gradually, in small steps and one detail at a time. Young people had difficulty in making a distinction between the change that was taking place in their environment and the change in their own individual lives from childhood to adults. The new technology of everyday life was revolutionary for parents who had recently returned from war to peace but was taken for granted by their children. The family home in an apartment house near the city centre, with electricity, central heating, running water, refrigerator, washing machine, telephone, radio and finally television, was for the young an ordinary bundle of necessities. The country life of their grandparents without such facilities seemed strange and antediluvian. The private car expanded the spatial scope of individuals, changed urban structures, made possible the growth of major cities, helped to concentrate production and distribution of commodities and thus propelled the growth of consumption possibilities further. All this happened fast, but from an individual's perspective the change was piecemeal.

Ideological reasons contributed to the difficulty of seeing the change. European labour movements had for more than one hundred years, fought against want and wretchedness, to match working-class aspirations of decency with the dignity of autonomy and intimacy in consumption. American trade unions incorporated in their ideology elements from the populist radicalism of rural areas, which always has been critical of big cities, white-collar idleness and capitalist profiteering (Dubofsky, 2000; Hofstadter, 1955). Admitting that the new urban life was an improvement could have undermined their credibility and in any case required a radical revision of their doctrine. The improving quantity and quality of mass consumption items available were confusing and aroused suspicion: was misery really being eradicated, was life really getting easier for the masses, or was everything just trickery and the reality behind it as wretched as before – albeit in a new way?

Malthusian pessimism

The ambivalence regarding the new consumer affluence was articulated in the tension between the two variants of critical awareness of modernity, rationalist and Romantic, which were discussed in the two preceding chapters. As we have seen, the rationalist consciousness was far from elitist – on the contrary, its ascetic dimensions were most successful whenever they met the approval of the organized working classes. This made it possible to represent the state as the executor of the general will of the people for their self-improvement as well as for the improvement of their conditions. Still, the asceticism had a Malthusian morality attached to it. Thomas Malthus has been the emblem of repressive economic liberalism since the publication of his *Essay on the Principle of Population* ([1798] 1993), where he argued that income support policies such as the Speenhamland Act would only lead to increased misery through population growth. The sexual instinct is greater than the instinct for nutrition and leads always to birth rates that exceed the growth in food production. Hunger is the mechanism that holds back the population size, which tends to expand geometrically whereas food production can, at the maximum, grow arithmetically. Economic development automatically generates new needs, and wretchedness inevitably results.

The ascetic critics of affluence in the post-war Western world similarly argued that economic growth in capitalism in fact generates more needs than it satisfies, and thus results in misery. The need-generating factor was no longer population growth but the qualitative requirements of the labour force. In fact, the key issue in Western social policy since the First World War had been insufficient fertility (Therborn, 1995: 38–9), which was one of the important arguments in favour of supportive social policies. According to the orthodox Marxist version of the ascetic criticism (*Der Staatsmonopolistische Kapitalismus*, 1972: 276–80; Mehnert, 1973: 51–67; Autorenkollektiv, 1974: 115–31), affluence in mass consumption is illusionary, since workers pay for it with more intensive input in the labour process, in training and in providing for the future generation of workers. The surplus value that is squeezed out of labour increases with increasing productive capacity of capital, and in fact the rate of exploitation goes up, contrary to what might be deemed from improving working conditions, from shorter annual working time, from almost universal attendance at public secondary schools and exploding tertiary education, from better social security and health care, and from the unforeseen wealth of home technology and commodities that became available to ordinary wage earners. The *reproduction deficit* – the minus-marked balance between the requirements placed on the reproduction of labour power and the workers' income (salaries and state assistance combined) – was accompanied by the increasingly alarming environmental calamity that began to be felt in the late 1960s. Finally, global exploitation jolts Third World countries into misery, making them dependent on the raw material markets in advanced economies, on the one hand, and on their industrial products, on the other, which leads to an unrecoverable path of underdevelopment (e.g. Frank, 1969).

The Romantic critique of use values

Colin Campbell (1987) began his seminal work on the Romantic ethic of capitalism from his bewildered observation of the thirst for the imaginary, strange and hidden true self amidst the student radicalism of the 1960s in Britain and the USA. In France, the 'artistic' critique of mass consumption made claims for self-realization, authenticity and freedom around the events of 1968 (Boltanski and Chiapello, 2005: 521–52). In British (Cohen, [1972] 1980; Martin, 1981) and American youth culture (Roszak, 1968 [1995]; Bell, [1976] 1996) the Romantic ethos was important from the start. In the Nordic and German-speaking countries, it actually had relatively little weight in the build-up stage of the student radicalism in the 1960s and only became important later. The key issues emerged first from the rational side of the modern ideals – progress, universalism and the potential capacity of the national state to procure justice, given that it meets the ideals of the *Rechtsstaat*, the political philosophy that in the Nordic countries has been integral to the nationalist movement (Slagstad, 1998).

The differences in the argumentation about alcohol and drug policies are again a striking example. As discussed in the previous chapter, transgression and intoxication have always been important in Romantic intellectual movements, for example, in literary circles in England in the late eighteenth century (Taylor, 1999), or among the American 'Lost Generation' writers in early twentieth-century Paris (Room, 1984), or among the post-war Existentialists (Arppe, 1998). These movements were exponents of the Romantic sense of history, frontline fighters of the modern consumer society against Puritanical bourgeois boorishness.

In contrast, when the alcohol control systems in Norway, Sweden and Finland were liberalized in the 1960s to allow the more deregulated retail of beer in grocery stores in the mid-1960s, the arguments of the young generation had very little to do with liberating the self or seeking the imaginary, not even with the pleasures of drinking. The justifications were based on first, the public good, and, second, equality. For example, the Swedish Students Federation, quickly followed by the gymnasts, argued in 1965 that if beer was of better quality (i.e. had higher alcohol content) and was more readily available, students would stop drinking vodka and other strong drinks, and social problems would be reduced. Equality, on the other hand, would be assured in this way since the limited network of alcohol monopoly stores discriminated against the rural population and – it was said – against the working class (Sulkunen, 2000: 79–80).

It is paradoxical that in Nordic and German-speaking social science the Romantic criticism was adopted only later, with the new wave of Marxism in the 1970s. On the surface, this new interest in the works of Marx was a stern affair, a critical intellectual praxis relying on serious social science rather than personal, moral and aesthetic judgement. But underlying the often technical complexity of the argument, a Lawrencean style of Romantic criticism can be detected. The tenet of that argument, too, was that despite the growing availability and cheapness of commodities, advanced capitalism cannot answer the real, authentic needs of consumers and society. But what are 'real needs'? The Romantic answer to the question was different from the neo-Malthusian one.

American over-production/under-consumption theories of the early 1960s were well known and fed into the Romantic critique. For example, Kenneth Galbraith (1962) had diagnosed the affluent society to be inept in directing resources to satisfy needs. The market favours private consumption of commodities, notably the private car, at the expense of collective goods such as public transport. With a more devotedly Marxist approach, Paul Baran and Paul Sweezy (1966) assessed that American late capitalism tended towards unfree markets manipulated by monopolies. These economies are cost-efficient but not price-flexible: industrial corporations are interested in their costs but not willing to cut prices, which would increase demand. Surpluses accumulate in excessive profits, which cannot be further invested. The spending of the surplus is the key to maintaining monopoly capitalism in function, and sales promotion – advertising, brand development and planned obsolescence of products – is one answer to this.

The new Marxian critique of bourgeois consumption in the 1970s was not satisfied with the critique of monopoly capitalism; it searched the corrupting effects of capitalism in the commodity form itself. It recognized the principle that Marx developed in the *Grundrisse*: production not only produces the object of consumption for the subject; it also produces the subject for the object:

> Production also gives consumption its specificity, its finish ... the object [of consumption] is not an object in general, but a specific object which must be consumed in a specific manner, to be mediated in its turn by production itself. Hunger is hunger, but the hunger gratified by cooked meat eaten with a knife and fork is a different hunger from that which bolts down raw meat with the aid of hand, nail and tooth. Production thus produces not only objectively but subjectively. Production thus creates the consumer. (Marx, [1859] 1973: 88)

The capitalist mode of production therefore corrupts not only the material world of consumption but also consumers themselves. An influential German example of theorizing consumption from this starting point was W.F. Haug's (1971, see also Lindner, 1977) analysis of commodity aesthetics (*Warenästhetik*). For capitalist production, it is inessential whether commodities actually meet a need; to serve their function in capitalist accumulation they only have to meet a paying hand. For this, every marketable commodity must give promises of its use value with its packaging, design and brand image. As capitalist markets develop, the value of usefulness gets increasingly detached from the original use values; *Schein* (appearance) becomes more important than *Sein* (real nature of the thing). The commodities are encrusted in a shell of imaginary use value that only serves the purpose of circulating exchange value.

The critique of deformed use values encompassed not only consumption – it was attached to a wider philosophical and ideological interpretation of Marxian theory of value as a theory of capitalist alienation, a bridge between his political economy and his philosophical humanism (Schanz, 1974: 97–8, 103–6; Pohrt, 1976). Helmut Reichelt argued that the commodity form chops products of labour into two separate things: representatives of abstract exchange value and objects of consumption, or use values. According to this variety of Marxism, sometimes called *capital-logic*, commodity theory should be seen as a dialectical demonstration of Marx's early views of alienation to the effect that capitalism turns labour into a hostile instrument of repression against its own subject. It was a meta-theory of capitalist social relationships as well as a theory of the immanent historical development of capitalism. (Reichelt, 1970: 17–27, 73–89, 126–50) Oskar Negt (1973) and Alfred Krovoza (1976) similarly argued that *Capital* should not be seen as an economic theory but as a theory about the repressive force of the value form, which extends to the hub of social relationships. Wage labour breaks time and personality into segments and desexualizes human relationships. The emancipating interest of knowledge to reveal the repressive capacity of the dual value form sometimes acquired revolutionary vehemence, as in the writings of the student radical Hans-Jürgen Krahl:

> The emancipation of the human species is no longer possible by unveiling the ruling class in persons ... We must divulge Things – the debris which late capitalism produces and in which its social relationships are crystallized. The commodity form in which use values already display the signs of its death bears in it the tendency of its extinction. The package has taken a final victory over the

product – the use value is dead. We consume advertising when we eat and drink, we nourish ourselves with them. We must denounce things in order to allow people to enjoy them. Things that are not what they pretend to be are institutions – objective non-spirit (*objektiver Ungeist*). Also the concept of *Charaktermaske* has melted into air: behind masks there are no longer any faces (Krahl, 1971: 84, my translation)

At the end of the day, the Marxian vocabulary was, after all, of no great help in making moral and aesthetic judgements on the astounding new wealth of commodities more scientific and objective. The Marxian critique of political economy simply has not a great deal to say about use values. If the whole theory of capitalist reproduction in its complexity is of little relevance for understanding how commodities get their use values in consumption, even less helpful is its mere nucleus, the abstract theory of the value form, in understanding this. Its philosophical re-readings by the young generation of Marxian social scientists in the 1970s hardly veiled the underlying Romantic, even Lawrencean sensibility of emancipation from the constraints of the System, which spoils the satisfaction for which it has produced the means.

The political economy of signs

The semiotic turn

The engine of capitalist accumulation is the production of value in the labour process and its circulation in the market and in consumption. To participate in the circulation of value, every commodity must bear *some* use value, i.e. answer to a demand or satisfy *some* 'need'; otherwise also the exchange value – abstract labour – that it represents, gets lost. The question is about *how* use values get attached to commodities. This question belongs to the theory of goods (*Warenlehre*) which Marx throws out in the early pages of *Das Kapital* from the body of the value form without further ado.

'Malthusian' critiques of capitalist reproduction attempted to found also use values (and not only the exchange value, or price) of commodities in work, ignoring that already in Adam Smith's time consumption was only marginally related to needs emerging from work. Circuitous theorizing about the 'labelling effects' of the commodity form on use values and on consumer subjectivity were no less convincing. Marxian *capital-logical* critique of the commodity form attempted to rescue the theory of use values from the labour theory of value but failed. Neither needs nor their repression can be explained by the capitalist accumulation process itself. Attempts to establish such explanations lead to nothing other than imperious moralizing. Behind the 'value form' prowls, derailed and repressed, the same *homme bourgeois* who was to be emancipated from his character masks in the first place by the critique of political economy as a reflexive alternative to positivist bourgeois social science. Obviously, no theories of advanced capitalism, and even less the original Marxian theory of capitalism, can be translated into a sociological theory of consumption, and least of all into an emancipating diagnosis of mass consumption society. Such diagnosis calls for a theory of culture or meaning. The dearth of such a theory in the work of Marx was a key factor that turned away the generation of social scientists who were interested in reinterpreting it as an instrument of sociological emancipation in contemporary capitalism, as witnessed later by one of its influential advocates in Scandinavia, the Danish philosopher Hans-Jørgen Schanz (1996).

Although the Marxist critiques of the consumer society were proposed as a critical alternative to positivist social science, they nevertheless represented the mainstream idea of 'society' as a 'thing in itself', with its laws 'sui generis' without equivalent in human consciousness, cunningly conditioning both social life and the ideas we have about it. Instead, the new post-Marxist sociology of consumption involved a major shift also in basic social theory, incubating in the wings of the semiotic turn in sociology (Giddens, 1979). The ingredient from which it constructed its ideas about the uses of things was *meaning* rather than need (of humans) or functioning (of the system). Meaning, of course, was by no means a new theme in modern social theory. But when Giddens (1979) declared that the master trend in social sciences of the twentieth century is to recognize that people know a great deal about social life, this sounded fresh and useful especially in the study of lifestyles and consumption practices. The uses of things cannot be reduced to their capacities to satisfy consumers' preconditioned needs, of which people are either unaware, or which are unaffected by their awareness of them. They cannot be explained by the functioning of capitalist accumulation either. Users know a great deal about what they want and what they do with things, and this knowledge interacts with the satisfaction they get from consumption. An important part of this satisfaction is that objects in use transmit messages about the users and their relationships with each other. They have symbolic as well as material functions. Objects are socially constructed *in use*, not only socially produced in the labour process. The political economy of production must be replaced by a political economy of the sign, as Jean Baudrillard (1968) declared in one of his early books.

Giddens wrote that people know a *great deal* about social life. This is important: we must have many kinds of knowledge about social relationships, language, institutions, the meaning of gestures, etc. in order to act coherently and understandably in our social roles and contexts. But we *do not know the social world completely* – no one could, because there is no such thing as the complete social world. Meaning is not a property of things; it is not even a property of language: words, phrases or utterances. It is an ephemeral relationship between objects, their producers, marketers, users – and non-users. Use value is always something extra, beyond needs and functions but also beyond encoded meanings and decoded interpretations; something that nobody controls. Pasi Falk (1994: 93–150) has said that we always consume 'supplements' to the objects we use. Another way of saying it comes from Bruno Latour (1993): the translation of needs and technologies of production (knowledge) into objects and their uses is always imperfect and contingent. A third way to express the same idea comes from the French semiotician Eric Landowski (2005), who has said that the most meaningful interactions among people, and between people and things, are always risky because they are not completely predictable. They leave room for interpretation – and misinterpretation. No plan can control it and no sociology of knowledge can, even in principle, predict the outcome.

Let me take a simple example from consumption of commodities. A certain kind of chair in a living room communicates, and we need knowledge to interpret the message. The chair is for sitting (human body structure explains the basic shape of chairs), but it also says something about the owner's wealth, about their taste, and probably thereby about their social position and cultural background. We know this because we recognize the style and associate it with other styles and other kinds of people who pre-fer those styles. But styles are cunning: they change in time, they depend on technologies and economies of production and distribution, and they also are sensitive to the context. What people recognize and appreciate in a specimen depends on how well they know the conventions of its style, its history and its relationship to other styles, and on how they contextualize it. This is what Bourdieu ([1979] 1984: 114–15) meant by the term 'cul-tural capital'. Some people may recognize in a painting just 'a man with a golden helmet', others know and find it more relevant that 'this is Rembrandt'. Placing the chair in a certain way in a context, for example, a Rococo chair in a modern room, is using its styled properties for commu-nicating, perhaps giving it a special status as a piece of a family patrimony. All artful objects – consumer items are designed and therefore 'artful' – are in this way both specimens of a style as well as representative objects in themselves. They represent the need or function they serve (for example, sitting) and they represent their style and its relationships with other styles.

Expressive authenticity

The illusions of representation

From this perspective, the question of the use values becomes the question of representation. Do we have to reverse the radical assumption of politi-cal economy that commodities represent abstract labour rather than needs and desires, and what would be the consequences of such a reversal? Since commodities *are* exchanged and there is 'order in the world of riches' in the sense that the exchange takes place in markets with at least somewhat pre-dictable prices, do we have to conclude that people do have comparable desires, that 'in our bodies we feel the same hunger and our hearts obey the same desire for prestige'? In that way we would return to the Romantic anthropology of the 'authentically human', as the *capital-logical* criticism of the consumer society did – inadvertently – when it rode out to rescue use values from the inexorable laws of capitalist accumulation. Or do commodities represent needs, albeit inadequately, that are socially constructed in a deterministic way in the labour process, as in the 'neo-Malthusian' orthodox Marxist critique? Neither the anthropology of authenticity nor deterministic constructionism seems tenable to me within the framework of semiotic sociology, which would see the world of commodities in the light of signification rather than utility. The residue of the 'supplement' is too wide; the imperfection of the translation between needs and the language that objects speak is too significant.

As to the anthropology of authenticity, Theodor Adorno ([1964] 2003) already dealt it a death blow in his vehement critique of German Existentialism, especially Karl Jaspers and Martin Heidegger, in his pamphlet *The Jargon of Authenticity* in 1964. The Existentialists, pretending to perform a critique of the dehumanization of man in industrial society through celebrating the sense of self-realization, in fact provide nothing but a defence and ontological justification of the social conditions of domination in capitalism. Such a philosophy leaves no room for asking in what way society and psychology allow human beings to experience themselves authentically:

> The societal relation, which seals itself off in the identity of the subject, is desocietalized into an in-itself. The individual, who himself can no longer rely on any firm possession, holds on to himself in his extreme abstractness as the last, supposedly unlosable possession. (Adorno, 2003: 95)

As nobody is beyond the conditioning effects of both biology and historical social conditions, Heideggerian Existentialism gives us meagre consolation: we can always gratify ourselves with

> [the] stale reminder of self-identity as something which gives distinction, both in regard to being and meaning. This 'unlosable' element, which has no substratum other than its own concept, the tautological selfness of the self, is to provide the ground, as Heidegger calls it, which the authentic possess and the inauthentics lack. (ibid.: 53)

The authentics stipulate what it is to be human, believing that their stipulations are not dependent on the language they use, presenting the authentically human as an invariable 'super-natural nature-category'. In this way, the Existentialist defence of authenticity becomes mere jargon, a form of magical expression, as if by senseless repetition it could regain what Walter Benjamin called the 'aura' of the original work of art, which gets destroyed in the culture of mass reproduction. The critique of alienation slithers away from Existentialist ontologies of Being and the self to the suspicion of mass production and mass consumption and to a regret of dissolving (class) differences. This is why Adorno considered the jargon of authenticity to be a defence of capitalist relations of domination in the disguise of philosophy.

In Existentialist usage, this self-sanctifying authenticity decays into a mumble of empty declarations instead of a real critique of the social conditions that both produce the potentialities of human emancipation and repress them. According to Critical Theory, the task of philosophy and social science is to reveal this contradiction. The capital-logical Marxism in search of authentic use-values in fact endeavoured but failed to continue that kind of immanent critique in its pursuit to show in what ways the capitalist commodity form not only disfigures the objects of consumption but also constitutes the subjectivity of those who use them.

Immanent critique of lifestyles, in its turn, tends towards untenable constructionism, when it is consistently applied. Bourdieu criticized this kind of constructionism in his arguments against the objectifying determinism of traditional class theory. To reveal the contradictions between emancipation and repression one needs to have an intellectual position to make judgements that are not themselves cluttered by the labelling effects of capitalism, or in Bourdieu's terms, by the interests of the game. Adorno, as well as Bourdieu himself, was committed to the modern ideal of intellectuals' exteriority to society (Wagner, 2001b: 21–31), from which a sociological critique of consumption, culture and also intellectual practice was to be possible, and from which the distinction between low and high culture could be maintained. Both went through great trouble in defending this position, Adorno with much less success than Bourdieu.

Judgements on what is authentic and what is socially constructed, as if from an outsider's position, depend on the idea of representation. If needs, lifestyles and tastes are claimed to be socially determined, even when they appear to result from personal authentic choice, they are seen as signs that *represent* the social condition from which they are issued, whether participants themselves recognize the representation or not. One should be able to distinguish the character masks from the faces behind them. In Adorno's critique of mass culture, the distinction between representations of the authentic and the constructed still lurks behind the logic of immanence.

However, Hans-Jürgen Krahl's comment quoted above was prophetic in its insight that 'behind the character masks there are no longer any faces'. In the process of saturation, a real crisis of representation took place. When the principles of justification of industrial capitalism become saturated, relations of representation break down, and vice versa, when relations of representation blow apart, the discourses of justification stop making sense. This happens in three ways. First, the signs of belonging and difference become ambiguous. As Bourdieu argued, class *habitus* is neither dictated by objective class positions nor is it freely chosen by individual action. The ambivalence itself stresses the value of agency as a principle of dignity and greatness. We are always worried about being interpreted as acting out of necessity whereas we strive to present ourselves as agents of free choice. Second, however, the search for autonomy and intimacy as principles of dignity and greatness becomes self-defeating because the search in itself is a structural necessity issuing from consumer capitalism. Third, therefore, the sense of progress, the modern principle of the common good as expansion of autonomy and intimacy, becomes confused. What in our lifestyles today could represent progress if nothing represents group identity or the authentic self either?

The American cultural theorist Fredric Jameson (1998) has argued in his critique of representation that in modern art the primary representation – what a painting shows, for example ('this is a soldier with a golden helmet') – is dominated by the aesthetics of form, the way a painting is related to a style ('this is Rembrandt') and by the originality (the 'aura') of the work and its author; or by the charismatic ideology in Bourdieu's ([1979] 1984: 28–32) terms. Finally, the work of art only represents 'art', the institution. Mere silence can represent 'music' as in the sonata for piano 4'33' by John Cage where the pianist does not play a single note. An empty room may represent 'graphic art', or a reel of more than 5 hours showing nothing but the face of a sleeping person represents the 'art of the cinema', as in Andy Warhol's film *Sleep* (1963). According to Jameson, in post-modern culture, art no longer represents anything, it becomes a pastiche, imitation that only represents itself as a source of unmediated pleasure. There is no authenticity behind a representation because there is no representation, or representation turns into mockery of itself. The distinction between low and high, between sublimation and desublimation, between elaborated and banal, or between serious and fun, can no longer be maintained.

Similar critiques of representation have been presented by Jean Baudrillard (1976; 1981) who has argued that in the world where every-thing is manufactured, prepared and imitated, the search for correspon-dence between the model and the original is futile and presumptuous. What matters is the effect in itself. Representation becomes a simulacrum that participates in what is represented – for example, it is not meaningful to attempt to make a distinction between political reality and its media rep-resentation, since both are indispensable parts of the same reality. This is very close to Bourdieu's idea of the field, where the value of investments and profits in a game have no fixed relationship to what they represent (in terms of physical satisfaction, use values or aesthetic perfection) outside the relationships of the game itself.

Displaying difference

In the same way, representation becomes illusionary in mass consumption. The amplification of choice into a principle that permeates the whole way of life – even of the most deprived – is not a simple and mechanical out-come of the multiplication of possibilities. It is a mode of mundane con-sciousness, of which the discourses from the pulpits of post-modernity or philosophical critiques of representation are academic articulations. The critiques of use values from the Marxian starting points were theoretical failures largely because they did not account for the fact that the con-sumer liberation has been real with real consequences. Authenticity, which modern consumers seek, is *not behind the mask* of socially conditioned choice, it is *in the mask itself.* The authentic person cannot find herself by looking deep into her inner constitution as a representative of the human race, or of a social group assigned to her by the laws of social differentiation, or even as a unique individual with the true self. Authenticity must be constantly *expressed* and reproduced, tested and adjusted to reactions from others.

Choice is the currency of this expressive authenticity. While it is true that it occupies an enormously important role in our lives today, this does not mean that it did not exist before, nor does it mean that it would be in unlimited supply to everyone now. People have always had room for individual variation, as the literature on fashion shows, even before and certainly after the commercial success of mass-produced industrial clothing. Objective constraints on most people's lives have not been lifted. Food, shelter, security, health, mobility, knowledge or need for sympathy and love, are now as indispensable as they ever have been in less affluent societies. Most people do not have enough money, time or cultural capital to make choices between other than a limited variety of options as to what to eat, what to wear or how to spend their leisure time. The reverse may be the case. Vast masses of consumers in the wealthiest nations today spend their modest household budgets on a relatively small selection of standardized commodities, which is shown by the success of downscale (*bas-de-gamme*) distribution chains such as LeaderPrice, Walmart, Lidl, etc. It is the *sense* of personal choice that is experienced as authenticity, and this sense must be exposed for others to see. Intimacy presupposes distinctness, which you can see in the fastidiousness of the poor more clearly than in the pretentious imprudence of the rich, and it is the vulnerability of this displayed intimacy that makes people so apprehensive about their personal autonomy.

When the range of actual possibilities to translate needs into objects and practices is limited, 'even the meanest labourers' – or those who are excluded from the labour market altogether – are expected to make selections. Research on people who depend on social assistance shows that living below the poverty line is strenuous because it requires extremely careful budgeting, and the slightest unexpected expenditure spirals one's whole life out of balance. The penalties are ruthless: shame over shame, guilt and further loss of autonomy from what already is only marginal, and the greedy hand of want searching for yet another need to be suppressed.

For those who have more resources, the mass consumption market is a cunning instrument to boost the imperative of choice. Many of the innovations introduced to mass consumption since the 1970s emphasize liberation: home-making machinery give us more free time; transportation technology, mobile phones, mass tourism, ethnic foods and international mass communications give us liberty to displace ourselves either in person or in imagination. These innovations, combined with reforms that make working life more flexible and less secure, are important supports for our contemporary mundane consciousness. As consumers want different experiences for leisure, they are offered 'adventure trips' or 'survival courses'; if consumers want more 'natural' food, they are offered eco-labelled brands, organic products, box deliveries directly from the farm, fair trade products, etc. The authentic gets wrapped in the commodity form quite easily and is no more an alternative to it than 'do-it-yourself' represents an alternative to the market of DIY products. Increased freedom does not necessarily mean time taken off from household duties. Cooking becomes a hobby, homes become more complicated and demand more attention, and hobbies in the traditional sense are easier with better equipment but take more time to learn. Differences offer more choice, but more choice does not necessarily mean more freedom.

Many critics of mass consumption have emphasized that the amplification of choice is not in fact how the mass consumption market seems to operate. Manufactured differences offer fleeting individuality at most. 'The satanic mills of industry', as Adam Smith described the early industrial production, have become gargantuan systems of robots and automatic production lines that with very little physical human effort turn out consumables for huge parts of the world's population. Once a technical innovation has reached the critical mass of users and minimal standards have been agreed on, products become very similar. Transmission of digital information, appliances for handling digital sound and picture, the rest of household technology, cars, bicycles, clothes – everything that is meant for mass consumption – converges towards a very narrow range of standard solutions both from the producers' technical point of view and from the point of view of the users' consumption practices. This is even true for food. No matter how wide the selection of available foods becomes, what is on the ordinary family menu tastes pretty much the same no matter where it was purchased, for what price and under what brand. Even between different countries the differences between pork chops, lamb chops, beef, milk, butter and most staple foods are not great. Price differences, in so far as they reflect product quality at all and not, for example, the methods of distribution, service or other adjuncts, are probably related not to usability but to the choice of materials or assembly techniques that may affect the life span or servicing needs of the product but have very little to do with its usability (e.g. television, telephone transmission, cars, etc.). Even organic food has more ethical than nutritional or gastronomic added value over other industrially produced food.

However, the imperative of choice is there, amplified in three ways. First, what one consumes is related to the whole way of life. Not having a car implies urban residence close to the necessary services; being a vegetarian is a choice that only those can make who have a sufficient assortment of vegetarian foods at their affordable disposal (and often more time for cooking than mixed diet eaters); and whatever else one's

113

choices are as a consumer, they have implications on the use of time. Second, the amount of information that is available about our consumption possibilities overwhelms ordinary consumers' capacity to actually take it into account. This is the case with technical appliances – most drivers, for example, know next to nothing about how their cars function and are not advised to service them – but it is even more the case about anything we absorb into our bodies. Only experts can have informed opinions of the millions of different kinds of molecules that are part of our food, drink, the air we breathe, the water we drink, not to speak of the substances we need for medical treatments. Nevertheless, we are obliged to make choices according to our convictions, trusting this or that expert view or considering the matter too insignificant to be bothered to know. These choices become part of our expressive authenticity; in the worst case they might even cast doubt on our capacity to exercise our reason and free will as sovereign knowledgeable consumers. And, third, the mass consumption market is dazzling in its capacity to generate the need for choice between practically nothing except the brand. Over-production and under-consumption theories (such as Haug's theory of *Warenästhetik*) are probably wrong in arguing that the function of marketing and advertising is to create artificial needs.[1] Marketing does not sell commodities but produces choice. It *does not create* but *usurps* a need, but it is not a need for the commodity itself; it is a need to assure oneself and others of being an agent of choice. In doing so, marketing is not a waste of resources but an indispensable production cost of the consumers' expressive authenticity. One must be a fairly well-trained expert to make olfactory or gustatory perceptions to distinguish brands of similar wines or beers, the most brand-sensitive classes of articles among ordinary consumables. The fact that so much is written about these differences, and so much money spent on branding in general in the mass consumption market, proves that the *appearance* of difference itself is more important than what underlies it.

Manufactured originality

The search for inner authenticity seems to be labour lost, be it for the ontological self, for human nature or for naturally or socially produced differences in taste. We live in a world of appearances, deceptions and illusions definitely, and no standard for objective critique is available. Yet modern consumers are destined to seek the original behind the appearance. 'Discover' is one of the most frequently used words in contemporary advertising: 'Discover the virgin nature of the Seychelles', 'Discover *Café East*', 'Discover the comfort of ...', 'Discover the inner hero in you', as if somewhere out there, behind the appearance, in the unknown (to you), there was something real, a reference, other than your own unmediated experience. Discover your own pleasure – and show it!

The experience of originality in ordinary consumption is part of the sense of hierarchy or self-respect discussed in the preceding chapter. The middle-class bar regulars whom we interviewed revelled in their sense of being avant-garde discoverers and explorers of new possibilities. Their experience of authenticity and public intimacy, of an inimitable immediacy of their controlled and sterile sociability, was for them a sign of their competence and self-control that they felt they had, in contrast to others who did not have the free will that they exercised. In this sensibility they were typical modern consumers who, although well aware of the impossibly short cycle between the unforeseen and the outdated, as well as of the artificiality of all difference and even more of the futility of searching one's true self in their lifestyles, nevertheless keep discovering and exploring. But what they explore and discover is not 'authentic' in any other than a self-referential sense: they are discovering their own pleasure. It is as if the self-assigned *aura* that in the late nineteenth century belonged to the work of art, and in the early twentieth century to the Existentialist, now belongs to the consumer. The originality of his or her experience is personal, yet no longer private. The *aura* is public and demands recognition. The discoveries of intimate pleasures must be exhibited and the moral barrier around them must be transgressed.

Since the original and the appearance are so easily confused, also this aspect of the hierarchy is very sensitive to symbolic violations. By analogy with Jameson's diagnostics of representation in modern art, the choices in contemporary mass consumption represent choices themselves and are therefore uncertain, beyond verification and exposed to disparagement. Let me again take an example from the middle-class pubs where we did fieldwork. The regulars were as tight about being pushed into social contacts as they were about being excluded from them. Their sense of intimacy was a sense of being hygienically separated from others and re-connected to them by their own choice and free will, keeping a distance. In the same way they sought milieus and appreciated styles that were different from the ordinary and *original*, in other words, *authentic*:

Pete, engineer (M): But I'm quite sure they weren't marble statues, they must have been some sort of mock marble. And obviously someone had gone to a great deal of trouble to figure out what they would look like and what kind of atmosphere they'd create.

Jere, real estate broker (M): I suppose what they're trying to do by building that sort of posh interior is to attract a different kind of clientele ... the workers were no longer coming so they said, hey, there's much more money in this segment so let's try to make our place more appealing to these people who've got all the dosh. But it's all so plasticky, it's like plastic walls all round, and so you go in and try to identify yourself with that sort of environment, which I suppose is what they're using to try to attract customers.

Johan, manager (M): What we're trying to say here is that we prefer the real, genuine stuff rather than all this pink velvet.

Marianne, secretary (F): I've always enjoyed *Speaker's Inn*, for instance; I used to go there quite often, I think it's a really nice place, it's a nice Jugend-style pub and they had live music there and people from different social classes, it's quite lively and genuine in there and often these

places you have that are there for just one purpose, you know like these Italian places, I mean
it's pretty formal and relaxed. (Sulkunen, 1992: 92)

Bar owners and designers have to attract customers; the fitments of the bar
form the instrument to achieve the desired end. Awareness of this aroused
trepidation among the patrons that they were being used as an instrument
to serve the interests of others. Artificial names and décor were seen by the
regulars as manipulation that mocks their desire for the authentic, ruining
their pleasure and pride as subjects who discover, make, or create their own
social space. The suspicion of deceit makes them feel like tourists who find
themselves behind artificial stages set up for them to create a back-stage
illusion, usurping their ambition to 'discover', to find the unique and original behind the usual front-stages made for visitors. The patina of old
objects that, according to McCracken (1988), constitutes identities, turns
into an imaginary nostalgia, longing for a past that nobody has ever lost
(Appadurai, 1997: 77). Nostalgia without memory is a hopeless search for
authenticity, which escapes every effort and turns into an experience here
and now without reference, a pastiche or manufactured impression. It
could be a very distressing experience without the attitude that one of our
interviewees expressed: 'For me, the appearance is the original.' That is
post-modern Stoicism.

Intimacy made public

The new consumer society brought with it much more than an unforeseen
variety of possibilities to consume. It was the flipside of the new capitalist
spirit in working life, which Boltanski and Chiapello (2005) have deemed
to be the response to the crisis in the bureaucratically organized regulatory
capitalism of the post-war decades. The Romantic critique of industrial capitalism was easily absorbed by the consumer market, which found no difficulty in adapting to 'alternative' lifestyles or consumption patterns. There
was, nevertheless, a moral barrier around pleasure that needed to be broken. The post-war discourse of frugality and rationality to advise consumers
in home-making gained a companion. Now television programmes and
columns in dailies on food, drink and sexuality appeared that had not seen
the light of day before. In the Nordic countries, major newspapers started
wine, beer and gastronomic columns in the early 1980s. Beer drinkers' societies were founded starting in 1971 when the Campaign for Real Ale
(CAMRA) was established, followed by similar associations in other countries soon after. Since the early 1980s, regulations on alcohol availability have
been relaxed in most parts of the world, except for restrictive legal limits of
blood alcohol concentrations of drivers (Sulkunen, 2000: 27–85).

It is not insignificant that the Lost Generation or the Sartrean intellectuals
who exposed their private life to the public through the media presented
themselves as outsiders and forerunners of a new morality. They paved
the way for the youthful radicalism of the 1960s and the consumer revolution of the 1970s and 1980s. They broke the bands with which the

modern social movements had contained pleasure in the private sphere and introduced the idea, first shocking, that satisfaction from consumption could be publicly presentable and even an object of serious discourse. They acted with their aura as cultural intermediaries from an external position that they had gained by their activity in the legitimate artistic, philosophical and literary fields, and constructed a model for emancipation through consuming in public. They articulated what Bell called the cultural contradiction of capitalism between the Romantic ethos of consumption and the ascetic ethos of discipline and sobriety. Their radicalism transferred intimacy from the private sphere of life to the public, confusing the distinction so that media personalities' private lives become a public matter, which again might be a very important reference in many people's private lives.

Still in the last third of the twentieth century, the breakdown of the moral barrier between public and private was a sensitive issue. 'Breaking taboos' around sexuality, emotions, mental disorders and many other questions was the business of youthful artistic, often left-wing students and intellectuals,[2] arousing moral panics among the older generations, as Stanley Cohen's study ([1972] 1980) of the media reactions to the 'mods' and 'rockers' demonstrated. It was a scare that concerned the stability of the Protestant moral order. The platform was the mass media, particularly television, as in a scandal that occurred in Sweden, again over alcohol. In September 1983, the Finnish author Jörn Donner and two Swedish writers Anderz Harning and Jan Guillou appeared on a direct prime time Saturday show on the Swedish public television channel tasting 21 different whiskies in one hour (with the natural and visible consequences, of course). The next day the national daily newspaper *Aftonbladet* published a three-page illustrated report on the show and on viewers' reactions: '[the writers] were drowned in phone calls after the show yesterday. Not by angry viewers, no, they only received applause. – It is ridiculous to say that it is foul to booze (*supa*) in Swedish TV, Anderz Harning opined' (*Aftonbladet*, 4 September, 1983). The barrier restricting pleasure to the private realm had been broken.

The breakdown of the moral barrier around private pleasures was important in cultural terms but it had political consequences as well. Whereas the state until now had been entrusted with extensive powers to regulate lifestyles in the interest of advancing the common good, now lifestyle issues became a challenge, not only to the state's authority to take a stand in moral issues but to the justification of the welfare state as a whole. This is the topic to be addressed in the next chapter.

Notes

1 It has been known for at least three decades that marketing expenses respond to the business cycle reactively rather than proactively. In a recession they go down, not up, and in the high phase of the cycle investments in marketing increase, although demand is already high (Kim, 1992; Kotler and Armstrong, 2006).

2 In Finnish socialist radicalism of the 1960s, consumption and particularly alcohol policy aroused lively interest. The first consumers' column with critical comments and questions for producers and commercial chains ('Why is the margarine produced by the Socialist Co-operative more expensive than the brand produced by the competing capitalist firm?') was carried by the Socialist independent magazine *Ajankohta* in 1968 (Sulkunen, 2000).

7

The Welfare State in the Consumer Society

Our contemporary social order is built on the ability of self-determination, by giving citizens a collective right to self-governement. And this not only in political terms: every person in our modern society stands more than ever alone. She no longer has an intimate, narrow circle of solidarity to rely on, like the family, the village or the church. She must therefore be able to plan her conduct and have visions about her living possibilities as well as make many more decisions on her own responsibility.

(Alva and Gunnar Myrdal, 1935)*

'The welfare state has become a problem for us'

The shift from industrial to consumer capitalism shattered the principles of justification on all fronts, in particular, the social bond, and the political bond especially. When the autonomy of individuals from traditional ties seemed almost complete, a new wave of reflections arose regarding the role of the state. After about one hundred years of consensus on the need to compensate for the shortfall of the free market through state intervention, neo-liberal arguments have suggested that capitalism now needs the state even less than anti-mercantilist capitalism did two hundred years ago. The state should safeguard the operation of the market, but beyond that its interference is harmful. Public services and income transfers have come under special attack. Critics have maintained that such interventions constrict free consumer choice, constitute a bureaucratic dead weight on society, attract monopolistic usurpation and are a risk to political and civil liberties. Such criticisms have continued since the first fiscal crisis of the 1970s, caused by suddenly increased oil prices and slack economies in most Western countries. In the Nordic countries the criticism reached its second peak after the banking crises of the late 1980s and early 1990s. An influential Finnish civil servant wrote in 1993:

The welfare state has become a problem for us, and its operations and loss of value basis block Finland's way out of the trouble, turning against welfare. The state has grown into an over-sized machinery, which is expensive, inflexible and authoritarian. Public administration interferes in many ways with people's lives. Business firms and economic activity have been regulated through stiff norms and various directive idelogies. Public services have been

---

* My translation

centralized and normatively homogenized. Citizens are patronized and made dependent on public assistance. Taxes have become intolerable. Transfers exploit people's work efforts to the benefit of others, and their initiative and responsibility for their own lives have been destroyed. The welfare state erodes true morality. Instead of cultivating community and shared responsibility, public administration destroys it and turns to its opposite. (Hautamäki, 1993: 135, my translation)

The welfare state has become a problem for researchers as well. The criticisms have not disabled the welfare state: contemporary capitalist countries have kept their income maintenance systems and their public services in health care and social affairs at stable levels. It is one of the most intriguing paradoxes of advanced consumer capitalism that the criticisms, although launched by the powerful media and important politicians, have had so little impact on what actually has happened in the welfare state structures and on the mundane consciousness that supports them. If the media, politicians, and many expert social scientists alone had their way, we should have seen the radical dismantling of the welfare state structures some time ago and should expect their final demise soon. According to some experts, individualistic 'rent-seeking' leads to suspicious means testing, cheating and erosion of citizens' loyalty to the state (Sørensen, 1998). Permanent unemployment, massive poverty in some countries, government budget deficits, international competition at the lower end of the labour market, erosion of working-class politics and the collapse of socialism should lead us to believe that the era of the welfare state, at least of the Nordic type with a strong emphasis on universalism, income solidarity and public services, is now over.

Yet researchers report very little change. The austerity discourse since the Thatcher–Reagan period in the Western countries has not been accompanied by the privatization of education, health or social services, at least not to a point where the system risks a breakdown. Public support for health services continues to be strong. Education is not even threatened, many personal services to families and old people continue to be publicly provided or at least publicly funded. For example, Swedish attempts to liberalize day care and education à la Milton Friedman by offering vouchers to parents has not led to the extensive use of privately offered services (Stephens, 1996: 47). In stark contrast to neo-liberal policy initiatives, the role of the public sector in health care systematically increased in Europe until the late 1980s and continues to dominate relative to the private sector, especially as regards financing health care as a whole, and in the provision of intensive and long-term inpatient care. The exceptions are Poland (and probably the rest of the new EU members) and Belgium (Maarse, 2006).

Many other similar examples could be given. Privatization has actually cut back state-funded social services in several countries only in public housing (Kosonen, 1995: 70–7). Also infrastructures, including transportation, energy, communications and security, have to some extent become commodified, partly within the state structure, partly privatized. National broadcasting monopolies that earlier were considered vital strategic vehicles of national unity have been partly opened to commercial competition (Therborn, 1995: 121–36).

Despite efforts to cut back state budgets, public social security and health expenditures as a percentage of gross domestic product continued to increase even after 1980 in Western countries (Esping-Andersen, 1996a: 11; Iversen, 2001: 46). The vocabulary to describe adjustment needs in the research literature is rich and telling: retrenchment, recalibration, cost containment, recasting, restructuring, and modernization. However, as Diane Sainsbury (2001) concludes in a review of the research, only piecemeal change has been observed, although some of the new rhetoric may indicate a transformation in the logic of welfare services.

The stability is usually attributed to popular opinion. The evidence has continued to be relatively strong and uniform that public opinion firmly supports the welfare state's income maintenance programmes and public services (Taylor-Gooby, 1985; 1995; Svallfors, 1989; 1996; Haller, et al., 1990; Allardt, et al., 1992; Pettersen, 1995; Roller, 1995; Brook, et al., 1996; Svallfors and Taylor-Gooby, 1999; Jaeger, 2006). Comparative studies show that in most Western European countries they enjoy majority support, which is strongest in countries with low relative levels of public spending (Pettersen, 1995; Taylor-Gooby, 1995). A Swedish study showed that even distrust in the state's capacity to provide income maintenance and public services does not translate into scepticism; on the contrary, it leads to increased demands for resources for this support (Edlund, 2006). There is some expert disagreement on whether social security systems are actually converging in Europe (Castles, 1993; Ploug, 1994; Kosonen, 1995; Haataja, 1996; Rauch, 2007), but political electorates support harmonization upwards rather than downwards, and therefore European integration as such is hardly a threat to the welfare state.

In public opinion surveys, criticisms about the welfare state's functions are directed at its insufficiency and poor performance rather than excessive generosity, and more so in terms of coverage than in terms of replacement levels or of service quality (Cnaan, 1989; Svallfors, 1989). The more marginal the population who benefits, the less popular is the service or support. Thus means-tested social assistance is the least popular of all income maintenance schemes (Pierson, 1991: 168–71). So something is wrong. Either we should not trust what we hear in the evidence, or we do not hear the right things in the critique.

Decommodification

The most influential conceptual analysis of the welfare state among social scientists is Gøsta Esping-Andersen's (1990) decommodification theory. Its clarity is very convincing. It argues that the welfare state is needed to support those who are unable to earn their living by working. Capitalism is fundamentally a system of commodified labour power. It is sold on the labour market and wages are spent on commodity markets. However, for several reasons, no society will ever survive complete capitalization. If workers are nothing more than commodities, they will likely destroy the system. Unprotected dependence on the markets will marginalize a part of the population permanently, and in any case temporary disruptions in market participation due to illness, parenthood, old age and unemployment are unavoidable for most people. Finally, unabridged commodification would only be possible if workers were isolated individuals competing with each other, which has not been, is not and will not be the case in industrial societies. As Walter Korpi (1978) has stressed, the role of the politically organized working-class in establishing the Nordic type of the welfare state cannot be underestimated. In some form union activities and working-class politics are still viable today and will undoubtedly continue to be so (Esping-Andersen, 1990: 35–54).

The decommodification functions of the welfare state implement a partial disengagement of the labour power from the market through income maintenance programmes, equalizing transfers and public services. In what way and to what extent this is organized through the state depends on three factors: (1) (working) class mobilization; (2) class coalitions; and (3) the legacy of institutional structures in society. Not all welfare states are decommodifying to the same extent, and they do it in different ways. The continental European welfare state type is 'service-lean and transfer-heavy' (Esping-Andersen, 1996b: 67). Transfers are based on contributions rather than need or citizenship, which means that they aim to guarantee accustomed status and earnings rather than redistributive ambitions. The continental welfare states – Esping-Andersen calls them the corporatist type – have a more contractual character than the Nordic systems, and they are therefore also more consensual and resistant to change. They presuppose a labour market and a family system where one (male) breadwinner is predominantly responsible for dependants; these states are inefficient in preventing poverty exactly because of their weak decommodification capacity (ibid.: 66–7). In contrast, the Nordic welfare states are strongly decommodifying in preventing poverty traps, but are nevertheless directed to sustain high labour market activity, especially by women, by providing public services. These services employ women directly, and they help harmonize fertility and work.

The usual explanations, suggested by specialists, for the stability of the decommodifying welfare state are based on the assumption of rational interest articulation by welfare beneficiaries. The welfare state nurtures employment interests among administrators and public service providers. It strengthens the neo-corporatist mechanisms of consensus-building and stability. Finally, the welfare state clients are not easily persuaded to support the abolition of their benefits, especially in so far as the middle classes are among them in large numbers. In the Nordic countries, the economic independence of women is largely due to these benefits. Furthermore, it is difficult to envisage that they would be willing to forgo their role in the labour market, which is – paradoxically, in view of the term – strongly dependent on the 'decommodifying' functions of the state (Pierson, 1991; Esping-Andersen, 1996c: 261–7). Göran Therborn has stated the conclusion even more strongly: 'A radical anti-welfare state party or coalition will find it virtually impossible to succeed under democratic rules of universal suffrage and rights to industrial action' (Therborn, 1989: 62).

These are impeccable reasons to expect the firm status quo to continue. But does this mean that nothing at all is changing or that the impression of a welfare state transition in Western countries is merely an illusion, which can be expected to evaporate as the neo-liberal tide ebbs by itself? To answer these questions we must go back in history, both of the welfare state theory and of the Western capitalist states in a wider perspective. 'Wider' means two things in this context. First, when researchers talk about the welfare state, they tend to place most stress on what the state spends on transfers, somewhat less on what it provides in terms of services, and modestly on the effects of all this – but a lot on what people think about it. Very little interest is shown in *what 'the state' actually is*: an institution, organization, structure, power and action. This is discussed vigorously in the context of public administration and juridical discourse, but little in the context of welfare policy. Second, surprising as this may sound, the concept of welfare itself has been almost completely neglected in 'comparative welfare state research'. I, too, must leave my discussion on the first of these topics to another context and concentrate on a few points about the second.

The gap between the shattering ideological consciousness and the stable public opinion supporting the status quo could be explained by the insufficient precision in the use of terms. Even an author as sensitive to theoretical nuances as Christopher Pierson (1991: 180) occasionally falls back on rather sweeping expressions such as 'public expenditure' that 'squeezes out the choices of private consumers'. Public expenditure on what? In what choices would consumers be interested, to sacrifice tax-paid public services free of charge at the point of delivery? How much would they be willing to pay for such freedom of choice? It is my view, too, that the presumed 'crisis' of the welfare state is related to the new consumer society, but this relationship is complex and entails an array of moral quandaries in people's everyday life. These perplexities concern their images of themselves, of justice and of their relationship with society, especially the state.

Planning for the growth of the nation

The foundations of the 'social question' were laid in the mid-nineteenth century, after the catastrophic consequences of the initial free reign of capitalist market economy. However, the construction of the European welfare state, as we know it today, coincided with and was functional with respect to the rapid industrialization in the early part of the century, and it was greatly accelerated by the Second World War. For some authors, like

Harold Wilensky (1975), welfare state growth is an almost automatic and indispensable concomitant of industrialization. Others have stressed the importance of universal suffrage and especially the political role of women; some have attributed the evolution to socialist or social-democratic political influence. Pierson (1991: 7–101), for example, has reviewed the literature and there is no need to rehearse the arguments here. There is no uncertainty that the turning point in welfare state construction was the post-war 'reconstruction period' that soon turned into the Cold War.

A fundamental starting point for understanding the consciousness of the crisis is to see that the Keynesian welfare national state (KWNS) found in the USA, Canada, North-West Europe, Australia and New Zealand, has been a continuation of the third modern ideal besides progress and universal individualism: the *nation*. According to Bob Jessop (2002: 73–81), the distinctive contribution of this state formation was its capacity to manage, displace or defer the contradictions of capitalist accumulation within the nation. It was a configuration of the national economy, the centralized national state, national citizenship ('nationality'), national culture and national identity (as against ethnic, gender or class contradictions). The welfare state builders of that period were amazingly convinced of – and in agreement with (Pierson, 1991: 125–37) – the catalytic powers of the centralized national state. Sir William Beveridge, the 'designer' of the British welfare state, declared that the reconstruction period signalled a new era of economic policy thinking, where the Ministry of National Finance was no longer a cameralistic book-keeping treasury, but an agent of national economic planning, with wide responsibilities not only for the public outlay of the state but also for the outlay of private citizens in consumption and in business investment (Beveridge, 1944: 177). Its aim was no longer to minimize public spending, but to optimize all spending in society, in regard to available labour power by means of 'manpower budgeting'. The state budget should be measured to maintain full employment, but not to exceed the national manpower capacity. The Keynesian principle of full employment was translated into income equalization in social policy and growth was its primary objective. The dreadful memory of the deflationary pre-war recession was reflected in the concerns to avoid underconsumption cycles. The influential Finnish social politician Pekka Kuusi summarized one of the principal welfare state arguments in his landmark drawing on Kegnesian economic theory. He argued that:

> Transferring consumption possibilities from the rich to the poor implies in itself that flexible spending on luxuries will decline and the much more inflexible spending on necessities will be strengthened. The preconditions for developing general production will be consolidated, if we can rely on the invariable demand for food, clothing, housing and other necessities that will remain stable from one year to the next. (Kuusi, 1961: 61)

The lessons learned from the success of the war economy were considered to prove the benefits of government participation in industry and its investments, in public direction of consumption with regulated prices, in labour market bargaining and in planning man-power mobility. The publicly guaranteed supply of food was no longer necessary, but government retained an important role in providing housing and energy. These lessons slithered into welfare state theories and bred a comprehensive planning ideology. The 'spectacular achievements of the wartime planned economy' (Beveridge, 1944: 120) measured by the GNP and employment were used as an argument that the economy in peace also could benefit from state regulation, and not only by means of income redistribution. The anti-mercantilist liberals of the late eighteenth and early nineteenth centuries had already stressed that in industrial capitalism the state must be centralized. Now the new functions of the state made national centralization even more necessary. Non-marketable goods and services such as the infrastructure, traffic, land use, education and health, needed central planning to secure a balanced regional development. The central administration of the state was, according to the Beveridge Report, necessary for this, and the local governments were left with the execution of national plans. Any suggested considerations of autonomy for England, Wales and Scotland were ruled out of the question (1944: 165).

The old idea that welfare growth would alleviate class conflicts, and that elimination of misery would stop hatred, was an integral part of the welfare state thinking in the reconstruction period. The ultimate purpose of the welfare state was to transform the society of production to a consumer society where some people could choose not to work, but nobody would be forced into lasting unwanted unemployment. The universalism of social insurance and income equalization policies was based on the two guiding principles of European welfare policy: first, economic progress and, stability, and, second, the centrality of the nation–state. Citizenship rather than need or individual contribution was to be the basis of rights to freedom from Want and Idleness (Titmuss, 1976: 124–36).

However, this is only half of the story. The other half is a story of the moral foundations of the state's authority over citizens, and vice versa.

The state's debt to citizens

French republicanism and the rise of 'the social question'

Montesquieu was probably the first to articulate the principle that society incurs a debt to its needy citizens simply by having them as its members: 'A few alms given to a naked man in the streets does not fulfil the obligations of the state, which owes all the citizens an assured sustenance, nourishment, suitable clothing, and a kind of life which is not contrary to health' (Montesquieu, [1748] 1989: XXIII, xxix). This duty has been written in many constitutions, declarations of human rights and political documents since then (Castel, 1995: 190), and it seems also to be written in the hearts of welfare state citizens who give their strong support to pensions, health insurance, minimum standards of employment, health care, income and other conditions of well-being, organized, funded or at least guaranteed by the state. It is the *source* of this duty and the *objectives of its fulfilment* – which we now cover by the rather euphemistic global term welfare – that have undergone a change in public consciousness: theoretical, ideological as well as the mundane awareness of the present.

The first major change in the justifications of the capitalist state took place in the latter part of the nineteenth century. Jacques Donzelot (1984) has argued that in France the 'social question' could only be born after the dissolution of republican contractualism around the 1848 Revolution. Before that time, republicanism itself was believed to be the solution to the problem of inequalities. If everybody had equal rights to make contracts, and equal rights to participate in politics, the state would automatically become the servant of the people, as Rousseau had taught. The gist of the post-revolutionary critiques of contractualism was that the Rousseauian fictive individuals were either completely at the mercy of the state or completely alone in facing the miseries placed on them by capitalist exploitation. The idea of 'society' that was neither the state nor its isolated member-citizens had to be invented. After the successful destruction of pre-modern communities, guilds and orders of many kinds in the post-revolutionary period, a new type of solidarity needed to be found and adapted to the differentiated industrial division of labour. Donzelot writes that in industrial society the Rousseauian state was either too much or nothing: if the state's duty is to give work and subsistence, this will destroy the basis of private ownership capitalism and lead to socialism in the Marxian sense. Alternatively, the state would have no space in society at all and leave it to the mercy of its own fatalisms (1984: 67). The bourgeoisie and the political right defended the latter position, but the proletariat and the peasants, too, experienced the state as a blood-sucking usurper. The theoretical and practical non-existence of 'society' mediating between the individual and the state explains the co-existence and complicity of anarchism and totalitarianism in the post-revolutionary period. The Republic was no longer a solution, but was itself a problem.

Durkheim's great political significance, according to Donzelot, was his success in introducing the idea of the priority of the social vis-à-vis the state and the individual. Both states and individuals are social facts produced by the bonds of solidarity, which themselves are conditioned by the extended division of labour in modern society. Among Durkheimian political commentators, the most interesting from the contemporary perspective was, first, Léon Bourgeois, the illustrious politician of Left Democracy, and, second, Léon Duguit, the sociologist of positive law, and Durkheim's disciple. For Duguit, the state is only one community among others, with the special function that it codifies in law what already exists as the moral order of society. Its function is not to represent a Rousseauian general will, but to nurture and serve solidarity. Whereas Duguit was in favour of a weak and decentralized state (sometimes he was called 'The Anarchist of the Chair'), Bourgeois supported a centralized and extensive state, but for similar reasons. He incorporated the Montesquie principle of the duty of the state into a doctrine that anticipates Esping-Andersen's view of the welfare state: 'Through the actions of the state society commits itself to correct the evils it inflicts from the defects of its own organization' (quoted in Donzelot, 1984: 111). Whereas liberalism has turned the individual into an *instrument* of progress, for 'solidarism' the individual, co-operating in organic solidarity with other individuals, is its goal and justification.

The normative state

In Britain or in the Nordic countries, republicanism never was a similar problem, probably because the pre-industrial moral communities were never dissolved. They continued their existence, first, in local and then increasingly in national political movements. Aage Sørensen (1998) has argued that the origin of the welfare state in Prussia and Denmark and Norway was the merger of absolutist rule with Pietist Protestantism in the seventeenth century, which established a militaristic state apparatus with a supreme value on obedience. The King was the head of the Prussian and Danish state churches that became effective instruments of administration and moral education of the population. Pietism was favourable to popular education under clerical supervision, but moral obedience was also generated by poor relief legislation, of which the Copenhagen Poor Plan of 1799 was the culmination. A similar proximity of the state and the people was characteristic in Sweden and in Finland.

Literature on the nineteenth-century social movements indicates that moral reformers, especially among the working class, used the state quite successfully for moral regulation. Its emergent parliamentary institutions justified state action not only in extending the rights and benefits of citizens but also in claiming moral obedience to the secular authorities. Regulation of sexuality and drinking, improving living conditions and civilizing the working poor, were duties entrusted to the state, supported by strong popular movements. Hygienists, charity workers, churches and religious groups found ready and well-functioning solidary communities to work with, whereas in France these groups were more specialized and expert-driven, which partly explains the vulnerability of their efforts. This difference apart, the social policies were similar in two respects in late nineteenth- and early twentieth-century European societies. They were, first, policies about the life and welfare of the population, conceptualized as 'bio-power' by Michel Foucault (1991) in his famous lecture on 'Governmentality', in contrast to disciplinary power to assure the subjects' loyalty to the sovereign. Second, they shared a normative character that Foucault described with the metaphor 'pastoral power'. Pastoral authority, the shepherd, knows the herd and its needs, leads it from one meadow to another, and cares for the lost sheep. These metaphors describe perfectly the welfare state until the last third of the twentieth century because they stress that the function of social policy was, besides the well-being of the population, the consolidation of social order. In contrast, they are incompatible (as I shall show in the next chapter) with the neutralized principle of risk management today.

The new concern about social order through well-being turned attention from deviant or rebellious individuals to the size of the population, its health, hygiene, sexuality, and mental fitness. Its manners and ways of thinking, too, were conceived as products of good government. We should say, more precisely, that it was a policy about *national* populations; populations require limits and the territory of the nation was increasingly important in the definition of a society, as the 'century of peace' (Polanyi, [1944] 1957: 3) after Napoleon drew to a terrible close in the nationalistic war in 1914. A new biological anthropology emerged to explain and control the risks of degeneration in mid-nineteenth-century Europe, and this concern continued to dominate social policy thinking well into the Second World War and beyond. Besides the protection of work safety and the ten-hour working day, it had normative implications on the moral regulation of consumption and sexuality that would be almost unthinkable today. In concrete terms it consisted of restrictive alcohol policy,[1] control of sexuality,[2] and above all in pro-natal and eugenistic family policies, which culminated in the family and child assistance programmes before and after the Second World War (Weeks, 1985).

'Improving the quality of human material'

The population question

Without a population policy, nationalism is impossible. Without the nation, there is no population policy to worry about. These are trivial truths, but they are the key to understanding the history of the welfare state in the 'short twentieth century' as Hobsbawm (1995) has christened the period between the First World War and the fall of the Berlin Wall in 1989. The health and welfare of civilians and military alike were strategic resources in the two world wars that were motorized and organized to meet the standards of industrial efficiency, but required nevertheless huge armies of men, mobilized for years to fight in extremely strenuous circumstances. However, the population needed to be also morally educated to constitute a nation, and that was as true for the conditions of peace as much as for war. Material needs were not the only target of the fight against poverty and social misery. Higher causes were at issue. Even William Beveridge himself, for whom the 'Plan for Social Security is first and foremost a method of redistributing income' (1942: 170), declared that 'Want is only one of five giants on the road of reconstruction and in some ways the easiest to attack. The others are Disease, Ignorance, Squalor and Idleness' (ibid.: 7).

The 'population question' arose, first, in a quite literal sense concerning the size of the nation. The population losses of the First World War signalled the fact that modern military technology required both well-trimmed organization and millions of men. Fertility had declined already in the nineteenth century and populations even stopped growing, notwithstanding the increased life span in the 1930s at least in Austria, England, France, Germany, Norway and Sweden. These concerns survived and were reinforced during the Second World War, and they reincarnated in the family policies of the reconstruction period. Second, the population question concerned the role of the individual family as the unit of reproduction, consumption and redistribution of income in the labour market. The nuclear family, not its individual members nor its social environment – the community or the extended family – became the standard unit of 'the social' throughout the salaried working class. Whatever income maintenance programmes, health or social services were introduced, the family and the programmes' effects on the family had to be accounted for (Walby, 1997: 166–79). An important example is that family allowances were an integral part of welfare state construction everywhere in the post-war years. Pro-natal national policy was not limited to encouragement with assistance schemes; it penetrated deep into the moral content of life. A brochure of The Family Federation of Finland instructed married couples in this way in 1949:

> As most things and inventions in the world, also birth can be used for good and bad purposes. It is bad whenever the number of children is restricted for selfish reasons of personal comfort, or exaggerating one's difficulties. In family formation it is a wrong starting point to make 1 to 2 children for the personal pleasure of the parents. It is more valuable to consider what you can sacrifice for your children than to offer them something from overabundance. Many parents have bitterly grieved at the grave of their single child or otherwise toward the eve of their life, regretting their excessive child restriction that had been dictated by their fear of life. (Rouhunkoski, 1949: 2, my translation)[3]

Four children per family was the ideal norm.

The family was politically important also for idelogical reasons. The Second World War and its aftermath intensified the political rhetoric of freedom in defence of non-socialist but planned capitalism. Full employment was to be achieved, according to Lord Beveridge, subject to the proviso that essential citizen liberties are preserved: 'freedom of worship, speech, writing, study and teaching; freedom of assembly and of association for political and other purposes ..., freedom of choice of occupation; and freedom in management of a personal income' (Beveridge, 1944: 21).

The locus of these freedoms was the individual family, and it would be only a slight exaggeration to say that the normative debate on lifestyle in the formative years of the welfare state was about adjusting the ideals of individual freedom to ideal models of independent families. As Foucault (1991: 98–102) formulated it, the patriarchal family was turned from the model of governance to its instrument and object. Free management of personal income meant in Britain, first and foremost, maximum security of employment for the male breadwinner; next to that was income maintenance in case of his discontinued earnings, and, finally, women's economic independence from their husbands in case of illness, widowhood or divorce (Beveridge, 1942: 5–19, 122–7).

In the Nordic countries, the issue of women's individual freedom was more complex. Alva and Gunnar Myrdal, in their early report on the Swedish population question (1935), presented not only a plan for stopping the ongoing decline in the birth rate, but a comprehensive welfare state programme. Its aim was to improve the quality of living conditions of families through rational birth control, improvement in education, free school lunch, public day care, improved housing conditions, hygiene and medical care, parent training and, of course, an equalizing system of family allowances. Although the question was about the problem of the declining population, the underlying vision of progress and modernization was aimed at promoting individualism. The last third of their book argues that 'The immediate direct task of a prophylactic social policy is to create improved human material' (Myrdal and Myrdal, 1935: 215–45, my translation). Modern life places higher quality requirements on citizens, and central among them is that:

> Our contemporary social order is built on the ability of self-determination, by giving citizens a collective right to self-governement. And this not only in political terms: every person in our modern society stands more than ever alone. She no longer has an intimate, narrow circle of solidarity to rely on, like the family, the village or the church. She must therefore be able to plan her conduct and have visions about her living possibilities as well as make many more decisions on her own responsibility. (ibid.: 309, my translation)

In this, they echoed the socialist views of the Second International, for example, those of its wartime President, the Belgian socialist and temperance advocate Émile Vandervelde. Vandervelde had insisted that the aim of social policy is not only to keep working-class people out of misery, but to educate them to take responsibility for their lives as individuals. For the Myrdals, individualism meant self-responsibility, but also the right to political and legal citizenship, and, above all, the right to an individual biography – to choose a career or the right to work, in the French revolutionary tradition – according to personal preferences and abilities independently of class background. The Myrdals proposed that scientific personality testing for occupational fitness should be extensively used, and they should be further developed to help individuals in this difficult choice. Both horizontal mobility between occupations and vertical mobility between classes are signs of a sound and healthy society (ibid.: 318–33). Families should be provided with help in educating their children to meet the new requirements for individual independence and the necessity to make choices.

One issue of the new family life was of special importance to the Myrdals. That was women's employment outside the home. They argued against the conservatives that women have always been hard-working in the rural economy, taking care not only of the home, but also of many tasks on the farm. Progress in household technology in urban conditions left ample free time for women, and the Myrdals ridiculed the bourgeois model of filling up that time with excessive shopping, sports and beauty care, less constrained ('*vidlyftigare*') eroticism, social activities and charity, albeit also with intellectual preoccupations. A more natural way of employing the women's energies liberated from useless household work was to turn to the labour market; a long-time necessity for the poor, but now also a meaningful and rational option for those middle-class women who by that token can improve their living standards (ibid.: 372).

Employment outside the home was not an unchallenged ideal of women's liberation in the Nordic welfare states, however. The celebrated Finnish social democratic politician Miina Sillanpää was thinking about 'the housemaid question' and about the army of impoverished female factory workers at the turn of the century, when she declared in 1925:

> If we want to keep women at home, then we must say that only co-operation between men and women can create such tolerable economic and social conditions that mothers can completely devote themselves to keeping house and taking care of the children. (Sillanpää, 1925, quoted in I. Sulkunen, 1986: 84, my translation)

The Finnish social-democratic movement joined the bourgeois women liberationists in the 1920s to demand freedom from 'double slavery' for women, claiming new rights of motherhood over children and valorizing a clear sexual division of labour where women are devoted to the home and men are the breadwinners. Furthermore, it should be recognized that work in the home also requires skill and training. If that is not done, any improvements in working-class life will be impossible and class hostilities will continue, as another social-democratic liberationist, Laura Harmaja, said:

> If house and home cannot be properly taken care of in working-class families, the improvement of working-class conditions in other respects is of no use ... So the dissatisfaction and bitterness towards society will be maintained, because all these ventures for improvement have actually been not completed, they have stopped at the point where the use of income starts to contribute to the satisfaction of human needs. (Harmaja, 1928, quoted in I. Sulkunen, 1986: 83, my translation)

The idea that women's liberation implies participation in the labour force equal to men was adopted by emancipatory movements only in the post-war years in Finland across the political spectrum (Jallinoja, 1983). Finland was, in fact, an exception less than Sweden. The war had brought women into the labour force, like it or not, and the post-war reconstruction made their participation necessary in countries with retarded industrialization. It is arguable to what extent the service orientation in the Nordic welfare states as a whole was instrumental to this effect. According to some researchers (Julkunen, 1994: 197), the high degree of women's participation in the labour force was achieved *in spite of* lacking public services, not *because* public services, especially child care, made it possible.

I have discussed the debates on the 'women's question' at length to underscore that the construction of the welfare states, especially in the Nordic case, before and after the Second World War, was laden with normative ideals of the good life. The normative issues went into much greater detail than full employment and women's participation in the labour force as such. Parents' training programmes, child care counsellors, and home economics or hygiene classes in schools taught mothers and also fathers how to care for themselves and their children. National primary and secondary schools had centrally planned curricula. Food policies attempted to harmonize scientifically based nutritional requirements with agricutural interests (Jensen and Kjærnes, 1997). Consumer policies aimed not only to protect consumers from fraud and unfair trade practices, but also to direct consumption patterns towards rational goals (Ilmonen and Stoe, 1997). Public housing policies defined standards for homes, sometimes in some detail, determining what kind of rooms a family should have, how large a kitchen it needed and how it should be equipped, and so forth (Frykman and Löfgren, 1985: 140–77).

The target of all these regulations was the modern private family. Its reproduction functions had expanded from the simple production of 'human material' to the production of civilized individual citizens, capable of independent management of their lives and their future families, but also of their own romantic pleasure. All this was to be adjusted to the national interest and to the public good, especially to controlled population growth. Therefore, the moral regulation of sexuality was a key issue in the construction of the post-war welfare states. Contraception technology advanced rapidly and the pill was introduced into general use in the USA in 1960 and later in the decade in Europe (Therborn, 2004: 290). The romantic ideal of personal love had been shimmering in the shadow of national defence, depression and war, but in the post-war period it was ready to attack the solemn culture of rights and duties. As Armas Nieminen, another Finnish authority on social policy and family planning in the 1950s, put it: 'Eros joined the absolute morality of justice' (1951: 234), meaning that the pleasure of sexuality was becoming accepted independently of fertility, but only within marriage. This was a precarious task: individual pleasure, notably of women, was to be elevated to an unforeseen respectability without forfeit to the national interest and the public good.

From needs to resources

Consensus and critique

Class conflicts in post-war Western Europe were waged on issues of distribution and industrial relations, not on the meaning of progress in lifestyle and consumption. Individualism, both in the sense of equal citizenship rights and in the sense of freedom to manage one's income in the framework of the private family, was the keynote of this idea of progress.

Educational policies were expressly designed to supply adequately skilled labour force to the growing economies, and consequently to maintain high mobility both vertically and horizontally. These aims were not contested by conservatives; on the contrary, one of the most important Cold War anti-socialist arguments was equality of opportunity in the West, as opposed to the repressive – and increasingly failing – equality of result under the social-ist regimes. The state-driven change implied also geographic mobility, from rural to urban areas and from underdeveloped regions to industrial growth centres. Life became family-centred in the newly built urban housing areas, and the ideal of a personal home with a living room and a television set, separate bedrooms and a private kitchen furnished with modern household technology turned from a dream to concrete reality for millions of Western people by the end of the 1970s.

There were critiques, of course, already at the initiation of welfare states. It has often been observed (Pierson, 1991: 49) how close the underlying reasonings between left and right critics were in the crisis period since the 1970s. The same can be said about the critics in the halycon days of welfare state ideology. The most relentless early conser-vative critic of national centralism and planning economy in the West, Friedrich von Hayek, based his argument in *The Road to Serfdom* ([1944] 1962), much cited in the Nordic countries in the 1960s, not on eco-nomic theory, but on the moral and sociological value of individuals as the source of norms. Allocating particular benefits cannot be based on general and impartial rules even in theory; in planned economies, the state is given the discretion over what needs are satisfied, not only to what extent different distributive interests are served (ibid.: 55, 76–88). Only countless individual free interactions can constitute the kind of community that is required to support a non-totalitarian state, a just dis-tribution of goods and resources and an efficient economy for procuring them.[4] Von Hayek was not against state participation in the economy in cases where they cannot profitably be produced in the capitalist system. And of course, the market economy needs an intelligently designed and continuously adjusted legal system (ibid.: 29). What von Hayek and the neo-liberals who today follow his opposition to 'collectivism' ignored is that their individualism was also the ultimate goal of the designers of the welfare state.

There was another type of early critique of the welfare state that also was influential in the Nordic countries at the initiation of the welfare state. It was opposite in its political orientation to Hayek, but significant in stress-ing the autonomous and original value of community as opposed to the state. This type of critique was exemplified by D. H. Lawrence's ideas of the state and the individual. Although an author from working-class origins, he did not see the state as a counter-force to the devastating influence of industry and commerce on community. The Lawrencean critique, which we now so often rediscover transformed into official discourses of flexible soci-ety, empowering, the contract society, communitarianism or the like, gave expression to a deep underlying suspicion of the state. It was therefore directed against social democracy, but it was nevertheless working class in its ardour for community and in its vehemence against bourgeois hypocrisy. These themes have been important in the British and in the Nordic working class cultures since the late nineteenth century.[5] They are the font of the Romantic sense of history, which lives on in what Luc Boltanski and Eve Chiapello call the 'artistic' in contrast to the 'social' critique of capitalism. Whereas social critics grumble about injustices, insecurity and wretchetness, artistic critics bemoan

> [t]he lost sense for beauty and grandeur effected by standardization and commercialization, not only of everyday things, but also objects of art (bourgeois cultural mercantilism), even humans. It bewails the objectifying will of capitalism and of bourgeois society to regiment, to dominate, to suppress humans to a work prescribed by the profit motive while it invokes hypocritically a morality that opposes the liberty of the artist. (Boltanski and Chiapello, 2005: 84)

The clumsy term is justified as regards the critics of capitalism in the maturing years of the welfare state. This kind of criticism was hostile to the state; therefore it did not translate well into positive social science or into politics of the left, but flourished among free, artistic intellectuals instead. It was influential in countries where the intellectuals maintained a distance from the state. This was the case in Denmark and in Norway. In Sweden and Finland, the ideals of civilization and progress through rational planning bonded intellectuals to the state and to the labour movement; consequently, there was little room for Lawrencean individualism beyond literary circles (Longum, 1997; Nielsen, 1997).

The Romantic or artistic critique of capitalism turned up in social scientific assessments of the welfare state only with the arrival of the consumer society, in the 'crisis' consciousness of the welfare state. Towards the end of the 1970s, feminist writers and anti-capitalist Marxist theorists launched mounting criticisms, arguing that the welfare state contributed to the 'transcapitalization' of society.[6] With state support, commodity relations penetrate the private sphere to the benefit of the capitalist system of reproduction and class reconciliation. The thrust of these arguments was dissatisfaction with the state that sustains an excessively standardized morality about consumption and family-centred lifestyle. It is recognizable in the commentaries by many feminist authors such as Elizabeth Wilson, whose landmark book *Women and the Welfare State* (1977) criticized the normative sexual politics embedded in the welfare state ideology. Traces of it appear also in the works by Klaus Offe, Jürgen Habermas and many others inspired by Critical Theory (Pierson, 1991: 50–101). It shares with its liberal (and now neo-liberal) counterpart an element which is more important than their abstract individualism, namely the germs of the idea of moral neutrality of the state, an idea which in the Nordic welfare theory is known as the 'resources theory'.

The 'resources theory' in welfare research

The underlying roots of the consensus about the welfare state were much stronger than the apparent differences on distributional issues, on union power or on state ownership of industry, let alone opinions about 'socialism'. The welfare state was meant to break traditional ties between people to make them autonomous individuals, but as it matured, it also nurtured anti-authoritarian ideals and cultivated alternative lifestyles. This is where the system started to crack even before its edifice was completed. As early as the end of the 1950s, youth cultures celebrated 'non-traditional' anti-family values and lifestyles. Social groups formed to defend the rights of lifestyle minorities and deviant subcultures. Socialist intellectuals sought out autonomous anti-bourgeois working-class cultures, but it took a while before sociologists joined them.[7] They were challenging with increasing force the 'civilizing education' of manners, which to the young generation seemed nothing better than parochial bourgeois boorishness.[8] Pluralism and diversity in the name of freedom and equal rights became catchwords among the post-war generation liberals.

In the aftermath of 1968, experts on the welfare state translated the pluralism and diversity into a 'resources theory'. Researchers, most influentially Sten Johansson (1970, 1971) and Erik Allardt (1975), began to coin welfare concepts that were 'value-free', like the state should be. The concept of welfare became neutralized. Erik Allardt formulated the principle by saying that welfare policy is 'not aiming to promote the good life; its function is to eliminate vile circumstances and bad consequences' (1998: 123–33). Experts refused to investigate welfare in terms of objective *needs* and their satisfaction through public policy. They declared that income maintenance schemes and services should supply welfare as a *guaranteed resource* to satisfy individual aspirations, but the content of that welfare should be determined by each individual according to his or her values and preferences. In British welfare state sociology, this view has been promoted by John Keane (1988).

It did not take long before the welfare state itself incorporated these criticisms. Official policy found the solution to the value problem in 'community work', youth work, and in preventive or promotional activities concerning health, social order, crime or exclusion. Associations and citizen groups, often understood as the 'third sector', have been expected to accumulate 'social capital' in local communities. They should solve the double problem of the classical welfare state: maintaining full employment and social security while also promoting individual freedom of choice. Through the 'communities' the state should leave it up to people to decide for themselves how they prefer to deal with problematic life situations such as adjusting employment to parenting, or with illness, addictions, mental and social malfunctioning or old age. The Durkheimian idea of solidarity seems to experience a revival; now only it is very often recognizable as manufactured by programmes commissioned, designed, funded and managed by ministries rather than spontaneosly hatched within organic communities of the society itself.

The consumers' state

Unfortunately, whereas we have ample research on what people expect from the state in transfers and services, we have only occasional and scanty research available into what they wish the state to do about their choices. Coughlin's study (1980) summarizes research from eight countries saying that while expectations have increased in the area of state-assured conditions of life, 'survey evidence suggests a simultaneous tendency to support individual achievement, mobility, and responsibility for one's own lot' (according to Pierson, 1991: 169). However, there is little research into public opinion on the state's role in regulating private life.[9] The lack of data reflects a bias towards the calculative model of action in welfare state research. Survey studies capture best those aspects of the welfare state that are concrete and positive, such as pensions and sick leave coverage. The fear of paternalism is more abstract and intangible, but can in some cases be tapped by questions like the one posed by Svallfors: 'Public authorities interfere all too much in questions that should be left to individual citizens' (1996: 51). The percentage agreeing with this statement in Sweden increased between 1982 and 1992 by 30 per cent.

One well-researched area in this respect is alcohol policy. The Nordic alcohol monopolies were an integral part of moral regulation in the modern welfare state until the crisis of the 1970s. Alcohol policy polls measured people's willingness to accept beer and wine being sold outside the monopoly, in grocery stores with or without a special licence. The long-term trend has been towards liberalization, with a dramatic shift in the 1990s (Sulkunen et al., 2000). This is in no way related to the prevalence of alcoholism or public awareness of alcohol use as a social or health problem. There are other examples, like France, where the long-term trend in public opinion on the need to regulate alcohol consumption has gone in the opposite direction, while the support for state regulation of the market has been variable. These examples show that the stability of support for the decommodification functions of the welfare state has its counterside in the instability of support for the regulation of lifestyle and consumption.

The lack of research on what people think of the state is somewhat compensated for by observations on what the state thinks of the people, and of itself. The belief in national centralism is eroding. Since about 1980, the OECD countries have adopted new principles of public management, which seem to incorporate not so much the social as the consumerist critique of capitalism. The first initiatives in public administration reforms aimed at rollbacks and cost containment (Pollit, 1990; Trosa, 1999; Vignon, 1999). However, as the reforms have continued and evolved, the doctrine has become increasingly consumer oriented (Leroy, 1999; OECD, 2002). Devolution and decentralization aim to move decisions from central government, especially ministries down to service-providing organizations, departments and units and emphasize the role of regional and local governments. Public administration increasingly operates on the principle of accountable budgeting and competition. Local communities, which earlier executed national plans under the supervision of the central state administration, are now responsible for planning and resource allocation as well as for fulfilling the requirements set for them in legislation or in ministerial programmes. This shift in the principles of public management of lifestyle issues will be the topic of the next chapter.

Autonomy, intimacy and the state

Now I have identified the reason for the apparent contradiction between the crisis consciousness concerning the welfare state, on the one hand, and its indomitable stability and support, on the other hand. Understood in the narrow sense in which the research literature has discussed it, the welfare state has been built on the 'social' critique of capitalism. It corresponds to citizens' demand for security as well as to their sense of justice, today as before. However, the state is vulnerable to the 'artistic' critique. Just *how* vulnerable it is remains an open question.

Boltanski and Chiapello (2005) have shown that in industrial relations the two types of critiques, artistic and social, are contradictory. Capitalism responded to the crisis of the 1970s with flexible employment relations, project organizations, profit centres, networks, fixed-time contracts and individualized pay schemes. This was a reaction to artistic critiques of bureaucratic management, patterned after military organization. Without incorporating the artistic critique in this way, capitalism might never have seen the Silicon Valley and the third industrial revolution.[10] However, this was at a cost. Job security, the idea of a career, pre-fixed certainty of promotion, gradation of diplomas and bureaucratic (in the Weberian sense) measurement of merit had to give in, thus betraying the aspirations of the social critique that were the basis of 'organized capitalism' for the first two-thirds of the twentieth century.

In social policy, the two modalities of critique do not disagree with each other in the same way as in employment relations. We can easily incorporate expectations of security with Lawrencean claims for the self's 'fullness of being'. Without contradicting ourselves, we can claim the right to autonomy and intimacy at the same time as we claim our rights as creditors of the state, expecting coverage for pensions, for health insurance and public services. This is what the welfare state ideologists wanted us to be: self-responsible managers of our lives. There is no contradiction between the welfare state and modern individualism as such.

However, there is a tension *within* modern individualism in its saturated form. The consciousness of crisis of the welfare state that I described at the beginning of this chapter constitutes a powerful image of unfreedom. Many people feel that the autonomy and intimacy of individuals – the modern principles of dignity and greatness – are under threat. The welfare state is more likely to be experienced as intimidating the latter than the former. There is no imminent conflict between the roles of a consumer and a client of the state; on the contrary, these are very compatible experiences. It is no hindrance to being a free and autonomous consumer if medical help is provided by public rather than private health care institutions. For reasons of technical and economic expediency, making diagnoses and treatments are mostly performed in public hospitals anyway, even in France with a relatively large bed volume in for-profit hospitals (20 per cent) and almost no public services in primary health care (Maarse, 2006). In what sense will the commuter have more autonomy, if the train is run by a private company rather than by a public one? By what logic does a public school system destroy children's and their parents' initiative? In what way does the city hall destroy autonomy when it supports youth councils, parents associations or hobby clubs, and maintains association buildings or sports facilities, as it does in most European countries today?

However, autonomy presupposes sameness; rights and duties should be equal, and their distribution should be based on commonly understood standards of fairness. Property, sex, sexual orientation, ethnic background, religious beliefs or other particularities do not justify special treatment in law courts, hospitals, tax offices, or differences in the way welfare benefits are determined. They should not justify disrespect of other persons' rights. The postulate of sameness creates problems when particularities such as young or old age, handicaps or diseases, or other factors reduce persons' capacity to be responsible for themselves. But even in those cases, *maximum possible autonomy* is the ideal. This is why we have an increasing amount of codes of good conduct, regulations defining children's and old persons' rights, codes of research ethics and other rules to protect the autonomy of the weak.[11] In questions of sameness, negotiation is always possible.

Intimacy is more vulnerable and less negotiable than autonomy because it is built on difference. Physical and psychological constitution, ethnic identity, religious and political beliefs, emotions and chosen taste and style are inalienable elements of the authentic distinct self. These elements often clash with the principle of sameness. The right to wear Muslim scarfs or ethnic attire at schools, or claims for special rights by the disabled, are such difficult issues because the right to be different must be weighed against the right to be equal. The vulnerability of intimacy is intensified by the fact that it must be displayed in order to exist, and therefore it is exposed to public violations. Whether we actually aim at authenticity or not, we are judged by others, as if we did. No wonder many people now feel *fatigué d'être soi*, tired of being themselves, to use Alain Ehrenberg's (1998) brilliant expression.

Abstracted ideals of the good life

The welfare state supports individuals' autonomy, but in doing so it undermines their intimacy. *This* is where the crisis consciousness stems from, not from dissatisfaction with the decommodifying functions of the welfare state. Friction between autonomy and intimacy at the interface between the state and the individual is aggravated in the saturated society. We have no problems in accepting the norms of sameness, in fact, we take them for granted. Instead, when the state is felt to take a stand on our differences, it is experienced as exercising intolerable paternalism. The moral consensus about the good modern life, on which the modern welfare states were constructed, has disappeared. The notions of progressive population policy and the public (national) good have acquired the taste of a suspicious mixture in which totalitarian paternalism is blended with particular, often professional interests.

The state's response has been the same as welfare researchers' reaction to lifestyle pluralism: *abstraction of the ideals of the good life*. Health, well-being (or quality of life) and security are the three large baskets of goods that the state is expected to deliver to its citizens. Empowerment discourse in social work, emphasis on self-responsibility in public health, stress on communities and the third sector, and the rhetoric of decentralization, are symptoms of the saturated welfare state. The state still has the mandate to worry about lifestyle risk to the 'other', but it no longer has the mandate to determine the good life for the 'self'. To stay within this new limited mandate it must declare its concern, but deal out responsibility; it represents the interests of others and requests solidarity. This is the topic I am going to discuss in the next chapter.

Notes

1 Prohibitions in Canada, the USA, Iceland, Norway, Finland, and New Zealand; availability restrictions, taxation, and opening hours in other countries (Sulkunen and Warpenius, 2000).

2 Prohibitions of contraception in Canada, the USA, Sweden, Denmark, Netherlands, Belgium, France, Germany, Austria and Italy; later followed by positive pro-natal policies (Therborn, 2004: 252).

3 The Family Federation of Finland (*Väestöliitto*, literally, the Federation of Population), was founded in 1941 to support and implement pro-natal family policy by research, instruction and parental education. It is legally an association, but it is funded by the state (Rouhunkoski 1949).

4 The similarity of von Hayek's and Léon Duguit's views is not a coincidence – they both were influenced by the spontanistic Vienna school of right (*libre droit*).

5 See e.g. Hoggart ([1957] 1981) for England or Ambjörnsson (1988) for Sweden. It is no coincidence that Swedish working-class reading circles preferred Romantic authors.

6 The term, originally *Durchkapitalisierung*, comes from a German author Joachim Hirsch (1980).

7 The famous Birmingham Centre for the Contemporary Cultural Studies (CCCS) was started by literary critics (Raymond Williams and Richard Hoggart). In the Nordic context, ethnologists (Ronny Ambjörnsson, Orvar Löfgren, Jonas Frykman and many others) were important as well as the literary circles before sociologists entered the field.

8 This was the case in Nordic alcohol policy, which attempted to plant a fictive 'Continental' drinking style from the harsh cultural soil among young adults as late as in the mid-1960s (Sulkunen et al., 2000).

9 There are plenty of studies on changes in lifestyle attitudes. For example, a shift in attitudes towards sexuality and family life occurred at the end of the 1960s. Pre-marital sex, cohabitation

of non-married couples, contraception and homosexuality became more accepted in Western countries. In the 1960s and 1970s, public opinion also requested liberalization of the divorce legislation (Jallinoja, 1991: 153, 198; Therborn, 2004). However, these studies tell us almost nothing about what people think about the role of the state in these matters.

10 This view is affirmed by many experts of the network society; references and synthesis can be found in Castells (1996).

11 A powerful indicator of this trend is the 'basic rights' or 'secondary rights' movement in continental constitutional law. For example, the Finnish constitution of 1995 included economic, social and cultural rights in addition to the traditional procedural rights of *Rechtstaat* citizenship (equal political and legal rights) (Tuori, 2007).

8

From Pastoral to Epistolary Power

Clear! is a network for coordinating the resources of professionals, voluntary associations, parents and the rest of the citizenry. Its aim is to create a safety net for young people to advance their well-being and to decrease their substance use. Its guiding principles are high quality, voluntary activity, partnership, self-confidence and belief in the future. The focus is primary prevention, occasionally also secondary prevention.

(*Clear!* project, plan of activities, 2002)

The predicament of prevention

Welfare state research has largely ignored the concept of welfare itself, as discussed in the previous chapter. Now we turn to its second caveat, the state as an institution of power. Critics of 'neo-liberalism' attribute anti-state rallies to the conquest gained by the market over the public good, but there is more to the welfare state transformation than a simple roll-back or market-oriented ideology. The concept of welfare has changed from the normative ideals of the good life to abstract issues of resources and rights. This chapter will show that in the saturated society even this solution is not sufficient. The moral tie between the state and the citizens needs to accommodate the autonomy and intimacy of individuals. These are the principles of dignity and greatness that have attained full maturity in the discourse of justification. This re-bonding is written in the way the state is structured and its power over citizens is organized. Who decides, what, for whom and with what resources and techniques, sets a framework for *what can* be decided, especially in regard to lifestyle choices made by individuals.

From the cruel welfare state to persuasion

A few decades ago, European states still tried to guide citizens towards good manners, and they implemented social policies to improve the quality of their populations. The state took a normative stand on sexuality, women's employment, parenting, social manners and legitimate cultural taste. The techniques were harsh. Thousands of involuntary sterilizations on eugenic or non-medical (social) grounds,[1] thousands of alcoholics incarcerated in labour camps (Warpenius and Sutton, 2000), prohibition of contraception and repression of sexual minorities are illustrative examples of policies applied not only by the twentieth-century totalitarianisms, but also of the cruelty of the modern welfare state. The pedagogy applied to potential victims of vice was less harsh than smug, such as a state-appointed committee to select music permissible in bars in Sweden in 1956 (to prevent sexual indecency), state regulations on how many shots of vodka or glasses of beer could be served with and without a meal, or state committees to decide on the dress code for licensed restaurants (Tigerstedt, 2000). In Finland, the state even published official guide-books on good manners (Peltonen, 1996).

Today the state is no longer vested with authority over the good life. The welfare state stands steady on its two feet – social security and public services. But as individuals anxiously shield their autonomy and intimacy against symbolic violations, the state faces another kind of problem: the predicament of prevention. While affluence has liberated the vast majority of Westerners from the distress of choosing only what is absolutely necessary, it also has created a baffling moral responsibility about the consequences of the choice. We know a great deal about the detrimental effects of consumption. We have a potent technology to correct many of those virulent effects, but the cost of applying it may be very high. The effects spread, with a gravity ranging from a minor inconvenience like tobacco smoke at a bus stop, to contagion like the bird flu, or moral crazes like drug use. The cost is often damage to somebody's health, or to the environment. Many effects cannot be detected by consumers themselves, and thus they are helpless to contain them. Prevention of problems is an efficient way of cost containment, but it entails the collaboration of the whole population, not only those who are immediately concerned such as smokers, drug users, heavy drinkers, bulimics and other risk takers (WHO, 1986; Petersen and Lupton, 1996). Moral responsibility for prevention is diffused to wide segments of society, but in what way? Who should be responsible for the millions of premature deaths caused by tobacco, alcohol, obesity, motorized traffic, or by exposure to toxic substance in air, water and food?

Combining risk management with individual autonomy and intimacy is the predicament of prevention, the theme from which this book started. In this chapter, I shall show how states face this predicament with what I call *the ethics of not taking a stand*. This principle attempts to manage lifestyle risks through persuasion rather than law. Persuasion is couched in rational arguments about health, well-being and safety, appealing to everybody with moral neutrality. I am suggesting that Michel Foucault's metaphor of *pastoral power*, which so well describes the power of the welfare state, must be replaced with the metaphor of *epistolary power*, which describes the ethics of not taking a stand. It involves three aspects. First, it exercises control through abstract guidance from a distance by political bodies that send instructions and issue principles, warnings and sanctions. Control is implemented through *projects*, temporary organizations with specific targets, funding (usually public) measured to their estimated outcomes. Projects operate in partnership with national, regional and local actors, who may be public bodies, private enterprises or associations. Second, epistolary power shifts moral responsibility from the state to *communities and citizens* who are asked to operate without a centrally directed plan. Third, it seeks a balance between the right to satisfy specific individual desires and the principle that I call *consequentialism*. This is the idea that policy should be justified not by judgements of the intrinsic value of different lifestyles, but on the basis of what follows from them.

Pastoral power and its discontents

It should be repeated here that the new problem is not the invisible presence of risks themselves. The ethics of not taking a stand is the upshot of the restructured interface between the state and its citizens. It is a reformulated modality of what Foucault ([1976] 1979: 134–39; 1991) called *bio-power*, by which he meant a concern by modern governments for the life of the population. It consisted of both disciplinary techniques exercised by the school, by the army and by penitentiary institutions to educate and keep individuals in line, and demographic techniques to manage the size, health, hygiene and welfare of the population. Population was its object, but also its subject: the source of its legitimacy. This definition fitted in well with the welfare state policies until the last third of the twentieth century. The mode of operation of the welfare state was *pastoral*, to use Foucault's (1988; 2007: 115–34) second metaphor. Pastoral power is a relationship of care. The shepherd knows all the needs of the herd and attends to them all at once (Dean, 1999: 72–83). But such care produces outcomes that undermine its own authority, because it is not only a collective but also an individualizing power: the shepherd directs the whole flock, but he nevertheless cares for each sheep individually and gets them back if they escape (Foucault, 2007: 128).

The metaphor referred originally to the genesis of modern power, which Foucault called 'governmentality', in the sixteenth century in Western Europe. It nevertheless applies perfectly to the story I am telling in this book about power and lifestyle regulation since the French Revolution, and particularly from the late nineteenth to the late twentieth century. When nineteenth-century hygienists fought on all fronts to fight the invisible causes of contagion, they also instigated the idea of the dangerous touch, and gave form to the significance of personal distinctness in modern individualistic culture. When the temperance reformers set out to liberate humans from drink and dirt, they implanted in them the idea that every person matters and should be master of her and his own life. When population policies aimed at improving the quality of human material in the early twentieth century, they thereby also established norms of sexual responsibility and the institution of the private nuclear family. The post-war welfare states fought against Beveridge's Five Giants all at once; the result was not only freedom from want, disease and squalor, but also a universalized sense of individual integrity. These missions were embedded in broad agendas, the consequences of which we are witnessing in the democratization of the whole civilizing process.

Pastoral authority consists of three dimensions (Foucault, 2007: 115–34). The first is the principle of universality that includes everybody as part of the herd. 'There shall be one flock and one shepherd' (John 10:16). Inclusion means not only equality, but also individuality: the shepherd seeks out the lost sheep and keeps the herd together. Second, the shepherd directs the flock's movement, from the troubles of the worldly run of time to eternal salvation. He shows his people the direction they must follow, and the herd recognizes the shepherd's authority: 'I know those who are mine, and those who are mine know me.' The third principle is solidarity. 'I shall look for the lost, the lost sheep shall I bring back, bind the wounded, strengthen the weak; but the fat and the strong I shall destroy. I shall look after them as is right' (Ezekiel 34:16).

When the class-based social movements of the nineteenth and early twentieth centuries advocated social reforms, they disagreed about many things, but shared three underlying standards of judgement much like the principles of pastoral power: progress, universal individualism, and the nation as an inclusive frame of reference. There was a need for change because the future was to be better than the present; everybody should be treated on equal terms and held accountable for their choices. The parliamentary national state was the platform on which differences would be negotiated and the necessary reductions of individual freedom imposed. Progress, universalism and the state were unchallenged 'imponderables' of the critical awareness of the time, with both its legitimating and fault-finding functions. The ebullient faith in the civilizing capacities of the pastoral state, and the intrepid belief in a better future justified forms of state interference that today would be experienced as scandalous.

The potentialities of these pastoral imponderables have now come to their full maturity. The methods of the cruel welfare state seem abominable to us today, and also its goals have become self-contradicting. Few master trends from the period of industrialization would increase human happiness. More, cheaper, better quality food, bigger and better quality housing, improving and more comfortable mobility, more and richer availability of information and entertainment, longer and healthier life, better care for children and old people, etc., are wishes that are relatively easy to agree on, but all of them have two chastening caveats attached to them. The first is that every innovation to solve a problem tends to create a plethora of new risks. More of something usually means less of something else. Longer life often means less comfort and vice versa, more comfort means shorter life; more food may imply less health. Choices have become not less but more difficult, and any improvement is likely to make that difficulty even more salient.

The second qualm is about the pastoral mode of government itself. It involves obedience under the duality between 'clergy' and 'laity', the shepherd and the flock, but no obedience is possible without occurrences of resistance. Foucault distinguished five forms of resistance that culminated in the Reformation: asceticism, community, mysticism, reliance on the Scriptures and eschatology. The aspiration was to liberate the faithful from the guidance of the prophet, incarnated in ecclesiastical or in governmental authority on all five accounts. (1) 'Exercise of self on self and on the world' in asceticism sets the sinner free from the institution of confession and absolution, except in the eyes of God himself. (2) The laic community liberates the faithful from the sacraments of the church. (3) Divine presence in mysticism turns prayer and reading into spiritual experiences without clerical mediation. (4) Direct contact with the Spirit through the Scriptures sets the faithful free of ecclesiastical patronage. And, finally, (5) the advent of the Holy Spirit on earth, when he will return, spreads over the entire world so that a particle of him will be in each of the faithful and they will no longer need a shepherd (2007: 214).

In Foucault's treatise, these forms of resistance culminated in the Reformation, but the analytical distinctions apply perfectly to the history I am outlining in this book.[2] The individualizing effects of the pastoral welfare state have become pervasive. Exercise of self on self distends the sense of autonomous mastery, not in asceticism but in public display of pleasures. A new nostalgia about laic community has reappeared as a refusal of state control which treats citizens as if they were children with no will. Instead of following shepherds we look to our own authenticity, however illusionary, for salvation of our personal integrity.

Capitalism still needs the nation–state, but its principles and structures of responsibility have been altered. The sense of 'the common good' has become abstract and thin, and the national moral community has lost its strength. Nikolas Rose has even asserted that the end of societies has arrived: defining the 'good' that public policies ought to advance, and agreeing on common terms for such a discussion, is no longer easy (Rose, 1999: 98–136).

Projects: programmes, funds, contracts, partnerships and evaluations

The state's response to the conflict between private lifestyle choice and public interest is reflected in the structures and practices of public institutions. The doctrine of *New Public Management*, advocated by the Organization for Economic Co-operation and Development (OECD) since the 1980s, emphasizes devolved responsibility, local initiative, increased civic responsibility, competition, budgeting by results, and the use of private-sector service providers (OECD, 1995; 2002). Public management is seen as offering a flexible and effective alternative to old-fashioned bureaucracy (Clarke et al., 2000; du Gay, 2000). It is expected to neutralize and resolve conflicts in domains where there are radical differences of opinion, among experts and among citizens (Newman, 2000).

Many public services such as transportation, energy, communication and health care, have been privatized. As far as they are concerned, the critics of neo-liberalism are correct. But also in preventive social and health policy, public management stresses partnership, community development and cooperation. The hub of the new structure of governance is the *project* funded from specially designated funds rather than from the regular state or municipal budget. This requires a new form of administration: contracts between partners and the funding agency. To supervise the contract, the agency needs evaluation, and to set the targets and a standard of evaluation for the projects, a policy programme is necessary. This form of organization replaces traditional command structures with voluntary commitment, bargaining and trust. It no longer guarantees stability based on inspection and authority; instead, evaluation *ex ante* (reviews of competing project proposals) and *ex post* (reviews of outcomes) stress the competence, commitment and autonomy of the partners. This emphasis has moral dimensions far beyond the merits of the market as compared to the bureaucratic state. Let us take a closer look at a typical case of moral management in a post-pastoral state: youth work.

New public management of youth problems

Whereas modern lifestyle movements a century ago relied on the parliamentary state, the law and bureaucratic control, governance by projects aims to shift power and responsibility down from the central state to the project partners, and ultimately onto the citizens themselves. Transparency and direct mediation of the citizens' interests to policy programmes are the goals. The subjects of the state should no longer be targets of disciplinary action, but become agents of their own life, aided by the services of the public administration. What actually happens?

The case we studied in detail in Helsinki, Finland, was a project set up to prevent young people from taking drugs. The local context is not important; similar projects are found everywhere in Europe and North America, with similar goals, methods and organizations. The similarity originates partly from international programmes or strategies of drug prevention. For example, the EU drug strategy for 2002–2004 highlights cooperation and shared responsibility in preventive work (Council of the European Union, 1999). This orientation is incorporated in national drug strategies in Finland (e.g. Action Plan, 2003) and in the 2000 Drug Strategy for the City of Helsinki. In the same vein, national alcohol programmes highlight local initiative, multi-professional cooperation, citizen participation and voluntary partnership. The consciousness of the crisis of the welfare state of the early 1990s had already presumed that local administration and the third sector would have to step in to replace the central government in health promotion and preventive social policy. In response to these deliberations, an experimental drug abuse prevention project, let us call it *Clear!*, was set up in Helsinki, employed by the City of Helsinki and partly financed by the Ministry of Social Affairs and Health. *Clear!* had its own management, a separate budget and partners among associations as well as among private business firms. Its sponsors saw it as a pioneer of new European-style preventive social policy. It was started in the Northern City District in 1994 by a nurse who had earlier worked in an alcoholism clinic. *Clear!* was expanded into a city-wide project at the beginning of 2000, and established as a permanent structure three years later. Each of the seven city districts employed a prevention worker.

146

Initially, the organization consisted of the manager, a marketing director and an educational director besides the field workers. The formal power lay in the hands of a Board of Directors appointed jointly by the city administration, the police and the church. The declared aim of the project was to coordinate professional and voluntary work for the benefit of young people (see the epigraph to this chapter). It did not produce any educational programmes or materials of its own (Rantala and Sulkunen, 2006).

In the mid-1990s, a wave of illicit drug use hit Europe and also Finland, with an associated HIV epidemic, but the primary challenges were still tobacco and alcohol. Alcohol control was centralized in the state alcohol monopoly until 1995 when EU regulations opened production and wholesale to free competition, with only retail sales remaining under state monopoly (Holder, 1998). Restaurant and bar licensing and inspection gradually was relaxed. Action at the local level was the only possibility. The project's partners were youth workers, social workers, teachers, the police and parents associations.

But what to tell the partners was a problem. Drug use is risky, but so is advice about it. Although the official policy is 'no alcohol to persons under 18, and no illicit drugs at all', in practice, the situation in regard to alcohol or other drugs was ambiguous. Strict control of moderate drug use creates unnecessary exclusion and causes more harm than it eliminates. Alarm messages may destroy the most important support that children need: trust in their parents. (Sulkunen et al., 2004). Many officials are aware of these risks, but they fear public outrage if they are to appear too permissive. They do not know what to say:

> I have thought about it myself, but the fact is that we have no shared view. If we work as part of the city, we surely ought be clearer on that, too ... If a parent comes and asks, 'What shall I do now – my son says that cannabis is OK', what is our standpoint, or is it a personal matter? (field worker B; interviewed 25 October 2001)

Alcohol and tobacco are even more difficult issues. Smoking and drinking by teenagers raise public alarm, but field workers know that in fact youngsters have more problems due to their parents' than their own drinking. Research has shown that only multi-component prevention has a realistic chance of producing effects; mere information about the risks does not suffice. Preventive policies should restrict availability and involve the media to support local initiatives (Holder, 1998: 135–43). However, this requires much stronger political and moral resources than *Clear!* had at its disposal. It relied strongly on individual self-regulation and the sharing of responsibility:

> Should we perhaps start from the idea that there would not be so much state control? The control rather should lie in the family ... Individuals are very much masters of their own destiny, and there's quite a lot one can do about one's life. People have strength – when you just give them a chance to do something .... You have to try to find solutions actively, for bigger and smaller things. (Project Manager B; interviewed 6 September 2000 and 23 October 2000)

If drug problems are symptoms of a general malaise, then the road to their prevention should be improved welfare. However, the structural causes of exclusion, such as unemployment or gaps in the service system, are beyond field workers' reach. They can only offer partnership and empowerment, but courses in parental education or human relations skills reach mostly those who have greatest motivation for thoughtful parenting to begin with. The communitarian approach in prevention tends to exclude those who are in greatest need of support.

The managers' response was improved well-being and 'safety nets' to enable parents and children to face these dilemmas. But the problem remained. The project made information programmes and kits available to parents, some produced by very anti-drug-oriented NGOs, and were of the 'Just Say No' type. The field workers were aware that these programmes can do more harm than good, but felt that they had no other resources to offer. A further problem arose when parents should have been advised on their own behaviour. Too strict positions on smoking and drinking would have alienated many of those parents who most need help. One field worker summed it up: 'The most ethical stand, eh, that is, not to take a stand at all' (Field worker D, interviewed 1 February 2002).

Epistolary power

Guidance from a distance

The managers and field workers were not implementing a neo-liberalistic marketization of the state. Admittedly, drug prevention programmes such as Drug Abuse Resistance Education (DARE) (www.dare.com), or social skills programmes such as Parent and Youth Effectiveness Training by Thomas Gordon Inc.,[3] are produced by NGOs or private companies. Whether they are for-profit- or non-profit organizations, the diffusion of the programmes is market-based. Nevertheless, the market is only marginally related to the main problem, which results from the transformation of the welfare state itself.

The *Clear!* project represents the opposite of pastoral authority. The managers and the field workers thought of themselves as technical resources rather than representatives of moral authority; they did not believe they knew what their customers needed; and they had no capacity to support solidarity. Their mandate did not include outreach work to bring back the lost sheep, and they had no corrective role to bind the wounded. Their mode of governance was more like the epistolary role of the apostles, guiding from a distance the faithful who wanted to hear, giving advice for the road to salvation, but leaving the responsibility for following the advice to their public. The project form outside the political and bureaucratic structure of power represents the epistolary aspect of the ethics of not taking a stand, replacing universal inclusion with voluntary partnership. It offers provision for needs with advice and encouragement rather than disciplinary techniques, and it assures caring solidarity with information packages instead of laws and regulations.

Communitarian rationalism

Clear! illustrates how community, one of the fields of resistance against pastoral power outlined by Foucault, operates in the new interface between the state and the citizens. The project managers held strong views on the causes of social problems in contemporary society. They referred to 'our Zeitgeist' and 'late modernity', indicating that their everyday consciousness interacts with the consciousness of the sociological pulpits. They diagnosed Finnish society as work-intensive, pluralistic and fragmented by drastic social change. Parenting has become an extremely demanding responsibility but a lonely task. Life offers a multitude of alternative values and possibilities but no common framework for making choices. The resulting confusion tends to burn out professional educators and parents who are unable to provide security and support to young people. As if referring to Robert Putnam's (2000) book *Bowling Alone* (which they might well have read), the staff of *Clear!* thought that this isolation causes further malaise: social exclusion, disorders in adolescent development, mental health problems, crime and use of intoxicants:

> And then there's this cultural change. No village community or grandparent support, or a safety net for you any more. Too much has disappeared too fast, and all that cultural avalanche on top of it! Adult contacts around children have disappeared ... The late modern world is so chaotic for the youngsters that no individual can cope with it alone. Parents have the main responsibility, but cannot quite do it on their own. Cooperation thus is essential. Parents need special support in all this. (Project Manager A, interviewed 18 September 2000)

According to the managers, co-ordinated work among professionals and cooperation among parents will generate a new sense of community to replace the one that has been lost. They thought that the traditional village community had been replaced either by indifferent mass society individualism or by paternalistic and bureaucratic state control. Communitarian policy aims to revitalize and consolidate the sense of collective responsibility. The managers of *Clear!* believed that their task is to fill the social gap in a fractured and chaotic world. The programme gave financial support to community events organized by and for adults. Another activity was to offer free social skills training for parents. Those who were seen to need help most urgently were parents who have difficulties in maintaining contact with their children.

In contrast, the programme had little to offer to young people directly. It was believed that the best way to help them was to promote the sense of community among adults. This would buoy up general well-being in the locality, and that would enfold children in networks of caring and solidarity. The field workers cared for adolescents and children from an epistolary distance, and treated them as objects of concern rather than as subjects with their own views of a good life. They were seen as a fairly homogeneous group, whose alcohol and drug use was understood to be a reaction to problems in life, especially loneliness, feelings of insecurity, and inadequate parenting.

Like many youth and social work programmes in Finland, the managers of *Clear!* had taken their models from American and British communitarianism. American versions criticize liberal individualism and stress that 'the whole village' should cultivate the sense of duty in life, particularly concerning the family, sexual morality and consumption (Bellah et al., 1985; Badwahr, 1996). In contrast, European versions of communitarianism, 'the third way' between free market competition and bureaucratic state control (Giddens, 1998), are more strongly formulated as criticism of welfare state collectivism (Conway, 1996). Communities are expected to liberate individuals from excessive state paternalism, in the interest of freedom as well as to contain the cost of tax-funded welfare programmes.

Both types of communitarianism are relevant in the ideologies of community-based prevention such as *Clear!*. On the one hand, the community is seen to be the solution to individual isolation; on the other hand, it is a way of shifting moral responsibility from the pastoral state back to 'society'. It is assumed that within the small locality it is possible to reach a deliberative consensus concerning the needs and norms shared by all.

However, faced by the diversity of lifestyles in contemporary multicultural environments, it appeared that such consensus is possible only in a very abstract form, especially as regards alcohol use, drugs or youth cultures. The rhetoric of *Clear!* stressed parenting because in abstract terms everyone agrees that parents should bear responsibility for their offspring. Beyond that, it was difficult to offer solutions to 'the whole village'. For example, a seminar organized for parents adopted a Pact of Good Parenting: Ten Principles. The principles stress adults' responsibility for their children, the need for shared rules on how to deal with young persons, as well as the importance of security and care for them. All this is formulated in very abstract terms without specifying what kind of security, care or rules are meant. No stand is taken on how parents should deal with young people, what parents should agree about homecoming hours, what to do in case of smoking, drinking or drug use, or on any other aspects of parent–child relationships.

Communitarianism in the European sense has been proposed as an alternative not only to welfare state paternalism, but also as a critique of the neutral concept of welfare as a resource discussed in the preceding chapter. The resource theory is closely related to a principle of ethical philosophy called deontology.[4] This principle gives priority to considerations of justice over considerations of values and the good in public life. Policy should minimize the constraints that one person's good life puts on other people's rights to pursue theirs. Instead of taking a stand on the intrinsic value of lifestyles, even on risk-taking behaviour, public policy should aim its interventions to reduce *harm incurred to others*: to innocent children of abusive parents, to peaceful neighbours, to tax-payers, school teachers, upright pupils and others who wish not to be disturbed by lifestyles they would not have chosen for themselves. Since the practical applications of this moral orientation focus not on the moral worth of different lifestyles themselves, but only on their consequences for others I call it 'consequentialism'.[5]

Seyla Benhabib (1992: 68–88) has distinguished two communitarian critiques of consequentialism. The first critique she calls integrationist, because it insists that it is impossible to make judgements concerning what is right in politics on the basis of justice alone; values are inevitably involved, and they should be made explicit. Disadvantages of integrative communitarianism are that many values simply are not compatible; for example, forced marriages, or mutilation of girls' bodies by circumcision, violate the Western value of female personhood, but may nevertheless be a moral obligation for some religious groups. Accepting one set of values will lead to the exclusion of others and at least arouse conflicts.

The second critique of consequentialism, the one that Benhabib defends, she calls participatory communitarianism. She argues that communities can and should ensure that participants are free and competent to articulate their needs, and will negotiate reciprocally between conflicting values between themselves. Such negotiation can and must concern differences and bring to public debate also issues that are beyond universal rules of justice. In this way, value conflicts will be solved by citizens, not by the superior authority of the state (which it gets from voters). This is one version of the notion of 'deliberative democracy', influenced by Jürgen Habermas, Jon Elster, and John Rawls. The essential prerequisite of deliberative democracy is free communication, and therefore it is also called discursive democracy.

The project workers in *Clear!* were inclined to apply participatory communitarianism as a guideline (although they had no idea of the theoretical issues involved in the academic debate). They realized that without offending someone they could say nothing concrete about parenting, or about what to do in conflicts between parents and children, or about problems related to parenting with their adult neighbours. These are issues that should be left to the parents themselves. Therefore the discursive competence of the parents gained dramatic importance in the project. The Romantic nostalgia of the community was combined with a belief in individuals' rationality. As responsible adults, parents were expected to know who they are and what they want in life. They should be able to make independent decisions. Community work was to provide a platform for all concerned to make agreements such as the Pact of Good Parenting mentioned above.

Pastoral power exercised by the welfare state could not be trusted, and it was not felt to be efficient or fair, unless individuals cooperate in their own interest according to their own values. The faithful should know their own way to salvation and be confident with it. However, as the content of the Pact indicates, this tended to come to nothing more than a declaration of the principle of participatory communitarianism itself. Project Manager C formulated the attitude in this way:

Almost all education and courses we provide are based on the 'solution-oriented approach', meaning that I am my own master and that my own decisions have an effect on how I live my life. The training of social and human relationship skills begins from the reflection on who I am, what is important to me and what I want from life. Communication with others comes only after you know yourself, it only works after you really know who you are. (Project Manager C, interviewed 18 September 2000)

The communitarian paradox

Participatory communitarianism as applied in the case we studied was, although perhaps ethically sound, sociologically flawed in a paradoxical way. On the one hand, community is an alternative to paternalistic rules and restrictions that are seen to violate individual dignity, much in the same way as communities in the Reformation were opposed to the ecclesiastical authority over the sacraments. On the other hand, communities are emotional networks of attachment and consensus. They, too, are individualizing associations, but in order to form a social bond, they must have a common enemy and shared understandings of the good life. As Charles Taylor (1992) has stressed, communitarian morality depends on difference as well as similarity: shared conceptions of the good life and affective relationships between people who adhere to the same values. Constraints on the freedom of their members in communities of the faithful are much stronger than among people who belong together simply as citizens of the same welfare state.

Epistolary power is therefore as individualizing as pastoral power, but in a different way. Whereas the shepherd cares for each individual and brings back those who are lost, the apostle addresses his instructions only to the community of the faithful. Pastoral authority is inclusive and individualizing, apostolic authority is exclusive and communitarian. The flock is a group in which one gains individual value because one belongs to it; the community of the faithful is a group one joins and is attached to by the bond of personal faith.

The paradox is that communitarian solutions are sought to liberate citizens from pastoral state control, but then communities of the faithful require even more conformity from their members. Few parents groups are able and willing to agree on substantial principles of parenting, unless they are also bound by strong particularistic norms, for example, of a religious congregation. In practice, communitarian projects such as *Clear!* are simply too weak to create such bonds. Prevention workers do know that people cannot be engaged in community action on the basis of rights, without enemies on the outside. Abstract talk about youth's malaise or about the erosion of communal ties is not sufficient to initiate communitarian movements. Concrete action, on the other hand, can only focus on limited problems such as youth disturbances in a particular locality. More comprehensive conduct would turn into assaults on particular groups who would be labelled trouble-makers, which would make the excluding effects of the project too explicit.

Consequentialism, rules and normative neutralization

Epistolary power must find a solution between communitarianism and deontology (or consequentialism). These two principles, morality based on common values and morality based on consequences, clash in a society where individual autonomy and intimacy as principles of dignity and greatness have reached the point of saturation. Politics of values gives priority to differences and supports communities with particular varieties of the good life. Politics of consequentialism stresses people's right not to be harmed by other people's choices. It is an indispensable moral resource for public interventions into lifestyle. In lifestyle regulation there is a constant battle between goods and rights.

Epistolary power has three ways to reconcile goods (differences) with rights (sameness). The first method is to set up *rules* to define tolerable behaviour. Inter-governmental institutions, such as the EU, issue a vast mountain of regulations to ensure good practices, from animal welfare, to food safety to public health and justice. Governments design their own version of these rules and regulations. In the attempt to make room for difference while also guaranteeing rights, these rules tend to become increasingly detailed, specifying each case and constructing a rule to handle it fairly. The more multicultural our society becomes, the more detailed regulations and codes of good practices we need. These codes regulate sexual relationships within and outside marriage, custody of children after divorce, rights of homosexuals, rights of children, or rights of animals. The more complex the issues of regulation become, the more procedural the rules. The same is true of professional life: we have ever more detailed codes of conduct regulating research ethics, scientific assessments, relationships between professors and students, etc., and such rules are constantly extended into new domains of everyday life. The problem about such penetration is that no rules seem to guarantee justice. As Alain Wolfe (1989) has aptly pointed out, the debate on abortion that concentrates on the limit beyond which the foetus has become a person and thus has the right to live can never lead to ethically justifiable solutions in particular cases, which are always complex and depend on factors that often have nothing to do with such a limit (Benhabib, 1992).

The second method is *normative neutralization*, extensively used especially in health policy to avoid the complexities of rule-based regulation. Public health can no longer be limited to preventing specific diseases. Risks related to lifestyle must be included (Lupton, 1995). Even if we could decide when one is responsible for having damaged one's health with excessive drinking, smoking, eating or other things, we would not be able to arrive at consensus on whether or not such a person should be treated or not. In prevention, rule-based ethics is even more problematic. What restrictions should individuals tolerate in the interest of the public good? How could the rights of others be weighed against risk-takers' rights to choose? As in the case of *Clear!*, the answer is often 'empowerment': promoting and sustaining abilities to make the right choices, in terms of apparently neutral moral goals, of which 'health' is the most important, followed by security and well-being. Also these goals are issued from inter-governmental bodies, national governments and local administration. They take the form of policy programmes, like those that constituted the framework for the *Clear!* project, or they are issued as framing laws that set targets such as reduction of exclusion among immigrant population, improving occupational health, the educational level of adolescents, or assuring minimum levels of care and well-being for the elderly.

Normative neutralization is not the same as simple consequentialism or deontology. It does not pretend to solve the problem of lifestyle regulation on the basis of justice alone, regardless of individual and group differences. Instead, it sets up a *grid of common values* as the criterion of justification: health, well-being and security. These goals are vague and wide, encompassing a great diversity of images concerning human capacity to act autonomously, to care for oneself, and to choose between preferences. The concept of health itself has become almost meaningless. Health is not absence of a disease but a *degree* of normality: the maximum quality of life that care and treatments can offer in each condition, even with the presence of disabilities or chronic conditions such as cardiovascular diseases and, increasingly, cancers.[6]

The principle of normative neutralization underlies the shift in public health policy of many European countries in recent decades. Consumer policy has changed from normative standard-setting to market-oriented safety regulation (Ilmonen and Stoe, 1997). Morally sensitive businesses like gambling have been deregulated in many countries, but combined with attempts to protect minors and excessive harm to adults. In health policy, the emphasis is now on preventing ill health in general through information campaigns, instead of attempts to direct lifestyles to avoid specific diseases (with the exception of HIV and AIDS). In alcohol policy, the dominant preventive theory has been the so-called total consumption approach for several decades (Bruun et al., 1975). It argues that public policy should minimize harm from drinking, and that an efficient method is to reduce the amount of alcohol consumed by a population. This can be achieved by price increases, limitations of points and hours of sale, age limits and possibly advertising bans and warning labels (Babor et al., 2003). Although sales restrictions interfere with consumers' and market actors' liberties, they are morally neutral if they are addressed similarly to everyone. The value of drinking as such is not commented on, only public health matters.

Public health administration has become organized in general public health departments such as the French Haut Comité de la Santé Publique, which earlier consisted of separate institutes to prevent cancers, traffic accidents, sexually transmitted diseases and alcoholism. Vice control and normative regulation in the area of sexuality has become health promotion and risk regulation. Sexuality, lifestyle and consumption are everybody's own business and not of public concern. What justifies public policies in these areas is not behaviour but its consequences for health, well-being and security:

social costs, health care expenses, risk to others such as HIV and AIDS, street safety, etc. The neutralized principle only defines the targets in preventive public health work, but shifts the responsibility for the means to local actors, often in partnership with publicly funded projects. In drug policy, harm minimization has become the mainstream approach in Europe. Although drug use generally incurs penal sanctions, its consequences and risks to the general public are reduced by needle exchange and substitution pro-grammes, even though these programmes violate the principle that drug use is illegal (Tammi, 2007).

The victim's point of view

The third way to reconcile rights and goods is to adopt the *victim's point of view*. Normative neutralization does *not* mean that the moral basis of the state has become insolvent at the expense of pragmatic considerations. Whenever politicians, business managers or other public personalities are caught usurping their positions for personal gain, or otherwise betraying the public's trust, we react with outrage. In general, the media is more than ever filled with news and stories about violations of justice and trust. Let us remind ourselves of what Adam Smith thought about moral senti-ments and the social order. The *social passions* of generosity, humanity, kindness, compassion and mutual friendship and esteem make social life pleasant, but are not necessary for society to exist. *Selfish passions* are nec-essary for social life, since persons who do not care for themselves leave the care to others, and deserve no more respect than greedy persons. The third category, *unsocial feelings* of hatred and anger, are necessary for social order, because they are the foundation of justice, given that they are mod-erated by and measured to fit the gravity of the offence. The moral func-tion of the state for Smith was the creation of justice with such moderation of the unsocial feelings.

Smith's theory about hatred and anger is even more valid today than in his time. For example, while public administration is cautious about telling parents how to treat their children, neglect of parental responsibilities arouses anger and hatred, and our sense of justice demands that such heed-lessness be corrected, and possibly punished. We are in fact so accustomed to arguing about justice that we tend to ignore how normative the modern welfare states have been, in contrast to the state's contemporary reluctance to take a stand on the good life. We tend to abstract the issues of lifestyle regulation into issues of justice alone.

However, our contemporary sensibility of justice has a new emphasis. The British criminologist David Garland (2001: 121–2) has pointed out how the criminal justice system has adopted a completely new emphasis on the *rights of victims*. Whereas penal policy in the nascent welfare state addressed the causes of crime, it now gives priority to its consequences, and particularly to its consequences for the innocent. Victims were reduced to the role of the complainant and witness rather than a party to the proceedings. The criminal jus-tice system aimed to understand the needs of the offenders and to rehabilitate them, whereas the victims' interests were subsumed within the public interest. Correctional measures were taken in the interest of both the public and the offenders. Today new forms of restitutive justice are being put in place, including court-mandated compensation orders, victim–offender mediation, and therapeutic support for victims. The victims' role in proceedings is emphasized in several ways. Therapies for offenders highlight the impact of crime upon victims, and organized victims movements have gained an improved presence in criminal policy. In short, 'the criminal justice system strives to reinvent itself as a service organization for individual victims rather than merely a public law enforcement agency' (ibid.: 122).

A similar emphasis on the feelings of the innocent, the victims of natural catastrophes, sudden diseases, accidents or neglect, is apparent in the contemporary media everywhere. The feelings of the victims' near ones are publicized and highlighted, whereas offenders are not shown mercy. In criminal justice, the victim's point of view is related to an increasingly exclusive penal policy. Politicians demand harsher penalties and lower penalty thresholds, with consequent increases in the prison populations.

The project society

The victim's point of view, normative neutralization and increasing specification of rules, are ways that epistolary mode of power accommodates intimacy and autonomy in the saturated society. The victim's point of view attenuates the distinction between 'us' and 'them'. It does this by contrasting the innocent and the guilty, the virtuous victims and the devious offenders or apostates of their responsibilities. Normative neutralization aims to square claims for authenticity of the self with the right to autonomy of the other. Specification of rules is a way of reconciling differences and sameness.

The balance is difficult to find, and there is no universal solution. It is no coincidence that the case of preventive social policy that I used to illustrate epistolary power in this chapter was started as a temporary project, not as a permanent structure. The project is the organizational form that public policy takes when it applies the principle of normative neutralization to itself. It is an apparently neutral solution to the dilemma between good and right. It spells out a mixture of three answers to the lacking moral authority of the state: *abstractness*, *pragmatism* and the *emphasis on outcomes*. Abstractness of the goals – health, well-being and security – imposes a standard of prudence on individuals, justifying the necessary reductions of their freedoms by their own self-interest. It is as if these abstractions had returned to the vagueness of the hygienists before Pasteur, who were fighting contagion on all fronts. Anything that might promote health, well-being and security can be included in the projects' agenda, because in the end it is up to the individuals themselves to define the content of these goals.

The pragmatism in governance by projects was illustrated by the 'solution-orientation' of the managers of *Clear!*. Solution-oriented therapy or pedagogy is not interested in causes of problematic behaviour; instead, it concentrates on the effects of preventive action. The search for causes is, according to this perspective, not only a waste of time, but might also have negative effects. For example, criminals and addicts may turn explanations of their behaviour into vocabularies of blame neutralization. Solution-orientation, often translated as 'innovation', has been used in science and technology policy for decades. Public administration cannot determine research results or fix industrial strategies, but it can take a stand on goals and set measurable targets. Pragmatism in social policy expects new ideas to emerge 'at the grass-root level', among field workers and citizens. People are thought to be creative and the solutions need to be given space to develop and grow. Auditors evaluate these innovations to identify 'good practices'. Since human behaviour is the sum of complex factors, social work research should not seek explanations concerning clients. It is more useful to observe the effects of social work itself and choose the methods that seem effective and cost-efficient. The rhetoric of good practice leads to a sort of new social Darwinism. Clients and employees are free to invent new action models, mutations, and the fittest among them are chosen for additional refining.

Governance by projects has turned impacts and outcomes into key concepts that are applied everywhere, with a bearing on what constitutes relevant knowledge about society. When the aim is not to explain behaviour, nor even to understand the mechanisms through which the measures taken might have effects, but only their outcomes or impact, there is no need to understand alcohol problems, youth culture or deviant behaviour. Evaluation researchers can flexibly move from one substance area to another.

The project is the organizational structure that epistolary power needs to send its abstract messages to society. It takes the form of a contract between partners rather than a command structure that is universally binding. Contracts and partnerships are a type of political bond, not merely expressions of attitudes and will. They aim to engage citizens as individuals and groups in participation. Many forms of this ambition lead to the exclusion of those who cannot or will not co-operate. Others can be illusions with little practical significance. Nevertheless, the illusions are significant reflections of the saturated principles of justification that stress the importance of agency. The next two questions are, first, whether this emphasis on agency is well founded, or whether that is also only an illusion that barely covers up what critics of modernity have always feared most: the homogenizing mass society. Second, is the contractual form of the social bond to be taken seriously, against the dominant conviction of sociological theory, which for over a century has maintained that there is no such thing as the social contract? We now turn to this question in the two final chapters.

Notes

1 In Nazi Germany, 400,000 women were castrated. Totalitarian states have generally favoured involuntary sterilization, but it has been applied for racial reasons also in the United States, Canada and Australia, among other countries. It is well known, however, that also the welfare state forerunners, namely the United Kingdom, Sweden and other Nordic countries,

including Finland, coercively sterilized thousands of women annually even as recently as in the 1970s. (http://en.wikipedia.org/wiki/Forced_sterilization#Overview, accessed 27 January, 2008).

2 Foucault's genealogies are surprising in their mesmeric accuracy when placed in the contemporary context, although their original references are eruptions of modernity in the course of the 2,500 and more years of western civilization. His treatise of the pastoral mode of power and the forms of resistance to it is only one, albeit an exceptionally fitting example of this.

3 Thomas Gordon Inc. has developed a much used (in Finland) social skills training programme that places strong emphasis on distinctness and authenticity. The company credo declares:

> When you are having problems meeting your needs I will listen with genuine acceptance so as to facilitate you finding your own solutions instead of depending on mine. I also will respect your right to choose your own beliefs and develop your own values, different though they may be from mine. However, when your behavior interferes with what I must do to get my own needs met, I will tell you openly and honestly how your behavior affects me, trusting that you respect my needs and feelings enough to try to change the behavior that is unacceptable to me. Also, whenever some behavior of mine is unacceptable to you, I hope you will tell me openly and honestly so I can change my behavior. (http://www.gordontraining. com)

4 In ethical theory *deontology* means that moral (political) decisions should not be justified by substantive notions concerning values such as sexual orientation, sexual division of labour, family structure, religious convictions, or other considerations that are considered to be 'private'. Instead, it is a universal moral obligation to respect individuals' human rights, and this obligation must be met in ethically justifiable politics. In the moral theory of the American philosopher John Rawls (1993), this duty involves a fair distribution of resources.

5 In theoretical moral philosophy, 'consequentialism' refers to a principle according to which the moral worth of acts must be judged by their consequences. It is considered to be opposed to deontological approaches that stress people's rights (Scheffler, 1988). Although ethical theory does not concern us here, it needs to be said that I find any philosophical version of this doctrine contradictory. It presupposes that we should not judge acts in axiological terms, i.e. by their intrinsic worth; nevertheless, any assessment of the consequences, e.g. maximum utility to the maximum number, resorts to assessments of the goodness of the consequences. In the sociological sense in which I am using the term here, it refers to a structure of argumentation justifying public intervention into private life on the basis of others' rights. In this way, it is closer to deontological than to axiological ethics.

6 The expanded meaning of 'health' is reflected in diagnostic manuals such as the *International Classification of Diseases* (ICD) or the *Diagnostic and Statistical Manual of Mental Disorders* (DSM). They include an increasing number of diagnostic categories such as 'depression', 'pathological gambling' or 'sexual disorder' that are not diseases but syndromes of different degrees of severity, depending on how many diagnostic criteria a person meets (psyweb.com/Mdisord/DSM_IV/jsp/dsmab.jsp. Accessed 4 January 2008).

9

Inner-Directed or Other-Directed Character? Agency and Citizenship in Mass Society

How selfish soever man may be supposed, there are evidently some principles in his nature, which interest him in the fortune of others, and render their happiness necessary to him, though he derives nothing from it
except the pleasure of having it ... That we often derive sorrow from the
sorrow of others, is a matter of fact too obvious to require any instances to
prove it.

(Adam Smith, 1790, *TMS*: I.i.I.1–2, p. 9)

The demise of differences

Individualization has been the basis of the problematic of justification in
modern capitalism. It has three aspects: individual biography, autonomy and
intimacy. As Axel Honneth (2004) has pointed out, sociology has contained
a curious heterogeneity about the three aspects. These frictions were
nowhere better articulated than in Simmel's ([1900] 1990) writing on
metropolis, money and modern sociability. The autonomy granted by
anonymity and distance in the differentiated metropolis upholds the free
individual, but it also takes away the prop of other individuals that is necessary to recognize and pursue one's interests. To experience autonomy and
intimacy, the individual needs sociability but also a certain detachment in
relations to others. As autonomous individuals, members of modern society
must be treated equally, but their homogeneity also sometimes contradicts
their indispensable difference as unique persons. These tensions have materi-
alized in the state's role in capitalism, first, minimizing the state in favour of
the economic autonomy of wage workers and capitalists, then making it an
important institution to prop up that autonomy against traditional social ties.

The French Revolution and the economic liberalism that followed freed
the individual from traditional, political and personal constraints through
the right to work, thus making individual biographies possible. However,
this led to a complete loss of economic autonomy among the growing proletariat, unprotected by the state in the early nineteenth century. Since
then, the welfare state has supported the universal autonomy in the political, juridical and economic sphere, but that in turn has led to a point where
the state intimidates intimacy, as discussed in the preceding chapter.

In this chapter I shall discuss an important train of thought, the mass society theory, in which the tensions have been seen to result in a conflict between individualization and the sway of mass behaviour. According to this idea, we have come full circle to a point where universal autonomy of individuals as contract-makers has been attained but at the same time become also impossible. Democracy of individuals has an immanent tendency to turn into totalitarianism of the masses. Individuality has become both centrifugal and implosive: it gives individuals autonomy but also isolates them from communities that are necessary for them to act as historical subjects. It also leads to a loss of personal calling, real differences and meaning of life (Baudrillard, [1978] 1997). Peter Wagner (2001a: 74) has pointed out a similar ambivalence in the wider sociological literature on the post-modern condition between visions of contingency and the 'liberation of individuals from the bondage of institutional iron cages' on the one hand, and the resulting dedifferentiation, even destruction of the subject, on the other.

This is a frightening possibility. Has modern society destroyed the individual's capacity to accommodate the natural 'principles which interest him in the fortune of others, and render their happiness necessary to him, though he derives nothing from it except the pleasure of having it', to use the quotation from Adam Smith (*TMS*: I.i.I.1–2, p. 9) in the epigraph to this chapter? Such principles of sympathy presuppose that people experience distinctness and difference, but at the same time are not indifferent towards each other, even when interest in others serves no utilitarian purpose. Destruction of this capacity causes the sameness of everything, or to use the expression of Gilles Deleuze (1968), indifference of differences; it damages the mechanisms of the auto-production of society. Indifference makes it impossible to articulate interests and negotiate over them. It makes group formation extremely contingent and dependent on emotional adjustment to, if not identification with, what others feel and expect. Such societies are readily governed by powers that might not be themselves seen but that operate through charismatic leaders, usurping well-known laws of mass hysteria.

The mass society view is a certain kind of critical awareness of the present, to be found in everyday positions on difficult issues in lifestyle regulation as well as in the consciousness of sociological pulpits. Unquestionably, contemporary capitalism fosters individualism in all three ways described above. Anthony Giddens (1991: Chapter 3) and Ulrich Beck ([1986] 1992), among others, have argued that in late modernity, individualism has even become a *conscious project* at many levels. Does this imply, paradoxically, the inevitable end to individualism, a regression into mass society, and the rekindled risk of totalitarian mass movements? Is this the perspective from which political uncertainties, the rise of new social movements, street action and the malign circuits of exclusion and reinsertion should be interpreted? Is the democratic modern project doomed to fail due to its very kernel, the self-responsible autonomous individual?

The warnings of mass society theorists are more than warranted. In this chapter, I consider these questions through David Riesman's (1950) contrast between inner-directed and other-directed character in his book *The Lonely Crowd*, massively influential after its publication and still very relevant today, particularly in the context of lifestyle regulation. He argued that in affluent consumer societies like ours, people tend to orient themselves to the expectations of others. In their pursuit of personal happiness they need the approval of their peers, but on the other hand, they become indifferent towards collective goals as well as towards their inner selves. Individualism is a self-destructive force, and more than ever before, even in Riesman's own time, we can see its consequences today in the saturated society.

My argument in this chapter is that current forms and consequences of individualism should not be seen as polar opposites to their modern ideals and predecessors but as continuities, or more precisely, saturated transformations of them. The kernel of both is agency, which in the current politics of governance is stressed in the rhetoric of communities, projects, contracts, partnerships and self-responsibility – in short, the epistolary mode of governance that I discussed in Chapter 8. The victories won by modern individualism cannot be denied. In fact, Riesman's diagnosis evolves from rather pessimistic starting points in this direction, and its ebullient optimism about autonomy at the end of his book is more warranted than is often claimed by interpreters (e.g. McClay, 1994). My view is that his most sinister prognoses and interpretations of contemporary realities must be qualified but not dismissed. The dangers lie elsewhere than mass society theories would suppose. The contemporary malaise about individualism accounts for a new and specific type of anti-authoritarian conservatism, which we can observe in contemporary middle-class society.

Characterology

The mass society thesis

The American sociologist David Riesman (1909–2002) became an emblem of a generation of post-war liberals worried about the fate of the individual in mass society. As the classical sociologists had done, he saw modern society as inherently anti-traditional, breaking down the old social ties. But for him, anti-traditional individualism may be of two types. The first, 'inner-directed' character, corresponds to Max Weber's understanding of the spirit of entrepreneurial capitalism. The second, 'other-directed' character, develops when industrial capitalism becomes a society of consumption, dominated by the middle-classes and mass culture. Other-directness means that pursuit of self-interest and internalized patterns of conduct are replaced by yearning for approval by peers, and etiquette for maintaining class boundaries becomes less important than conformity within one's own group of reference. Growing autonomy turns heroic individualism into its opposite, fear of the many.[1]

Riesman, as well as his compatriot and peer C. Wright Mills (born in 1916), was among the first to extend the bipolarity between individualism and conformity to modern capitalism as a whole as its immanent potentiality. Their predecessors and teachers had seen it as an abnormality and deviation in the modern process. When class-based communities erode, as they must in consumer society, individuals become isolated ('atomized' was the evocative term), and unable to defend their interests. The social bond, or the social as such, is in danger of disappearing. This has an impact on the individuals' psychological constitution called *character*. The old Victorian concept of character became rampant in American critical social thought in the post-war years. It was widespread in psychoanalytical literature since Sigmund Freud's use of the term at the turn of the century. Its introduction into social theory owes much to Erich Fromm, who in an early paper (Fromm, [1932] 1991b: 119–35) was the first to apply Freudian psychoanalysis to sociology, in subject matter no less prominent than the spirit of capitalism.

The purport of the analysis of character was to establish a relationship between social structure – a thing in itself with its own objective laws of evolution, conflicts and integration – and what people feel, believe, want and claim about it; and what, consequently, they are willing and able to do to direct its course. Thus, Fromm criticized Freud's understanding of human nature for being biological and fixed; instead, he argued, human beings are both psychologically adapted to society and the laws of psychological adaptation in turn have an impact on social structure and change (Fromm, [1941] 1991a: 8–11). Hans Gerth and C. Wright Mills (1954: xvii) declared in the Preface to their masterpiece *Character and Social Structure* that when societies are on a stable course and proceed smoothly, 'human nature' seems to fit so neatly into traditional routines that no general problem is presented; men know what to expect from one another; their vocabularies for various emotions and their stereotyped motives are taken for granted and seem common to all. But when society is undergoing seismic transformation and men are pivots of historic change, they challenge one another's explanations of conduct, and human nature itself becomes problematic. Problems of human nature arise when the life-routines of a society are disturbed and when men are alienated from their social roles.

The post-war years made it plain that all traditionalisms to hand, those represented by rural American Puritanism, urban working class and old middle class, were being challenged from the ideological pulpits as well as in the micro-level experience of everyday life. In sociological writing, characterology was an attempt to *integrate the idea of human agency with the idea of social structure*. Structure is something to which agency must adapt. It is beyond the grasp of human will, competence, ability and even responsibility. Hence the expression *character structure* that is central in Fromm's work, in Riesman's book and that of Gerth and Mills. Character, unlike psychic dispositions and the organisms in which it is entrenched, is itself socially conditioned, but in its turn character structure forms the emotional and meaningful framework for social integration and change. Yet the search for human agency in social theory by characterologists tended to lead to abysmal observations about its demise in contemporary reality. Adorno's authoritarian personality, Erich Fromm's 'automaton', C. Wright Mills' cheerful robots and other similar 'character structures' are constructions that cling to conformity in a way that allows little room for autonomy and self-determination. On the contrary, these dispositions of meaning and emotion are fertile seed-beds for 'manipulatability' (Gerth and Mills, 1954: xvii), and societies dominated by them are easy prey for totalitarian leadership and drift with no orientation toward progress.

German and Russian totalitarianism in the recent past were the primary scare. The mass society theory was influenced by the German intellectual émigrés to the USA before and at the beginning of the Second World War, especially by members of the Frankfurt School and the Institute for Social Research established to continue their work in America (Tilman, 1984).[2] The most widely read mass society theorists, Riesman and Mills, were Americans and they had American influences as well, notably Thorstein Veblen and the Pragmatists, of whom John Dewey was important for Mills, and Georg Herbert Mead's interactionist social psychology for Riesman. Their critical awareness of the present was curiously backward-looking. Mills diagnosed their contemporary American society as 'over-developed' (Gerth and Mills, 1954), even 'post-modern' (Mills, 1959a: 166, 183). Although Riesman declared himself free of value judgments, his description of other-directed 'inside-dopesters' divulges a profound dislike for their trivial taste (Riesman, 1950: 302).

The themes, although not the terms, of characterology and the mass society theory reappear in European post-modern sociology two or three decades later.[3] Contingency, ambivalence or reflexivity, are terms that rummage around to grasp a culture that has become very individualistic, more organized around consumption and taste than around positions in the productive process. Social capital (or the lack of it), or community (or the lack of it) denote social structures in which right-wing political indignation looms as a larger threat to the remnants of broken working-class politics than the self-interested conservatism of the industrial bourgeoisie ever did.[4]

The other-directed character

Riesman's characterology provides a caveat that was typical in other mass society theories of the time: the absence of agency. Other-directedness *does not* imply passivity and alienation. Riesman stressed the endemic urge of modern citizens to see themselves as contracting agents and clients of bureaucracies rather than as passive recipients of benefits and services. Passivity and dependency are the form of alienation that the mode of governance I call epistolary power, aims to break. To take a rough example, current 'activation' policy exercised by welfare states uses self-responsibility techniques precisely to eliminate withdrawal from the labour market. Free will and competence are now at least as central values of justification as they have been for over one hundred years of modern (welfare) state construction. Before examining these issues in detail, we must first consider Riesman's characters closely.

Riesman's rendition of the mass society stresses consumption and taste. The God-fearing Puritan businessman, for whom work is a calling, is the paradigm figure of the inner-directed man. Among wage earners, alienated from the products of their labour, and with an interest in work only for the pay and other benefits it brings, the ethos is different. But even working-class people aspire to be inner-directed in the pursuit of their interests and in their respect for the 'hardness of the material', which they take craftsman's pride to form into good objects of use. In contrast, the new middle class works with symbols and with other people. Riesman's distinction between working-class and middle-class characters reverberates through Thorstein Veblen's analysis of the producer and predator mentalities. Veblen ([1899] 1961) had argued that producers have the 'instinct of workmanship', an inclination that develops later in human evolution than the instinct of appropriation, since it involves creation and learning. For Riesman, the middle classes exalt their skills in working with the 'softness of humans', for example, as sales persons trying to assume the perspective of the consumer, or when they act as foremen juggling with the management's interests and the interests of the employees. Instead of orienting themselves directly to the task at hand, they adjust themselves to other people.

Work orientation tones with a person's orientation to consumption and leisure. The inner-directed character either takes no great interest in them at all, or relates to them, too, as an area of achievement: at the minimum, they signify escape from work for recovery, but even better if they can be conceived as self-improvement through culture, acquisition of valued objects, establishing useful and prestigious social relationships ('a titled son-in-law from Europe'). For Riesman, Veblen's conspicuous consumers are in fact other-directed in appearance only, despite the vanity of their ambitions, since they are seeking to fit a role demanded 'by their station, or hoped-for station, in life; whereas the other-directed consumer seeks experiences rather than things and yearns to be guided by others rather than to dazzle them with display' (Riesman, 1950: 122). The instrumentality, as we might call it, a utilitarian and calculative disposition attached to consumption and leisure as the means of obtaining the admiration of others (as Adam Smith would have said), gives the lifestyle of inner-directed persons its impersonal quality – as impersonal as their production, which also is just a residue of their work.

Experimentality

In contrast, other-directed consumers yearn for experiences. The instrumentality of the inner-directed is replaced by what might be called experimentality – a kind of addiction to experience itself, an objectless craving. Experience has no ulterior objective or purpose; it is not elaborated in comparisons with other groups and their station in life – it is satisfaction as such and as useless in fact as it seems to be in appearance.[5] Experience itself, of sexuality or of food, for example, becomes public for the other-directed consumers, while its regulation shifts from norms or law to the person. Trendy cookbooks, for example, have become gossipy and describe less the techniques of preparing dishes than the 'fun' of making them; they tell amusing but useless anecdotes about their invention; or they avow the sociability of cooking and eating. Pictures no longer illustrate the phases of preparation to instruct the ambitious chef-to-be but present the outcome or the lay-out of the whole meal.

A similar airing goes for sexual pleasures. What earlier was not permitted for a courtesan is now required of a respectable middle-class wife (Riesman, 1950: 156).[6] It escapes Riesman's attention that public exposure of intimate pleasures in itself indicates an emphasis on agency. The other-directed character seeks to exploit sexual experiences not in order to break quantitative records of the acquisitive sex consumers like Don Juan, nor quite simply to obey the drive. Sexual experiences are sought for reassurance of being alive, as a willing and accepted partner. 'The other-directed person looks to sex not for display but for a test of his or her ability to attract, his or her place in the "rating-dating" scale – in order to experience life and love' (ibid.: 154–6).

Riesman's analysis from more than a half century ago applies to contemporary consumer societies remarkably well, but unlike other mass society theories, it highlights agency rather than passivity. To take one more example of his interpretation, it notes the cult of bodily adornment, much like the French post-modern sociologist Michel Maffesoli (1994), who has talked about the epidermic consciousness. For Riesman, as for Maffesoli, the concern for body shape and colour in mid-century America and end-of-the century Europe are unrelated to economic or social competition, and only marginally related to sexual conquest. For both authors, the comparisons of shade and hue of the skin open the personalities for inspection and introspection in the desire to share in the leisure agendas of the self-exploiting adult peer group. Epidermic consciousness is a consciousness of agency within the chosen collectivity.[7]

Experience, however unmediated in the Kantian sense, is not taste-*free* (although it might appear as tast*eless* in critical reflection). Even in mass society, people are not indifferent to what they believe others consider as good taste; on the contrary, approval by others is for them the most important source of meaning and emotion. However, peer groups in consumer societies do not form taste communities with group boundaries. Boundaries around class and any social roles tend to wear out: businessmen wear informal clothes to work, evening dresses are worn in graduation parties in working-class as well as in upper-class schools; adult and child roles tend to be mixed up, and social configurations in families become increasingly personal. Parents and teachers no longer require kids to comply with their authority; they must persuade and argue, which they also expect of children. For middle-class adults, it may even be difficult to distinguish work and play, as the sociability in both is much the same, talking and gossiping.

Mass media enlarges the sphere of peer group comparisons and brings them close to the little turns and tides of everyday life. Distinction is not coded for difference from other groups; it is limited to trivial difference among the peer group, sufficient to show a sign of personhood but marginal enough to retain the acceptance of like-minded others. Still, taste and the ability to recognize subtle differences matter, and require even more skill than traditional social hierarchies. It is not necessarily true any more that money talks. The differences in style are more subtle than signs of acquisitive power, and making these intricate distinctions depends on 'the talk of the town', which can barely be captured in the most gracious guide books of good living. They are not identifiable as names bearing authority on good taste. Symbols of wealth and family can hardly be turned into curricula of the most sophisticated boarding schools.[8] Riesman's own account strongly suggests that other-directed individuality places much greater stress on individuality than inner-directed, which is oriented to serious and essential group memberships and differences *between them*, not between individuals within the groups.

Political apathy and citizenship

The Tocquevillean tradition

The overriding concern in the post-war American literature on mass society was not consumption, lifestyle or the taste community as such, unlike in its more recent European form, but politics – or 'political apathy', to be more precise. The central question was how to explain the rise of Nazism, Fascism and Stalinism. The paradigm work on this subject was Hannah Arendt's *Origins of Totalitarianism*, where she advanced the view that the most active supporters of totalitarian movements were either isolated, apathetic individuals of the lower middle class or members of the mob, the *Lumpenproletariat*. The acquiescent family man followed the crowd to keep his head down for the sake of his near ones, unable to defend his interests in class-based political organizations. Totalitarian movements and regimes grow in the seedbed of classless societies (Arendt, [1951] 1973: 305–40).

Many liberal political scientists and sociologists adopted this view (e.g. Lipset, 1969; Bell, 1963). When class boundaries crumble, authority structures become tangled. Moral sources are no longer the elders of one's own group but one's peers and the mass media, neutralized to serve all tastes and interests without commitment to positions that might be changed tomorrow. Mass culture generates value standards that are uniform, levelled and simple; conformity is based on rigorous and well-sanctioned norms, but mass values are also fluid, i.e. easily changed. Populist belief in the uniform popular will is an unfailing element in any mass movement (Kornhauser, 1960: 43–51, 102–15).[9]

In Riesman's (1950: 40–2) characterology, the dominant emotion of other-directed persons is *anxiety*, whereas failure to conform evokes *shame* for traditionalists. For modern inner-directed individualists the dominant feeling caused by failure to meet one's ideals is *guilt*. In mass society, politics becomes a consumable spectacle, more attentive to the daily soap-opera of political personalities than to policy solutions on public issues. The indignation of 'inner-directed political inclinations in decline', i.e. conservative groups of the extreme right, has a fertile seed-bed in isolated constituencies with no stable identities. However, mass society for Riesman is not equivalent with totalitarian rule, but prone to turn into one. William Kornhauser (1960: 33) summarized it: 'Mass society is a condition in which elite domination replaces democratic rule. Mass society is objectively the atomized society, and subjectively the alienated population.' The risk arises from the fragility of social groupings around class, family and local community, and from the concomitant psychological anxieties.

This analysis is rooted in the work of Alexis de Tocqueville, the French liberal political analyst of the early nineteenth century, who had explained the success of American democracy by the strong political presence of intermediary groups. Tocqueville had a penetrating influence on liberal political theory of the time,[10] and also Riesman followed the Tocquevillean argument (McClay, 1994: 42–6). However, he made two original twists in this diagnosis that are interesting from today's perspective. First, for him, the lack of intermediary groups does not automatically imply strong centralized power, as was often assumed in mass society theories (Kornhauser, 1960: 58–9). On the contrary, Riesman's model of mass society is composed of a large number of more or less arbitrary veto groups – trade unions, the National Rifle Association, religious groups, many kinds of moralizers, and so on. They do not necessarily have solid common interests but sometimes they may. Power gets dispersed, and becomes invisible. His mass society is devolved and decentred.[11]

Second, the other-directed character is not in itself authoritarian, indignant, ultra-conservative or apathetic. It is anxious about being accepted by others, and this anxiety bonds the person to them in tolerant approval. Even the conservative press aimed at other-directed audiences avoids taking a fast and strong stand on social issues that might have to be reversed tomorrow. Tolerance is not indifference; on the contrary, other-directed publics are keenly involved in political events and debates, not as spectators but as insiders. Riesman calls them inside-dopesters. Other-directedness means that one has a great deal of social skills, of which the most important is to hold one's emotional fire. Whereas inner-directed politicians and moralizers aim to influence others, other-directed politicians aim to please and change their views to suit their publics. This everyone can do, or can at least try: one does not have to be a great orator or a social philosopher to feel part of the game. The important thing is to know what key people are doing and thinking in great-issue politics – and beyond! Politics is now the spectacle of consumption with glamour, no longer the dour sphere of power and its consequences (Riesman, 1950: 199–205).

Tolerance and agency

The idea that new middle-class culture breeds tolerance rather than moralizing is Riesman's great insight and a challenge to the view that mass society leads to submission and passivity. This insight leads in the direction that most versions of mass society theory, mid-century American or late-century European, have failed to pursue, namely that new middle-class consumer societies engender, support and generalize the position of the consumer also in domains other than the commodity market, notably that of the citizen. Consumers choose, decide, judge by their euros and dollars, enter into contracts and protect their rights. They are *agents*. Whenever they are agents in the state, they are less interested in legislating on what others should be and do than legislating on what they *must not do* lest they violate somebody's rights. The closer the victim is to 'me', the more assuredly he or she is innocent, or the less capable of defending its rights (children, disabled, animals, plants),[12] the more virtuous it is to ride out to rescue. On the other hand, while tolerance breeds sensitivity for justice to victims, this sensitivity is indignant towards offenders.[13]

Political apathy, for Riesman, unlike for C. Wright Mills, Erich Fromm, or William Kornhauser, is not a direct consequence of the new middle-class position and the other-directedness it engenders. Indifference may result simply from side-tracked traditionalism, or it may be related to too much comfort in life – why should citizens care about politics if life offers them satisfaction at work and in leisure anyway? Alternatively, their situation may be too depressing to raise any hope for improvement. In any case, rapid change in either direction endorses indifference. The risk of ultra-conservatism comes not from the indifference or tolerance of other-directed groups but from 'moralizers in decline', i.e. inner-directed people who see their values threatened by social change and pluralism. Such people feel indignant.[14] They experience their lack of fortune as unjust because they do not understand it; they feel bitter towards the city slickers because they envy their success and sureness of grasp, which they overrate and misinterpret as snootiness and slap-happiness towards their values. Especially suspect to them are intellectual liberals, whose tolerance is both a direct threat to their values and an indirect blockade to their efforts to set things back and right (Riesman, 1950: 196).

The fear of a right-wing backlash was shared by most liberals in post-war America (McClay, 1994: 256–60), and Riesman was also weary of totalitarian movements, but not because the other-directed middle class would be disposed to join them. Other-directed persons are trained to recognize a *fait accompli*, not resist it. In their anxiety about being accepted, other-directed persons tend to be loyal to whoever is in power, regardless of the orientation and use of that power. Acquiescence, not action, is what inside-dopesters are prepared for, and if they contribute to totalitarianism it is not by their apathy but by their tolerance.

The middle class

Riesman's book, as well as that of Gerth and Mills, started a new era in mass society theory. Until then, the scare had been in the past. Nazism, Fascism and Stalinism were seen as deviant pathologies of modernity. The mass society explanations of them looked to marginal groups. Riesman, Gerth and Mills, and later generations of mass society theorists looked at mass society as a normal condition of advanced or post-modern society. The structural position of the new middle class was the key explanation for this normality.

The new middle class was new in the sense of unforeseen and in the sense of recent. Never before in the history of capitalism had the labour market generated such a large segment of salaried employees with such an ambiguous position in the class structure and in the hierarchies of the workplace. In the USA, the white-collar class arose up in the 1950s. In Europe, the expansion took place about two decades later, speeded up by the welfare state construction in many countries, and followed by de-industrialization. This is why also American political theory from the 1950s is more relevant today than it was half a century ago. The salaried new middle classes are spread over the whole spectrum of occupational, educational and prestige hierarchies and in all sectors of the economy. Nothing distinguishes the executive from the secretary, or the head of a medical ward from the nurses, except their academic degrees and a *belief* that one is worthier than the other. Ascension must be legitimated by display of achievement and excellence but also quite often by personal qualities, of which the other-directed social skills are the most important. Somehow the beliefs in indispensability must be upheld and the differences in its degree must be made visible. Hence the importance of symbols of taste. Symbols are not just play, they are now more indispensable than ever for the maintenance of social organization and its hierarchies. The problem is that they now are also more contestable than ever before.

Solidarities in new middle-class societies are weak and fluid, group boundaries murky and easily challenged. The majority of the population belongs to groups that have little in common except that they are *not* peasants, *not* industrial workers or *not* part of the old elites. Whatever the grounds for advancement, and whatever the personal motivation to achieve it, the prospect of a career is always present. Much of one's value as a human being is invested in success. As Riesman points out, if one is successful in one's craft, one is often forced to leave it. The machine-tool man becomes a vice president for sales, the reporter becomes a columnist or a deskman, the doctor becomes the head of a clinic, the professor becomes a dean, the factory superintendent becomes a holding company executive (Riesman, 1950: 133). Middle-class anxiety is not limited to specific groups. It is a phenomenon related to a web of changes in the whole class structure in advanced capitalism. The new middle class concerns everyone. Status anxiety is translated into lifestyle patterns and consumption, and captures everybody much the same way. Consumption patterns are easily copied; hobbies and leisure practices are quickly diffused with the exception of a few practices that demand great amounts of cultural capital.

Riesman combines the two structural developments, the rise of the new middle class and the coming of the consumer society, in one single process, reinforced by the mass media, to conclude that other-directed anxiety tends to become the culturally dominant pattern in advanced capitalist society. The consequence, however, is not acquiescence and a consequent disposition to follow charismatic leaders. This may happen, but it is most likely among groups who are traditional in their values and feel them threatened by rapid cultural change. Or it may occur in small-scale business communities with inner-directed values in decline. For the large majority, however, anxiety is not about leadership or the future of society but about one's own autonomy and intimacy. It is defence of its own agency which is likely to mobilize the new middle class, whenever it is threatened by intolerance or illegitimate authority.

Autonomy and agency

Riesman was influenced by Erich Fromm, who in *The Fear of Freedom* ([1941] 1991a, first translated into English in 1942) leaned on the Freudian theory of separation anxiety. Many of the problematic assumptions of the American mass society theories stem from this source. According to Freud, the human being, in becoming conscious of itself as a separate individual, may experience unbearable aloneness, isolation and inferiority. In unfavourable circumstances, the anxiety leads to destructiveness, to the *sadomasochistic syndrome*, or to a tendency to conform up to a point of complete self-denial. When this happens in the character structure of a society, individuality turns inward to its malformed side. Independence from traditionalism turns to assimilation, dependence, even destruction, and annihilates the ideal of autonomy.

For Riesman, the most frightening and obnoxious way in which individuals are held captives of their own freedom is assimilation in the workplace where its effects also are least possible to prevent. The inner-directed boss never 'saw' his secretary, and the secretary seldom 'saw' the boss. Both were concentrated on the work, only brought together by the invisible hand to pursue their own proper interests, with a clear boundary between them. In contrast, other-directed (middle-class) workers are forced into 'false personalization' in their relationships with supervisors and subordinates; everybody at work appears as a client or a customer to everybody else. The work itself – typing, selling, buying or in general getting things done – becomes insignificant in comparison with 'glamorizing' and energies spent on emotional relationships with others. False personalization at work becomes a barrier to autonomy because

> it is this, not the technical problems of production still remaining, that exhausts the character reserves of the other-directed man ... as he goes around donating

his energies to the sphere of work in order to be rewarded with the badge of indispensability. (Riesman, 1950: 311)

In the end, all the self-perpetuating buzz and fuss makes people believe that their work is important.

Other-directed persons would not gain autonomy even if they did not suffer from false personalization, because they need others. Sociability for them is like an addiction, an end in itself without ulterior purposes. Not the unbearable feeling of aloneness and insignificance but the constant threat of the *inability to experience oneself as different from others in interaction with them* is what underlies the other-directed person's fear of not being an agent and master of one's life. Training children to tolerance leads to this over-socialized state of mind; but also to the minimization of barriers between work and leisure, and to a lack of distance between child and adult.

Riesman concludes his analysis with a happy ending, a section on 'autonomy' where he paints a rosy utopia of a new kind of individualism in the middle of mass society. Critics thought that this was incompatible with the analysis that went before it, and the worst part of the book (McClay, 1994: 264–5). It is true that the connection is not well made, but nevertheless there are insights in his thinking that help us overcome the theoretical stumbling blocks in mass society theory and make us better understand the kind of conservative liberalism that I have described in previous chapters.

Fromm's association of the separation anxiety with the sadomasochistic syndrome is one version of the friction between the three dimensions of modern individualism – biography, autonomy and intimacy – to which Axel Honneth has paid attention in the article I referred to at the beginning of this chapter. In the sadomasochistic syndrome, autonomy leads to the loss of distinctness and authenticity, what I have called the two aspects of intimacy. However, the friction should not be considered inexorable. The three dimensions of individuality should be treated as separate, mutually interdependent but not identical, sometimes compatible and in other cases pathological or distorted. Differentiation opens up biographical possibilities, and autonomy is required to make reflexive decisions on them. Reflexive autonomy requires consciousness of the authentic, distinct self, and its realization appears as expressive differentiation. This would be a cycle of compatible parts.

Other combinations are anomalies, deformations of the logical and healthy course of individualization. Excessive differentiation without autonomy leads to anomie, excessive autonomy without real differences leads to mass society. The mass society feared by the American post-war liberals was a self-imposed abnormality of modernity, which threatens to throw society back to totalitarian rule modelled on pre-modern despotism but worse, since it would be empowered with the immense organizational and technical capacities of modern industrial organization, as described by Zygmunt Bauman in his study of the Holocaust (1989). Yet these disfigurements may result from the logic of individualization itself, echoing Adorno's and

Horkheimer's argument about the 'self-destruction of the Enlightenment' in modernity.

Critical stress on the frictions demeans the *continuity* in individualization. Of course, one might argue that social differentiation no longer provides us with the possibility of building our own biographies around some imaginary *inner* selves; and we certainly do not need to fight for autonomy. We are *forced* to assume self-responsibility, which is expressed in the kinds of contracts, plans and codes to which we are expected to subscribe in the project society (cf. the preceding chapter). It has been argued by critics of mass consumption that consumer autonomy no longer spells anything else than manufactured difference between nothing. However, even if it is trivial in substance, it is nevertheless a difference sufficient to sustain the *sensibility of agency*, which is embedded if not always explicit in the folds of Riesman's analysis. As a consumer, the other-directed person is acutely aware of being a choice-maker, responsible and individually different from other members of the in-group. As a citizen, she is a political consumer and the state's client. As a worker, she is a personalizer and self-responsible agent; client or seller to everyone else. The other-directed person keeps looking for *sincerity* – if others want to exploit her emotions, the person expects those others to involve their own so as to treat her as a person, not as a means to their ends. This may be agency in emotional experience only, and it may have rather little bearing on the choices as well as on their consequences. Yet the fact that people claim to be recognized as agents of their own lives, and that if they do not claim it, it will very likely be imposed on them, has very much a bearing on the nature and on the dynamism of the social bond. However strong the powers of assimilation and similarity in contemporary contractual society, public discourse on citizenship centres on free will and voluntary agreement (in spite of the daunting necessity to direct the will in one way and not otherwise for public reasons such as keeping down health care expenses or ensuring security against crime and violence).

There is no theoretical reason to suppose that the other-directed character should not yearn for the experience of autonomy and intimacy. In this matter the conventional mass society theory tends to have a sticky quality. It argues that cheerful robots are cheerful, because *they do not know they are robots*, only that they are cheerful. The Frommian modern seekers of 'magic helpers' only *seem to defy authority and believe they are doing so*, while in fact they cannot live without the symbiotic attachment between the dominant and the dominated (Fromm, 1991a: 144). And so on. I call this a sticky argument because it imputes an unconscious motivation to actions and emotional experiences of others, and there is no room for counter-argument. Contesting the interpretation, especially by the subjects themselves, would only count as conscious rationalizations of a subconscious reality that is exposed only to the diagnostic observer. Refutations of the observation would only be taken as confirmation that the observation is correct.

Empirical conclusions on the potentialities of Western democracies will be badly misdirected by such sticky arguments. We will do much better if we take seriously the possibility that the sensibility of agency – implied if not fully explicit in Riesman's other-directed character – is the very material of which the social bond is constructed, not just a pretext for actual submission, an insignificant residual of lost individuality. We must understand it not as a limp leftover of modern individualism but as its continuation in its full, transformed and saturated form. Taking such a starting point by no means sends us to the camp of complacent affirmation; on the contrary, it opens up a way to assess the consequences of saturated individualism itself rather than deny its validity from the start.

As a demonstration of my point, I shall take up one concrete issue that has traditionally been misunderstood in the light of the mass society theory: conservatism.

Anti-authoritarian conservatism

The authors discussed in this chapter generally agree that the character structure in mass society is conservative; it has no faith in the realization of what exists only as a potentiality. For Fromm and for Arendt, it was authoritarian, submissive, hyper-conformist, even destructive, but this held only for abnormalities that result from imbalances in the process of individuation. For Mills ([1951] 1956: 353–4), Riesman, and Kornhauser, mass society involves conformity, easily seduced by invisible power. Admittedly, Riesman's other-directed persons are liberal in the sense that they are (excessively) tolerant, unable to uphold barriers between themselves and others because difference in general for them is unbearable and conflict even more agonizing. All authors stress nevertheless that mass society character structure worships the past instead of the future. Mass society conservatism is heir to the conservatism of early nineteenth-century Europe also in its irrationalism, anti-egalitarianism, anti-universalism and concreteness.[15]

But what could conservatism be in a society like ours, in which 'the past' has become abstract and arbitrary, in which no lifestyle can claim the status of continued normality? If no pastoral authority can define the good life for everybody, what is there to conserve? Is the conservatism of mass society only the desire to restore an imaginary tradition that has never existed, an attitude that Appadurai (1997) has called nostalgia without memory, a longing back for something nobody ever lost?

One aspect of conservatism has been the persistent or recurrent electoral success of extreme right or ultra-conservative parties in European and North American politics. These parties might have been a political reaction of the new middle classes against the welfare state, particularly against the tax burden it places on wage earners (Crawford, 1980). Evidence has not supported these theories. Val Burris (Burris, 1986) was obviously right when he concluded that no theory that ascribes either a liberal democratic or a conservative, even reactionary political attitude to the whole or lower new middle class, however defined, can be empirically correct. The political cleavage in contemporary capitalist societies cuts through the middle of the white-collar ranks. Where and how the line should be drawn is a complex matter, although Burris himself believes that it is the lower middle class that ends up on its liberal side rather than vice versa.[16]

As a global description, even such a view is probably wrong. Political thinking in mass society is rarely a unified system of opinions and attitudes – not even in the minds of political professionals. Political beliefs are rather like ideological dilemmas, as Billig et al. (1988) say, more or less incompatible postures for example, in the direction of authoritarianism as well as in the value of democracy at the same time.

However, full incompatibility is intolerable and consistent inconsistency is a burden. Mass society characterology is blind to the fact that even if real differences may be partly difficult to sustain, the interest in the experience and reputation of autonomy and intimacy is real. This interest involves a consistent logic of agency that explains contradictions and gives coherence to thought and action. Another name for this interest could be individual sovereignty. It is a common basis of the new middle-class mentality that allows for radicalism as well as acquiescence and conservatism. The emphasis on individual sovereignty gives a distinct middle-class tenor to any political orientation, left or right.

Let me illustrate this by returning once again to my study of new middle-class groups frequenting city bars in the middle of Helsinki (Sulkunen, 1992). Exchange dealers, financial advisors, clerks in banking and insurance; journalists, copy writers in advertising; teachers, nurses, dentists and doctors, these people would be classified as middle class, but with no class consciousness and very few objective characteristics to define their position in the class structure. You can meet similar people in public places in the business districts of any big city. They are particularly interesting for the study of the mass society character structure, because they are both anti-authoritarian and, in their own words, explicitly conservative.

Their conservatism could hardly be an ideological conviction, elaborated in theoretical doctrines. In our interviews, they did exhibit a high degree of cultural capital, but in ideological issues they preferred to talk about personal values rather than about political theories. Their conservatism was not moral or normative either. They were tolerant; themselves frequent drinkers, for one thing, and considered themselves liberal and even avant-garde in this matter. Their understandings of sexuality and marriage were not old-fashioned or traditional, if by that one means stability and monogamy. They were enthusiastic nationalists, yet they were also very proud of their cosmopolitan contacts, atmosphere and manners. Their views sometimes sounded authoritarian, especially in regard to 'down-and-outs'; but they were extremely sensitive to relations of power, especially to power exercised on them from the outside. They were opposed to equality claims that belong to labour politics; but again, they firmly defended their own job security and benefits. Their conservatism was something else than political, not related to whatever political preferences each of them might have had.

Albeit otherwise modest and tempered in their views, the one moral question in which they exhibited vigilance was their antipathy towards external control and paternalism over individuals, particularly over drinking in public. Any boundary at all between the pub and other parts of the public sphere aroused objections, exactly as with Riesman's other-directed persons. Formal (traditional) restaurants, with their rituals of entering, the doorman, dress codes, and seating at tables, rather than moving around as they liked to do in their own pub, were viewed as symbols of unwanted power. Those symbols cut off drinking places from normal, everyday public life. In their own relaxed pubs the body is made public and satisfied as it were, on stage, together with other members of the tribe but seen by outsiders as well. The quintessence of their middle-class individualism was the experience of *self-direction without barriers*, guided only by one's own good judgement of what is proper.

Their conservatism arose from their claim to dignity as autonomous individuals, with their sphere of intimacy displayed in public. It was associated with elitism in comparison with people who do not have the competence and will-power to exercise self-control. However, their sense of superiority did not involve a sense of holding power in society at large. The image they constructed of themselves was in the role of reacting rather than acting agent. Their relation to power was that of its clients when they are served – or its victims when they are let down. Their conservatism was superiority of those who are served, not of those who make decisions or bear responsibility for social issues. It was the detached conservatism of people who see the political system as incontestable and faceless, a structure without qualities or attributes other than the constraint it puts on its citizens. Combined with the sense of superiority, it is an *anti-authoritarian conservatism* based on *elitism from below*, a populist rather than a dominant disposition.

Elitism from below is a combination of dispositions belonging to the inner-directed sense of hierarchic differences, and to the other-directed sense of sameness, equality, even indifference. In so far as the character structures of mass society are based on middle-class experience, this is not so surprising. The new middle class lives in the middle of hierarchies, but it also places extremely high value on the autonomy and intimacy of the individual. Power can well be tolerated in middle-class life; it is felt to be humiliating only if it deprives sovereign agents, 'us', of the basis of dignity and greatness in the exercise of our most valued modal qualities: good judgement and free will. With respect to social hierarchies and authority in general, the new middle-class mind probably turns much easier in the direction of loyalty than disloyalty. However, in one respect it is unconditionally anti-authoritarian. Mutiny will occur whenever it is felt that a dimensionless power of the system cuts into the heart of its identity as sovereign individuals, as autonomous and competent adults.

The voluntary social bond

I have now come to the point where the elements of our model of justification have been discussed in the context of contemporary consumer capitalism – the principles of belonging and differentiation, the principle of the common good and the principles of dignity and greatness. I have also shown how the saturation of these principles is manifested in debates on the consumer society and the welfare state as well as in the ideology and practices of epistolary power in social policy. In this chapter I raised the question, is it possible that the saturation of modernity leads back to traditional authoritarianism, as American mass society theories envisaged? My conclusion, drawn from David Riesman's diagnosis of the other-directed character and supported by my own researches, is that however much we depend on the esteem and sympathy of others – in the Smithian sense – what looks like a mass society is nevertheless constructed on the principle of agency and on the political as well as moral anti-authoritarianism it entails. We are not directed by others, we *direct ourselves* towards them, finding their happiness as necessary to us as we believe ours is to them. The principle of agency requires that cooperation is voluntary, not programmed by habit or custom, nor resulting from blind adjustment to the will and habits of others.

The next and final question, to be answered in the following and last chapter of this book, is a classic one arising out of the key issues in modern sociology: can contemporary social order be based, against all our inherited theoretical doctrines, on voluntary agreements, that is, contracts? This is how it often seems, and this is also how the rhetoric of epistolary power represents the social bond. How real is this rhetoric, and what are its consequences, is the question to which I now turn.

Notes

1 The editor gave Riesman's book its title, *The Lonely Crowd*, not used in the text. But it is a good title for the content, anyway.

2 Besides Fromm, particularly important was Hannah Arendt's study *The Origins of Totalitarianism* ([1951] 1973). Theodor Adorno and Erich Horkheimer were key figures. Especially important was Adorno's 'immanent critique' of modernity as potential emancipation of man from nature, but actually a road to slavery and exploitation by the apparatus and the groups controlling it (Adorno and Horkheimer, [1947] 2002: xvii). The Marxian theory of alienation is recognizable in this stream of thought, although the Freudian (or Frommian) influence on characterology was even more important in the classical American mass society theories, as it was in Adorno's and his colleague's path-breaking social psychology in *The Authoritarian Personality* (1950).

3 I have discussed this tardiness and its consequences elsewhere (Sulkunen, 1992). The transition from the post-war industrial development to middle-class service economy took place two or three decades later in Western Europe than in the United States. Also the new consumer society emerged later in Europe, largely because of the war.

4 In European end-of-the-millennium *Zeitdiagnose*, these themes have not had quite the same grim overtones that they did in the American classics. For example, in the work of Ulrich Beck, Anthony Giddens and Scott Lash (1994), there is no concern about totalitarianism, despite substantial increases in electoral absenteeism; even less so in Michel Maffesoli's writing. Maffesoli's argument has been throughout that post-modernity marks the end of the modern individualism, which in itself was an illusion at best, a tragedy at worst, as the subtitle, *The Decline of Individualism in Mass Society*, of his *Time of the Tribes* indicates. On the other hand, the arrival of 'The End of the Social' has been declared in a pessimistic fashion by Nikolas Rose

(1999). One of the most popular advocates of the post-modern malaise has been Jean Baudrillard, whose' *Échange symbolique et la mort* (1976) diagnosed contemporary societies as systems of complete repression, with no other symbolic exchange remaining between society and the individual than death. In a more light-handed manner, he ironically satirized those who speak in the name of the silent majorities in *A l'ombre des majorités silencieuses ou la fin du social* (In the Shadow of Silent Majorities, or the End of the Social), which I quote for its characteristic and inimitable sense of humour:

> The term mass is not a concept. As Leitmotiv of political demagoguery it is supple, viscous, lumpen-analytic. There is no polarity between one and another in the mass. This is what turns into void and null any system that lives on distance and distinction between polarities. This is what makes it impossible to circulate meaning in such systems; meanings disperse in them like atoms in a vacuum. This also is the reason why masses cannot be alienated – there is no self and no alien any more. Mass without words is out there, to be spoken for by all its spokespersons with no history. What an admirable conjunction: those who have nothing to say and masses who do not speak. ([1978] 1997: 14–15, my translation)

5 This point has been made later in criticism of Bourdieu's analysis of the 'anti-Kantian aesthetics' of working-class culture, as a 'virtue made out of necessity' by Gerhard Schulze (1992). He argues that the immediate satisfaction one gets, for example, from the effortless working-class sociability (*Gemütlichkeit*) with beer drinking, simple solid food and songs, is as far from necessity as can be.

6 The same exposure of pleasure to public view appeared in Nordic alcohol policy countries thirty years later, around 1980 when newspapers, even television channels, began to run wine columns or oenological programmes. Beer societies were formed, cooking programmes started on television, and reporting on sexuality became common. Drinking, which previously had been exclusively discussed in terms of problems and problem prevention in non-fiction publicity, was now displayed as fun and sociable, and in some cases even advertising to this effect was allowed (Sulkunen et al., 2000).

7 Riesman uses the term 'peer groups' for the collectivities of comparison, Maffesoli calls them tribes. Both stress the voluntarily chosen quality of such collectivities, as well as the fleeting superficiality with which they commit the loyalty of their members (despite Maffesoli's misleading term).

8 Riesman's (1950: 78–83) analysis reminds one of the miraculous powers of Pierre Bourdieu's cultural capital, capable of performing alchemy on invisible sensibilities of distinctions and turning them into visible differences of class and power (e.g. Bourdieu, [1979] 1984: 94).

9 Hannah Arendt's ([1951] 1973) account of Nazism and Stalinism rests on the idea that the bourgeois-dominated class system broke down in Europe; and that Stalin intentionally destroyed the elements of intermediary political communities that had been formed in the course of the Bolshevik Revolution.

10 It still figures importantly for example in Robert Putnam's (2000) writing on social capital.

11 This theme is close to Horkheimer's theory of rackets (Schmid Noerr, 2002: 233–4), bureaucratically organized groups with no idea of the society as a whole, only pursuing their particular interests, or protest groups with no clear aims whatsoever (today we would speak of the 'street'). In a wider sense, the concept of de-centralized society has been important in late twentieth-century European social science literature such as Offe (1985), Lash and Urry (1987), and Boltanski and Chiapello (2005). In a different way, the dissolution of power in late modern society appears in the neo-Foucauldian literature, for example, by Nikolas Rose (1999).

12 An ingenuous appeal to this sense of justice for the defenceless appeared in the parks of Paris recently. A sign appealing to dog owners says: 'Please show respect to the plants – pick up your dog's shit.'

13 As discussed in Chapter 8, the criminologist David Garland (2001) has pointed out that re-emphasis of the role of the victim is associated with the new punitive penal policy that is replacing what Garland calls 'penal welfarism' (the welfare state's stress on rehabilitation and therapy instead of punishment).

14 Thomas Frank gives an excellent and detailed description of the kind of indignation that Riesman refers to, in his book on contemporary American bible-belt conservatism in his book *What's the Matter with Kansas?* (2004).

15 Karl Mannheim ([1986] 1997: 86–110) defined early nineteenth-century European conservatism in terms of: (1) its opposition to natural law thinking and rationality; (2) a personalized view of property; (3) concreteness; (4) a non-egalitarian (anti-universalistic) concept of freedom; (5) affection towards all that exists and consequent inability to accept the idea of progress; and, finally, (6) respect for the past, as the sentiment that 'in every point in our present that has come to be; its past remains within it'.

16 Several authors maintain that the middle class is in fact the principal support of the welfare state against neo-liberal politics (Esping-Andersen, 1990; Olsson, 1990). Furthermore, several studies indicate that the new social movements – anti-nuclear, feminist, environment, local, regional and ethnic – are mainly supported by new middle-class groups especially in France (Touraine, 1968; Monjardet and Benguigui, 1982; Bidou et al., 1983) but also in other European countries (Offe, 1985; Lash and Urry, 1987; Kriesi, 1989). Inglehart (1977; 1989) even suggests that the affluent middle class could turn the blurring class-based political system on a new course with two lefts instead of one: the traditional working-class materialist left and a new left that promulgates the values of post-materialism. Empirical research confirms this hypothesis partly (Offe, 1985; Kriesi, 1989), although the relationships between class, party and post-materialism seem to be quite complex (Weakliem, 1991). There are some new middle-class groups who participate in progressive movements and organizations, but others could not care less or would be openly hostile to them.

10

Re-inventing the Social Contract

The conception of the social contract is today therefore very difficult to defend, because it bears no relation to the facts.

(Emile Durkheim, 1893)

Dissolution of 'society'?

This book began with the predicament of prevention, which arises from the vast human capacity to control nature, including human biology and psychology, as compared to society's inability to regulate people's lifestyle. Technology and science can help us immensely to avoid risks and harm caused by lifestyle choices, but they are of little use without the co-operation of consumers and citizens themselves. The problems are of a moral sort. The institutions of contemporary society, the state, the family, the school, have insufficient moral resources to secure people's co-operation, at least not with the techniques we are familiar with from the history of capitalism in general, and from the history of the welfare state in particular. I would argue in this book that instead of introducing external factors to explain the difficulty, such as neo-liberal ideology, globalization or the take-over of the public sphere by the market, we must look at the internal development of the problem of justification in modern society itself. The predicament of prevention results, according to my thesis, from the full maturity of the three great ideals that have made modern consumer capitalism possible: progress, universal individualism and the nation–state. The saturation of these ideals has elevated the notion of agency to a key position for any understanding of the social process. Individuals are, especially in lifestyle politics, no longer just elements of a population, not only subjects of the state and the market, and no longer just carriers of the collective consciousness; they are judges and creators of their bodies and souls, and by that token, guardians of their own autonomy and intimacy against threats from all directions.

Essential elements of the theoretical baggage sociologists have received from the classics concerning 'the social' have become a burden in such a situation, an obstacle rather than an instrument for understanding politics and welfare in consumer capitalism. These include the notorious culture–nature dualisms, in particular, the traumatic relationship to biology and the body, from which sociologists suffer. Another load of sullied goods is sociologists' fixity on integration, order and co-operation, and our consequent focus on violence, conflict, war and evil, although these should need to be understood much more than benevolence, order and peace. These are issues that I cannot discuss here in any adequate detail, but what about the concept of society itself? Do we need to reject the idea of society as a self-perpetuating structure with its own laws of operation, in favour of a much more agent-centred view of the world? Has the self-policing modern society, which Adam Smith envisioned, now developed beyond the point where we can no longer meaningfully call it a society at all? If the idea of the society was, as Peter Wagner (2001a) has argued, to form a link between the household (the private sphere) and polity (the state and the public sphere), has the saturation of this link made the idea conceptually redundant?

William Outhwaite (2005) has very usefully identified three streams of critiques of the concept of society, which have appeared in the chapters of this book, too: (1) action theory that gives priority to agency over structure (e.g. Alain Touraine, Margaret Archer, Anthony Giddens); (2) post-modernism, which either emphasizes epistemic scepticism towards social science concepts in general (Jean Baudrillard, Gilles Lipovetsky) or is critical of the traditional ways that sociology has understood (modern) societies as disciplined social systems (Michel Maffesoli); and (3) a whole range of theorists who are critical of the underlying idea of the nation, which most sociological notions of society share at least implicitly and in the last instance.

One central idea about 'society', as we have received it from the classical period of one hundred years ago, is that it cannot possibly be based on a plan, nor can it be founded on a social contract. Durkheim thought that this idea is not only contrary to reason but can be proven wrong by facts. By and large, every branch of sociological theory has accepted this view. It has become so taken for granted that nobody – however sceptical of the notion of society – has ever questioned it, in spite of the fact that social contract theories have a much longer history behind them than modern sociology. Even in political theory, where the idea of contractual order was born, it is commonly thought that its preconditions, originally valid in circumstances where only the property-owning classes participated in the polity at the time of Hobbes and Locke, no longer hold in democracies with universal franchise (Macpherson, 1977: 271–7).

Yet contemporary societies increasingly rely on voluntary contracts between individuals, groups, organizations, enterprises, states and their organs or officials. Governments have asked themselves two critical questions. First, is this or that service or regulation really the responsibility of public administration? Second, is it really the state which should deal with it, or could the responsibility be delegated to private entrepreneurs, to regional or to local governments, communities and institutions such as schools, associations; or should it be trusted to citizens themselves? Declared objectives of a contract-based governance include 'doing more with less', 'managing or budgeting by outputs or by outcomes'; adapting services to customers' needs, focusing on clients, service orientation, accountability, etc. All these are virtues of the well-functioning competitive market. But even more relevant for my point in this book is that for public administration experts 'contractualism' is also a reaction to moral pressures: it intends to replace the paternalistic idea of an impostor state. According to them, the concept of the service state that only provides what its customers want is not a justifiable alternative. Why would services need to be provided by public authorities? A state that simply serves is as obsolete as a state that imposes. Contractualism implies not only contracting out public functions but dialogue in a more general sense: listening, negotiating, setting priorities and committing oneself and the other, in short, a relationship of partnership where citizens are expected to know best what they need (Trosa, 1999).

In this final chapter, I shall first discuss briefly the sociological critique of the social contract theory and will then ask: has something happened in social reality that makes this critique problematic or even inapplicable in our contemporary world? Should we really take contractualism seriously as a new kind of social bond not only between citizens and the state but as the foundation of the social order? This chapter argues that new contractualism cannot be explained simply as an expansion of the market at the expense of the state. The contract is an illusion, but an illusion that has real effects. It disguises relations of domination as voluntary partnership. It stresses agency to a point where autonomy is not only granted to but demanded even of those who have little or no capacity for it. The contract principle has real consequences not only on how societies govern those who are able to defend their autonomy and intimacy but also on how it pushes to the margins those who do not manage to classify themselves as 'us'.

The sociological critique of the contract

For modern sociologists, social order of any kind can in no case depend on human will and intention, let alone agreement between several individuals. In Durkheim's words:

> The conception of the social contract is today therefore very difficult to defend, because it bears no relation to the facts ... not only are there no societies that have had such an origin, but there are none whose present structure bears the slightest trace of a contractual organization. Thus it is neither a fact derived from history nor a trend that emerges from historical development. ([1893] 1984: 151)

For any will to exist and for any individuals to enter into agreements, society is always already necessary. Contracts are the result of society, not its cause, and as such a result, they can never become the basis of social integration without other types of mechanisms that are archaic, universal and not dependent on human volition. These other, non-rational and non-calculative elements constitute the 'social' proper, which makes it possible to speak of society as an entity.

It must be stressed that Durkheim argued more against Spencer than against the classical social contract theories of the seventeenth and eighteenth centuries. For them, the nexus of social integration had been the state, which needed a legitimating contract with the citizens. Whatever 'society' meant for modern sociology, it was not the same as the state. Even less so for Spencer. He considered voluntary co-operation and contracts as the only possible pattern of social integration in differentiated industrial societies. (e.g. Spencer, [1891] 1996: 3–23) He contrasted them with militant societies, which are based on military excellence, status, hierarchies and discipline. In primitive militant societies, individuals are egoistic; the course of evolution gradually but inevitably boosts the division of labour, creates mutual dependencies and trains people to co-operate. Spencer combined his organic model of industrial society with a *laissez-faire* liberalism so radical that it makes von Hayek, Friedman or Margaret Thatcher seem wimps. Any state interference in society, including public education, would introduce 'militant' elements into its structure, disrupt its voluntary contractual foundation and result in a loss of adaptability, innovation, freedom, satisfaction of needs and equality (Peel, 1992: 192–223).

The rise of the new contract society

When we look around in advanced western capitalist states – and this is a serious theoretical as well as empirical framing of the whole question – it seems that Durkheim was wrong and Spencer was right. After a period of strongly state-interventionist industrial development that lasted about three-quarters of a century in North America and Western Europe, our societies seem to fit the Spencerian co-operative mode, at least in appearance. Governance is increasingly based on contracts and voluntary co-operation. Of course, the market operates on the basis of contracts, as it always has. What is new is that the idea of contract has been adopted also in social policy as well as in sociological diagnostics of the contemporary social order. The 'gender contract' has been for many years a controversial but in many ways a nifty concept to look at the welfare state as part of the complexity of gender relations. The Finnish specialist in social policy analysis, Raija Julkunen, has extended the idea to relationships between age groups and coined the term 'age contract' (Julkunen and Pärnänen, 2005). By this, she means the outcome of a multi-party bargaining process concerning retirement pensions, activation, social insurance, public services, and other measures, which aim to keep the ageing population in the workforce longer, to control public expenses it generates, while also guaranteeing an acceptable level of welfare for it. This is a social contract in a very Nordic welfare state sense. However, the rhetoric and practices of governance that can be called new contractualism have a far wider scope, which may reflect the transformation of the idea of society at a deeper level.

Management by performance, outcome assessment, budgeting by results and a plethora of other administrative terms refer to a new type of administrative ideology and practice. They stress, on the one hand, transparency in resource allocation, and on the other hand, autonomy of the partners – municipalities, public officials and service producers (e.g. public universities) and their clients (e.g. students). Partnerships can be established between private enterprises, associations, trade unions, employers organizations, NGOs, local communities, the ministries, even with the parliament. Contracts are made between service providers and public funding agencies on the basis of competition, as in the business world. An increasing part of public funding is channelled through non-permanent projects. In public administration itself, planning takes the form of competition and contracts, and resources are allocated to cost centres on the basis of result, output, outcome, impact and evaluations of these. Much of this is everyday reality in academic life, but universities and research institutes are only a small part of a wide system of governance restructured according to principles most widely known as New Public Management. Luc Boltanski and Eve Chiapello (2005) have shown in their study of business management that a similar change has occurred within firms. Hierarchical planning and command structures have been replaced by flexible management, quality circles, autonomous profit centres and extensive outsourcing. The market has applied its competitive logic to itself.

What is more, the idea of the contract has been adopted in the relationships between individual citizens and the state, and even between citizens themselves. For example, in activation policy it is usual to make plans between authorities and the users of employment services. Parents, even children, are requested to sign plans and contracts with schools, even preschools, on the principles of education. Local communities are encouraged to make plans for prevention of social problems and agree on good practices of early intervention; authorities are advised to seek approval and commitment to these plans among neighbourhoods. Citizens are no longer seen as subjects of governance, they are – at least in appearance – voluntary clients of public services and partners in co-operation among themselves.

The contract without the prince

The pre-sociological idea of the social contract (until the end of the eighteenth century in the works of Hobbes, Pufendorf, Locke and Rousseau, for example), to which Durkheim was partly referring, emerged from the concept of 'political society', the centre of which was the prince. The centralized and hierarchical political order was expected to eliminate conflicts and disorder that spring from the selfishness and imperfections of humans (Hobbes) or to represent the general will – *volonté générale* – granted to him by the citizens (Rousseau). The nexus of the social order and morality was the state.

Quite to the contrary, our contemporary discourses on contracts are characterized by the absence of the prince – or of his functional equivalents in the modern parliamentary mode of governance. The discourse on contracts, partnerships, projects, plans, and voluntary commitments is intended to stress that the state is no longer a superior ruler nor centre of social integration but only one among several actors in a rhizome-like network. This kind of society,

Spencer had thought, would hold together all by itself, because everybody would be related to others by exchange, which requires contracts and trust. No superior authority is necessary, because it is in the mutual interest of exchange partners to respect the rights of their partners. Social integration follows automatically from the autonomy of individuals. The social bond consists of rational and calculative self-interest in co-operation. Altruism follows from egoism but is not necessary to social life; like Adam Smith, Spencer thought that altruism is an ornament of co-operation and makes it more agreeable and pleasant, not its origin as it was for Durkheim (e.g. [1893] 1984).

For post-Spencerian modern sociology, such a situation is unthinkable. Without the state and non-rational elements of the social bond, societies would indeed dissolve. Which are we to believe, then: that Spencer's vision was correct, after all, or that the contemporary social order is on weak grounds, as post-Spencerian sociology would claim?

Before drawing our conclusions, we should ask a critical question. Might it not be that the contemporary enthusiasm about contracts is a mirage delivered in a jargon of autonomy, comparable to the jargon of authenticity criticized by Theodor Adorno for having no foundation in reality other than conventional hypocrisy, or as we would now say, the banality of political correctness? Or could it be that it actually corresponds to the way people in advanced societies experience their relationships to society and to each other or at least wish that this were their experience about power: partnership instead of subordination?

It is generally agreed that the ideological basis of New Public Management is neo-liberalism, and in that sense it is part of the dominant political philosophy of advanced Western capitalism. However, to say this does not explain very much. It amounts to the argument that the new contractualism is a response to the expansion of the market to the detriment of the state; and that its extension to public administration is an application of liberalistic convictions about the utility of competition. This explanation is not wrong but it is too simple. Certainly, the scope of the capitalist state was exceptional in the three glorious decades of the post-war period, when the achievements of the war economy were filtered into the ideology of the planned economy of peace, which now has become an obstacle for global market-based expansion. I call this the ebb and flow model: it makes it appear as if the bureaucratic state were a balancing counter-weight to the market, and an expansion of the latter would require a retrenchment of the former, and vice versa. The half-truth of this model blocks our way to a real understanding of the complexity of the situation, and brings with it a number of misunderstandings regarding the consequences of the process.

In reality, the re-invention of the social contract involves a redefinition not only of the market–state relationship but of the principles of social integration as a whole, like the classical as well as the Spencerian contract theories also did. Today contractual relationships between separate and autonomous individuals penetrate all spheres of life, including child-rearing. As David

Riesman (1950) argued already half a century ago, parents and teachers no longer require kids to comply with their authority but they must persuade and argue, which adults also expect of children. The idea of the contract is so deeply embedded in our contemporary culture that when social problems occur, they are thought to result from an incapacity or unwillingness to assume the role of a responsible partner. Justice requires reciprocity, not dependence, and the weak should be educated to understand this. A pioneer case is the well-known integration contract (*contrat d'insertion*) introduced in France in 1988. Recipients of allowances commit themselves to look after their children, to find a place to live, to look after their health, and above all not to turn down employment opportunities (Messu, 1999). Similar contracts and plans have become the norm in most welfare and activation programmes in Europe. In Britain, unemployment benefits are granted on the basis of a contract that defines the terms of accepting work if offered (Pieters, 2003: 291–5). In crime prevention programmes convicts leaving prison after serving their sentence are often requested to sign similar contracts, and parole surveillance institutions have also been developed in a similar direction.

In a collection of studies of the Finnish public administration, which was published under the title *Projektiyhteiskunnan kääntöpuolia* (The Flip-side of the Project Society, Rantala and Sulkunen, 2006), we stated that the rearrangements of citizen–state relationships were not only a matter of re-commodification, contracting out, or streamlining the bureaucracy. A moral dimension was also involved. Especially in areas where lifestyle issues are concerned, such as preventative social policy, health promotion or youth work, official bureaucracy not only strives to engage and commit citizens but also to disengage itself from moral responsibility. We called this ethos 'the ethics of not taking a stand'. Citizens were literally seen as 'clients of the preventative or promotional work', as it is now called, rather than as subjects of control policy as it was called earlier. Like consumers on the commodity market, clients are expected to define their priorities and make choices. The contract society stresses agency and autonomy instead of governance and plan-based command structures.

Instead of futile jargon, managerial fad, or a neo-liberal ideological tide, the new contract society is a response to the sovereignty claims of the worker–consumer–citizen. In fact, we misrecognize the weight of these claims not because they are new, but because we take them too much for granted to realize that they have a history. They are the outcome of the democratization of the civilizing process that started at the time of the French Revolution. As shown by the work of Jacques Donzelot (1984), Robert Castel (1995), Pierre Rosanvallon (1990) and E.P. Thompson ([1963] 1980), the right to work, i.e. the right to enter into a labour contract, was the central issue in the conflicts of the post-revolutionary period, both in France itself and also in England. However, as the right to work was gradually extended, it became clear that capitalism as a system of contracts between free individuals was an illusion from the start. As Marx showed, the appearance of equal exchange – the labour contract – between the worker and the capitalist, the form of equivalent exchange, conceals the substance, which is a relationship of exploitation. Everybody knows that the consequences of early nineteenth-century liberalism were disastrous. In consequence, before the labour contract was fully liberated from the traditional ties of guild, community and personal dependency on the master, new ties were introduced in their place. However, it is a paradox for many that it was actually the state which proved to be the indispensable support for individual autonomy not only in political, civil and cultural life but also in the market. Regulations concerning occupational life were the beginning of the welfare state institution. In the words of the radical socialist Léon Bourgeois, the individual should be seen not as the instrument but the *objective* of progressive social policy (Donzelot, 1984: 111). The history of the welfare state has been the history of the growing autonomy of the individual.

Today we take the sovereignty of the worker–consumer–citizen so much for granted that it is difficult to conceive how seriously incomplete the state-driven project of universal individual autonomy was still at the end of the 1960s even in the Nordic countries, which nevertheless were its vanguards among Western European states. The paternalism of states' cultural and moral policies in their authoritative structures reflected the paternalism of the old bourgeois family. Their civilizing efforts in educating the masses were experienced as humiliating and bigoted against the working class, the peasantry and women. Even the right to work was a matter of negotiation and struggle for women still in the 1960s (Hirdman, 1989; Julkunen, 1994).

The world-wide uprisings of students in 1968 and the political activism that ensued were the turning point in the individualistic development. Also in the Nordic countries, 1968 was both literally and metaphorically 'a revolt against the father', in Gerard Mendel's (1968) words; and I would add, a revolt against a *discriminating* father. It was a revolt against the father in the literal sense because it was generational. It was a revolt against the father in the metaphorical sense, because it went against all forms of paternalistic structures of domination. And it was a revolt against the father also in the second metaphorical sense that the young generation actually was claiming the right to self-determination, which the young had been taught to respect by their parent generations. The revolt took the form of 'liberalism', or I would rather say tolerance, in cultural policy, sexual policy, alcohol policy, even in drug policy, in a wave of reforms that were brought to completion only by the mid-1980s. The reinvention of the social contract – in the sense I have outlined above – is a logical and inevitable outcome of this revolt.

The year 1968 was important for individual autonomy also in another way, at the very heart of the capitalist market institution, the business firm. In their study of labour relations, Boltanski and Chiapello (2005) show that working life was in full crisis in the late 1960s and early 1970s. An OECD crisis meeting held in Paris in 1971 observed that there was a serious motivation problem at all levels in industrial organizations throughout the member states. Bureaucratic management practices were felt to be offensive and paternalistic, and they resulted in poor performance, frequent labour conflicts and excessive absenteeism. In reaction, work organizations were reformed in order to give more room for autonomy, creativity, self-responsibility and internal control. Profit centres were created, cost awareness was increased and management training was directed on a more democratic and less bureaucratic course. Manuel Castells (1996) has argued that the IT revolution would not have been possible at all without the replacement of hierarchical management systems by the horizontal co-ordination of the network epitomized by the Silicon Valley. In a wide sense, 1968 meant that enormous numbers of well-educated anti-authoritarian young employees claimed autonomy not only as right to work, as citizens and consumers but within the workplace itself. The contractual form and its corollaries were introduced as a response to this pressure.

The dissolution of society?

On the basis of these considerations, what should we think about the suggested dissolution of society? In one respect the classical notion of the social remains intact beyond doubt. Nothing at all suggests the need to revise the Durkheimian view that no social bond, not to speak of whole societies, can be based on voluntary contracts alone. Nevertheless, the contract is not futile jargon. It is an illusion, but an illusion with the force of reality. In order not to minimize the weight of reality it lays on us, I call it the thick illusion of contract. It is like Bourdieu's *habitus*, which has the alchemic capacity into transform invisible structures of cultural capital into visible structures of class and domination (Bourdieu, [1979] 1984: 172). It disguises social relationships as voluntary agreements, while in reality they are products of circumstances that agents can do very little about, and they even know it. Yet the disguise itself has effects that should be the object of sociological analysis. It was indispensable for capitalism from the start; it is even more indispensable in its contemporary condition.

An obvious function of this illusion, like that of *habitus*, is to justify actual relations of domination in a way that meets the taken-for-granted expectations of autonomy and intimacy. The truth of the contract is to conceal the truth, which is not Durkheim's original altruism but power. In this way it works towards the integration of society, not towards its dissolution. However, we do not actually know very much about its effects on power relations, except in the more obvious extreme cases. For example, it is a dangerous delusion to assume that the contractual form alone would guarantee commitment and integration of populations already destined to exclusion. On the contrary, in our studies it became amply clear, as is to be expected, that the contractual form in many citizen–state interactions actually reinforces the vicious circles of non-participation (e.g. Määttä and Kalliomaa-Puha, 2005). We also know that in community work the key factor of success is the non-contractual basis of co-operation, however rational, goal-directed and calculative the organizational forms are. To take up a third type of complexity, the competitive form of public management may in fact produce new forms of command structures that undercut rather than reinforce the autonomy of participants. We know only too well how ossifying the new practices of budgeting by results and the requisite evaluations have been at universities, and the same is true in all other branches of public administration.

All these disillusions about the illusion may and should be expected to breed resistance and they require systematic study, including a reopening of the concept of power once again. Rather than go into that in more detail here I shall answer the question about dissolving society from another angle, which has even more far-reaching consequences for sociology and its classical concept of the social. The thick illusion of the contract means that the concept of society as an entity is no longer to be taken for granted.

The welfare state has been an individualistic project, and a very successful one. But it has also been based on the sociological concept of 'society' as an entity. Remember, for example, that the Myrdalian project started from a concern about the population question. Populations are always populations of some entities, and these entities have a double moral power. First, they impose a higher duty on their members to subject individual and group interests to common positive goals. In the case of the welfare state, these goals were industrialization, growth and the civilizing process. Second, they translate the question of justice into a question of equity among members of the entity.

The illusion of the contract redirects the sense of duty from the entity to the agency itself. To use the expression of Gilles Lipovetsky (1992), we live in a post-deontic society with one qualification. If citizens do not claim the role of agency, it will be imposed on them. Autonomy is transformed from a right to a duty. For example, programmes on released prisoners, small children or marginalized youth show that whenever individuals' will and competence to assume the capacity of agency are in doubt, the more intensely it will be required of them. The sense of justice, on the other hand, will be transformed from considerations of equity to considerations of the negative freedom of the other. We are no longer asked to respect the others' positive right to be rewarded according to merit; we are asked to respect their negative right not to be constrained by our actions. We are at liberty to do whatever we like with ourselves and our lives as long as we are not taxing the liberty of others to do likewise.

The illusion of the contract concerns not only individuals but all actors on the public scene, notably the public administration itself. In our book (Rantala and Sulkunen, 2006), we observed that public management by projects leads to horizontal and vertical segmentation of policy-making and knowledge structures. Accountability and frame budgeting solidify ministerial boundaries in a very profound way. Ministries are no longer seen as executive instruments of the Rousseauian *volonté générale* but as actors in their own right, and more: they develop into lenses through which society is seen one sector at a time, and the same framework is applied all the way down to the local community, to NGOs, the project workers and their clients.

What could and should sociologists do?

Despite my problems with the classical tradition, I still do adhere to it sufficiently not to believe that society is a plan. I therefore do not believe that sociologists can do very much about the illusion of the contract, even if they so wished. As a corollary, I do not believe we can do very much about sociology either, as it is a knowledge structure produced by the social conditions in which it is operating. Nevertheless, reflexivity is one of the exceptional merits of the profession, and it is appropriate to draw one conclusion in this regard. It is the following.

Many sociologists before me have observed that the emphasis in sociological research and publishing shifted in the latter part of the twentieth century from societies to practices. These studies have focused on consumption, sexuality, social movements, work experience, sports, the arts, etc. These sociologies have drawn on general action theory, semiotics, psychoanalysis, theories of communication, literature and taste, but they have had little need for the idea of society as an entity. A large part of what today is accepted as sociology but widely overlaps other disciplinary domains should properly be called *hexicology*, referring to the Aristotelian concept of *hexis*. *Hexis* is usually translated as state, disposition or possession. This term was an early candidate for Bourdieu's *habitus* since it reflects well the double dimension of being structured and social (in the sense of received) as well as structuring and active (in the sense of creativity). Such a new label would make visible and give a name to what already is an actual fact: disciplinary boundaries have changed.

I see this change as a natural consequence of the thick illusion of the contract and the related difficulty of understanding society as an entity. The state is our principal client, and the other, lesser one is the media. It is hypocritical to believe that our publics are simply recipients rather than generators of the knowledge structures we work with. Neither the media nor the state have any great use for the old sociological idea of 'society'. The media are interested in lifestyle issues and the moralities involved, the state organs are interested in the impact of their own actions. Sociologists are asked to develop indicators of 'the quality of existence' for correct targeting of priorities. We are asked to evaluate, to identify best practices, to measure outcomes and efficiency. We no longer have the societal alcohol question, the youth question, the women question, the population question, not to mention the social question. We no longer talk inclusively about social control, incorporating interactions between deviant and normal populations as well as the legal, penal, policing and social assistance systems in the same problematic. Instead, we have pension bombs, exclusions and inclusions, the prison population, the bullying problem in schools and work organizations, the drug problem, the obesity risk, etc., i.e. segmented problems that are defined in terms of a segmented public of specialized expertise. Hexicology, not sociology, is what they expect to hear.

I see nothing wrong with hexicology. On the contrary, a new name should help sociologists to realize the need to abandon some of the overload we carry in our baggage from the classical period such as the dualism between culture and nature, the fixity on social order and integration. The new name helps us to realize how specific to Western capitalism the sociological idea of society has been. On the other hand, it helps to understand how useful it still is in circumstances like Africa, Latin America, South-East Asia and some parts of Eastern Europe. In such conditions there can be no question of the dissolution of society, since in those areas societies have not yet been formed. The principles of justification – the social bond, the common good, dignity and greatness – are still under construction. There, the sociological tradition, as analysis of justification and as part of it, has a role and a function, although perhaps not exactly the same form as in the West. Given the nature of the process by which society is producing itself in those circumstances, it would be as unreasonable as it is unlikely that the sociology emerging from the process would be quite as fixed on integration and order as Western sociology has been, at the expense of inattention to war, disorder and evil.

References

Adorno, Theodor ([1964] 2003) *The Jargon of Authenticity*. Trans. K. Tarnowski and F. Will. London: Routledge and Kegan Paul.

Adorno, Theodor W., Frenkel-Brunswick, Else, Levinson, Daniel, Sanford, R. Nevitt et al. (1950) *The Authoritarian Personality*. New York: Harper Brothers.

Adorno, Theodor W. and Horkheimer, Max ([1947] 2002) *The Dialectic of Enlightenment: Philosophical Fragments*. ed. Gunzelin Schmid Noerr, trans. Edmund Jephcott. Stanford, CA: Stanford University Press.

Aftonbladet, 4 September 1983.

Allardt, Erik (1975) *Att ha, att älska, att vara. Om välfärd i Norden* [Having, Loving, Being; On Welfare in the Nordic Countries]. Lund: Argos.

Allardt, Erik (1998) Det goda samhället. Välfärd, livsstil och medborgardygder [The public good: welfare, lifestyle and civil virtues], *Tidskrift för Velferdsforskning*, 1(3): 123–33.

Allardt, M., Sihvo, T. and Uusitalo, H. (1992) *Mitä mieltä hyvinvointivaltiosta? Suomalaisten sosiaaliturvamielipiteet, 1975–1991* [Opinions on Social Security in Finland, 1975–1991]. Helsinki: Sosiaali- ja terveyshallitus, Tutkimuksia 17.

Ambjörnsson, Ronny (1988) *Den skötsamme arbetaren. Idéer och idealer i ett norrländskt sågverkssamhälle, 1880–1930* [The Conscientious Worker: Ideas and Ideals in a Northern Sawmill Community, 1880–1930]. Stockholm: Carlssons.

Anttila, Anu-Hanna (2005) *Loma tehtaan varjossa. Teollisuustyöväestön loma- ja vapaa-ajan moraalisäätely Suomessa 1930–1960-luvuilla* [Vacationing in the Shadows of the factory. Moral Regulation of Industrial Working-Class Vacation and Free Time in Finland, 1930–1960]. Helsinki: Suomalaisen kirjallisuuden seura.

Appadurai, Arjun (1997) *Modernity at Large: Cultural Dimensions of Globalization*. Minneapolis: University of Minnesota Press.

Archer, Margaret (1988) *Culture and Agency: The Place of Culture in Social Theory*. Cambridge: Cambridge University Press.

Archer, Margaret (2000) *Being Human: The Problem of Agency*. Cambridge: Cambridge University Press.

Arendt, Hannah ([1951] 1973) *The Origins of Totalitarianism*. New York: Harcourt Brace Jovanovich.

Ariès, Philippe (1962) *Centuries of Childhood: A Social History of Family Life*. New York: Alfred A. Knopf.

Arppe, Tiina (1998) Sanctification of the 'accused': drinking habits of the French Existentialists in the 1940s, in Marc Galanter (ed.), *Recent Developments in Alcoholism*, Vol. 14. New York: Plenom.

Arvidson, Lars (1985) *Folkbildning i rörelse. Pedagogisk syn i folkbildning inom svensk arbetarrörelse och frikyrkorörelse under 1900– talet – En jämförelse häftad med skyddsomslag*. Gleerup: Högskolan för lärarutbildning i Stockholm och Institutionen för pedagogik.

Augé, Marc (1978) *Symbole, function, histoire: Les interrogations de l'anthropologie*. Paris: Hachette.

Autorenkollektiv (1974) *Proletariat in der BRD*. Berlin: Dietz Verlag.

Babor, T., Caetano, R., Casswell, S., Edwards, G., Giesbrecht, N., Graham, K. et al. (2003) *Alcohol: No Ordinary Commodity*. Oxford: Oxford University Press.

Badwahr, N. (1996) Moral agency, commitment, and impartiality. In E.F. Paul, F.D. Miller, and J. Paul (eds), *The Communitarian Challenge to Liberalism*. Cambridge: Cambridge University Press, pp. 1–26.

Baram, Paul and Sweezy, Paul, M. (1996) *Monopoly Capital: An Essay on the American Economic and Social Order*. New York: Monthly Review Press.

Barbalet, Jack (1998) *Emotion, Social Theory, and Social Structure: A Macrosociological Approach*. Cambridge: Cambridge University Press.

Barrows, S. (1991) Parliaments of the people: the political culture of cafés in the early Third Republic. In S. Barrows and R. Room (eds), *Drinking Behaviour and Belief in Modern History*. Berkeley, CA: University of California Press.

Barry, Norman (1996) Understanding the market, in M. Loney, R. Bocock, R. Clarke, A. Cochrane, P. Graham and M. Wilson (eds), *The State or the Market: Politics and Welfare in Contemporary Britain*. 2nd edition, London: Sage, pp. 231–41.

Baudrillard, Jean (1968) *Le syst éme des objets*. Paris: Gallimard.

Baudrillard, Jean (1976) *L'échange symbolique et la mort*. Paris: Gallimard.

Baudrillard, Jean ([1978] 1997) *A l'ombre des majorités silencieuses ou la fin du social*. Paris: Sens and Tonka.

Baudrillard, Jean (1981) *Simulacres et simulation*. Paris: Galilée.

Bauman, Zygmunt (1989) *Modernity and the Holocaust*. Ithaca, NY: Cornell University Press.

Beck, Ulrich ([1986] 1992) *Risk Society: Towards a New Modernity*. Trans. Mark Ritter. London: Sage.

Beck, Ulrich, Giddens, Anthony and Lash, Scott (1994) *Reflexive Modernity*. London: Sage.

Bell, Daniel (ed.) (1963) *The Radical Right*. New York: Anchor Books.

Bell, Daniel ([1976] 1996) *The Cultural Contradictions of Capitalism*. New York: Basic Books.

Bellah, R. N., Tipton, S., Sullivan, W. and Swidler, A. (1985) *Habits of the Heart: Individualism and Commitment in American Life*. Berkeley, CA: University of California Press.

Benhabib, Seyla (1992) *Situating the Self: Gender, Community and Postmodernism in Contemporary Ethics*. New York: Routledge.

Berridge, Virginia (1990) The Society for the Study of Addiction 1884–1988, *British Journal of Addiction*, 85: 983–1087.

Beveridge, William (1942) *Social Insurance and Allied Services*. London: His Majesty's Stationery Office.

Beveridge, William (1944) *Full Employment in a Free Society*. London: George Allen and Unwin.

Bidou, C., Dagnaud, M., Duriez, B., Ion, J., Mehl, D., Pinçon-Charlot, M. and Tricart, J.-P. (1983) *Les couches moyennes salariées. Mosaïque sociologique*. Paris: Ministère de I'Urbanisme et du Logement.

Billig, M., Condor, S., Edwards, D. and Gane, M. (1988) *Ideological Dilemmas*, London: Sage.

Boltanski, L. (1982) *Les cadres. Formation d'un groupe social*. Paris: Minuit.

Boltanski, L. and Chiapello, E. (2005) *The New Spirit of Capitalism*. Trans. Gregory Elliot. London: Verso.

Boltanski, L. and Thévenot, L. (1991) *De la justification*. Paris: Gallimard.

Bourdieu, Pierre ([1972] 1977) *Outline of a Theory of Practice*. Trans. Richard Nice. Cambridge: Cambridge: University Press.

Bourdieu, Pierre ([1979] 1984) *Distinction: A Social Critique of Judgment of Taste*. Trans. Richard Nice. London: Routledge.

Bourdieu, Pierre ([1980] 1990a) *The Logic of Practice*. Trans. Richard Nice. Cambridge: Polity Press.

Bourdieu, Pierre (1990b) L'économie de la maison, *Actes de la recherche en sciences sociales*, 81–82: 34–55.

Bourdieu, Pierre ([1994] 1998) *Practical Reason*. Trans. Randal Johnson and others. Oxford: Polity Press.

Bourdieu, Pierre (1997a) Le champ économique, *Actes de la recherche en sciences sociales*, 119: 48–66.

Bourdieu, Pierre ([1997b] 2000) *Pascalian Meditations*. Trans. Richard Nice. Cambridge: Polity Press.

Bourdieu, Pierre ([2000] 2005) *The Social Structures of the Economy*. Trans. Chris Turner. Oxford: Polity Press.

Bourdieu, P. and Wacquant, L. (1992) *An Invitation to Reflexive Sociology*. Oxford: Polity Press.

Brennan, Thomas Edward (1989) *Public Drinking and Popular Culture in Eighteenth Century Paris*. Princeton, NJ: Princeton University Press.

Brook, L., Hall, J. and Preston I. (1996) Public spending and taxation, in R. Jowell, J. Curtice, A. Park, L. Brook and K. Thomson (eds), *British Social Attitudes: The 13th Report*. Aldershot: Dartmouth.

Bruun, Kettil (1985) Maktens centrum – centraladministrationen [The centre of power – the central administration], in K. Bruun and P. Frånberg (eds), *Den svenska supen. En historia om brännvin, Bratt och byråkrati [Swedish Drink: A Story of Boozing, Bratt and Bureaucracy]*. Stockholm: Prisma.

Bruun, K., Edwards, G., Lumio, M., Mäkelä, K., Pan, L., Popham, R. E., et al. (1975) *Alcohol Control Policies in Public Health Perspective*. Helsinki: The Finnish Foundation for Alcohol Studies, Vol. 25.

Burris, Val (1986) The discovery of the new middle class, *Theory and Society*, 15(3): 317–49.

Campbell, Colin (1987) *The Romantic Ethic and the Spirit of Modern Consumerism*. London: Basil Blackwell.

Castel, Robert (1995) *Les métamorphoses de la question sociale. Une chronique du salariat*. Paris: Fayard.

Castells, Manuel (1996) *The Rise of the Network Society*. Cambridge: Blackwell.

Castles, Francis G. (1993) Changing courses in economic policy: the English-speaking nations in the 1980's, in Francis G. Castles, (ed.), *Families of Nations*. Aldershot: Dartmouth.

Chombart de Lauwe, Paul-Henry (1977) *La Vie Quotidienne des Familles Ouvrières*. Paris: Centre National de la Recherche Sciéntifique.

Clarke, J., Gewirtz, S. and McLaughlin, E. (2000) Reinventing the welfare state, in J. Clarke, S. Gewirtz and E. McLaughlin (eds), *New Managerialism, New Welfare?* London: Open University Press and Sage.

Cnaan, Ram A. (1989) Public opinion and the dimensions of the welfare state, *Social Indicators Research*, 21: 297–314.

Cohen, Stanley ([1972 1980]) *Folk Devils and Moral Panics: The Creation of the Mods and Rockers*. Oxford: Basil Blackwell.

Conway, D. (1996) Capitalism and community, in E.F. Paul, F.D. Miller and J. Paul, (eds), *The Communitarian Challenge to Liberalism*. Cambridge: Cambridge University Press, pp. 137–63.

Coughlin, Richard (1980) *Ideology, Public Opinion, and Welfare Policy*. Berkeley, CA: University of California Press.

Council of the European Union (1999) *European Union Drugs Strategy (2000–2004)*. Brussels: Council of The European Union. Available at: www.emcdda.org/multi media/actionplan/cordrogue64en.pdf. Accessed 19 January 2004.

Crawford, Alan (1980) *Thunder on the Right*. New York: Pantheon.

Crompton, Rosemary (1998) *Class and Stratification: An Introduction to Current Debates*, 2nd edn. Oxford: Polity Press.

Dean, Mitchel (1999) *Governmentality: Power and Rule in Modern Society*. London: Sage.

de Beauvoir, Simone (1963) *La force des choses*. Paris: Gallimard.

Decorte, Tom (2001) *The Taming of Cocaine: Cocaine Use in European and American Cities*. Brussels: VUB University Press.

Deleuze, Gilles (1968) *Différence et répétition*. Paris: Presses Universitaires de France.

Dennett, Daniel (2004) *Freedom Evolves*. London: Penguin Books.

Der Staatsmonopolistische Kapitalismus (1972) Berlin: Verlag Marxistische Blätter.

Dingle, Anthony Edward (1980) *The Campaign for Prohibition in Victorian England: The United Kingdom Alliance, 1872–1895*. London: Croom Helm.

Donzelot, Jacques (1984) *L'invention du social. Essai sur le déclin des passions politiques*. Paris: Fayard.

Dorchester, David (1884) *The Liquor Problem in All Ages*. New York: Phillips Hunt.

Douglas, Mary (1966) *Purity and Danger: An Analysis of the Concepts of Pollution and Taboo*. London: Routledge.

Dubofsky, Melvyn (2000) *We Shall Be All: A History of the Industrial Workers of the World*. Abridged edition. Chicago: University of Illinois Press.

du Gay, Paul (2000) Entrepreneurial governance and public management: the anti-bureaucrats, in J. Clarke, S. Gewirtz and E. McLaughlin (eds), *New Managerialism, New Welfare?* London: Open University Press and Sage.

Durand, Gilbert (1960) *Les structures anthropologiques de l'imaginaire*. Paris: P.U.F.

Durkheim, Émile ([1893] 1984) *The Division of Labour in Society*. Trans. W.D. Halls. Basingstoke: Macmillan.

Eder, Klaus (1993) *The New Politics of Class. Social Movements and Cultural Dynamics in Advanced Societies*. London: Sage.

Edlund, Jonas (2006) Trust in the capacity of the welfare state and general welfare support: Sweden, 1997–2002, *Acta Sociologica*, 49(4): 395–418.

Ehrenberg, Alain (1998) *La fatigue d'être soi*. Paris: Odile Jacob.

Eisenbach-Stangl, I. (1991) *Eine Gesellschaftgeschichte des Alkohols. Produktion, Konsum und soziale Kontrolle alkoholischer Rausch- und Genussmittel in Österreich 1918–1984*. Frankfurt and New York: Campus Verlag.

Elias, Norbert ([1939a] 1978) *The History of Manners: The Civilizing Process*, Vol. 1. Trans. Edmund Jephcott. New York: Pantheon Books.

Elias, Norbert ([1939b] 1982) *Power and Civility: The Civilizing Process*, Vol. 2. Trans. Edmund Jephcott. New York: Pantheon Books.

Eriksen, Sidsel (1996) *Stationsbyens samfund* [The Station Town's Community]. Grinsted: Overgard boger.

Erikson, Robert and Goldthorpe, John (1983) *The Constant Flux*. New York: Clarendon Press.

Esping-Andersen, Gøsta (1990) *The Three Worlds of Welfare Capitalism*. Cambridge: Polity Press.

Esping-Andersen, Gøsta (1996a) After the golden age? Welfare state dilemmas in a global economy, in Gøsta Esping-Andersen (ed.), *Welfare States in Transition: National Adaptations in Global Economies*. London: Sage.

Esping-Andersen, Gøsta (1996b) Welfare states without work: the impasse of labour shedding and familialism in Continental European social policy, in Gøsta Esping-Andersen (ed.), *Welfare States in Transition: National Adaptations in Global Economies*. London: Sage.

Esping-Andersen, Gøsta (1996c) Positive-sum solutions in a world of trade-offs? In Gøsta Esping-Andersen (ed.), *Welfare States in Transition: National Adaptations in Global Economies*. London: Sage.

Eyerman, Ron (1994) *Between Culture and Politics: Intellectuals in Modern Societies*. Cambridge: Polity Press.

Eyerman, R. and Jamison, A. (1991) *Social Movements: A Cognitive Approach*. Cambridge: Polity Press.

Falk, Pasi (1994) *The Consuming Body*. London: Sage.

Fischler, Claude (1990) *L'omnivore. Le goût, la cuisine et le corps*. Paris: Odile Jacob.

Fitzgerald, John L. (2002) A political economy of "doves", *Contemporary Drug Problems*, 29(1): 201–39.

Fleischacker, Samuel (1999) *A Third Concept of Liberty: Judgment and Freedom in Kant and Adam Smith*. Princeton, NJ: Princeton University Press.

Foucault, Michel (1966) *Les mots et les choses. Une archéologie des sciences humaines*. Paris: Gallimard. English translation (2001) *The Order of Things: An Archaeology of the Human Sciences*. New York: Vintage Books.

Foucault, Michel ([1976] 1979) *The History of Sexuality, Vol. I. An Introduction*. Trans. Robert Hurley. London: Allen Lane.

Foucault, Michel (1987) *The History of Sexuality, Vol. II. The Use of Pleasure*. Trans. Robert Hurley. London: Penguin Books.

Foucault, Michel (1988) Politics and reason, in L.D. Kritzman (ed.), *Politics, Philosophy, Culture: Interviews and Other Writings, 1977–1984*. London: Routledge.

Foucault, Michel (1991) Governmentality, in G. Burchell, C. Gordon and P. Miller (eds), *The Foucault Effect: Studies in Governmentality, with Two Lectures by and an Interview with Michel Foucault*. Chicago: The University of Chicago Press.

Foucault, Michel (2007) *Security, Territory, Population: Lectures at the Collège de France, 1977–1978*, ed. Michel Senellart. Houndmills: Palgrave Macmillan.

Fourastié, Jean (1979) *Les trente glorieuses*. Paris: Fayard.

Frank, André Gunder (1969) *Latin America: Underdevelopment or Revolution?* New York: Monthly Review Press.

Frank, Thomas (2004) *What's the Matter with Kansas? How Conservatives Won the Heart of America*. New York: Henry Holt and Co.

Fromm, Erich ([1932] 1970) *Crisis of Psychoanalysis*. New York: H. Holt.

Fromm, Erich ([1941] 1991) *The Fear of Freedom*. London: Routledge.

Frykman, J. and Löfgren, O. (1985) *Modärna tider* [Modern Times]. Lund: Liber.

Fuglum, Peter (1995) *Brennevinsforbudet i Norge* [The Spirits Prohibition in Norway]. Trondheim: Tapir Förlag.

Furst, Lilian (1969) *Romanticism*. London: Methuen.

Galbraith, Kenneth (1962) *The Affluent Society*. Harmondsworth: Pelican Books.

Garland, David (2001) *The Culture of Control: Crime and Social Order in Contemporary Society*. Oxford: Oxford University Press.

Geertz, Clifford (1973) *The Interpretation of Culture*. New York: Basic Books.

Gellner, Ernest (1983) *Nations and Nationalism*. Oxford: Basil Blackwell.

Gerth, H. and Mills, C.W. (1954) *Character and Social Structure*. London: Routledge and Kegan Paul.

Giddens, Anthony (1979) *Central Problems in Social Theory: Action, Structure and Contradiction in Social Analysis*. London: Macmillan.

Giddens, Anthony (1984) *The Constitution of Society: Outline of the Theory of Structuration*. Cambridge: Polity Press.

Giddens, Anthony (1991) *Modernity and Self-identity: Self and Society in the Late Modern Age*. Cambridge: Polity Press.

Giddens, Anthony (1992) *The Transformation of Intimacy: Sexuality, Love and Eroticism in Modern Societies*. Cambridge: Polity.

Giddens, Anthony (1998) *The Third Way*. Cambridge: Polity Press.

Goldthorpe, John (2002) 'Occupational Sociology, Yes: Class Analysis, No: Comment on Grusky and Weeden's Research Agenda', *Acta Sociologica*, 45(3): 211–17.

Goldthorpe, J. and Marshal, G. (1988) Intellectuals and the working class in modern Britain, in David Rose (ed.), *Social Stratification and Economic Change*. London: Hutchinson.

Goldthorpe, J. and Marshal, G. (1992) The promising future of class analysis: a response to recent critiques, *Sociology*, 26: 381–400.

Greimas, A.J. and Courtès, J. (1979) *Sémiotique. Dictionnaire raisonné de la théorie du langage*. Paris: Hachette.

Gronow, Jukka (1997) *The Sociology of Taste*. London: Routledge.

Grusky, D. and Sørensen, J. (1998) Can class analysis be salvaged? *The American Journal of Sociology*, 103(5): 1187–234.

Gusfield, Joseph (1955) Social structure and moral reform: a study of the Woman's Christian Temperance Union, *American Journal of Sociology*, 61: 221–32.

Gusfield, Joseph (1963) *Symbolic Crusade: Status Politics and the American Temperance Movement*. Westport, CT: Greenwood Press.

Gutzke, D.W. (1989) *Protecting the Pub: Brewers and Publicans against Temperance*. Suffolk: The Boydell Press.

Haataja, Anita (1996) Vaihtoehtoiset sosiaaliturvastrategiat: esimerkkinä työttömyysvaikutus, in Olli Kangas (ed.), *Hyvinvointimallit, niiden toiminta ja kannatusperusta* [The Models of Welfare: Their Functionality and Support]. Helsinki: Sosiaali- ja terveysministeriö.

Hacking, Ian (2004 [1999]) *The Social Construction of What?* Cambridge, MA: Harvard University Press.

Haller, M., Höllinger, F. and Raubal, O. (1990) Leviathan or welfare state? Attitudes towards the role of government in six advanced Western nations, in Duane Aldwin et al. (eds), *Attitudes to Inequality and the Role of Governments*. Rijswijk: Sociaal en Culturel Plaanbureau.

Harmaja, Laura (1928) *Perheenemännän taloudellinen tehtävä* [The Economic Mission of the Housewife]. Porvoo: WSOY.

Harrison, B. (1971) *Drink and the Victorians: The Temperance Question in England, 1815–1978*. London: Faber and Faber.

Haug, Wolfgang Fritz (1971) *Kritik der Warenästhetik*. Frankfurt am Main: Suhrkamp.

Hautamäki, Antti (1993) Spontaaniin yhteiskuntaan – hyvinvointia ilman valtiota [Towards the society of spontaneity – welfare without a state], in J. Andersson, A. Hautamäki, R. Jallinoja and I. Niiniluoto (eds), *Hyvinvointivaltio ristiaallokossa. Arvot ja tosiasiat* [The Welfare State in Turbulence: Values and Facts]. Helsinki: WSOY.

Hayek, Friedrich von ([1944] 1962) *The Road to Serfdom*. London: Routledge.

Helsingin huumestrategia (2000) *Helsingin huumestrategian 1997 tarkistaminen ja ajantasaistaminen*. [The Proposal of the Drug Strategy Committee for 2000, City of Helsinki]. Helsinki: Helsingin kaupunki.

Hirdman, Yvonne (1989) *Att lägga livel till rätta. Studier on den svensk valfardstatem [To set life right. Studies on the Swedish welfare state]*. Stockholm: Carlsson bokförlag.

Hirsch, Joachim (1980) *Der Sicherheitsstaat. Das "Modell Deutschland", seine Krise und die neuen sozialen Bewegungen*. Frankfurt am Main: Europäische Verlagsanstalt.

Hirschmann, Albert O. (1977) *The Passions and the Interests: Political Arguments for Capitalism before Its Triumph*. Princeton, NJ: Princeton University Press.

Hobsbawm, Eric (1995) *Age of Extremes: The Short Twentieth Century, 1914–1991*. London: Acabus.

Hofstadter, Richard (1955) *The Age of Reform*. New York: Vintage Books.

Hoggart, Richard ([1957] 1981) *The Uses of Literacy*. New York: Penguin Books.

Holder, H. Kühlhon, E., Nordlund, S. et al. (1998) *European Integration and Nordic Alcohol Policies*. Aldershot: Ashgate.

Honneth, Axel (2004) Organised self-realization: some paradoxes of individualization, *European Journal of Social Theory*, 7(4): pp. 463–78.

Hume, David ([1748; 1751] 1998) *Enquiries Concerning Human Understanding and Concerning the Principles of Morals*. Oxford: Clarendon Press.

Ilmonen, K. and Stoe, E. (1997) The production of the 'consumer' in Nordic consumer political discourse, in P. Sulkunen, J. Holmwood, H. Radner and G. Schulze (eds), *Constructing the New Consumer Society*. London: Macmillan.

Inglehart, Ronald (1977) *The Silent Revolution*, Princeton, NJ: Princeton University Press.

Inglehart, Ronald (1989) *Culture Shift in Advanced Industrial Society*. Princeton, NJ: Princeton University Press.

Iversen, Torben (2001) The dynamics of welfare state expansion: trade openness, de-industrialization, and partisan politics, in Paul Pierson (ed.), *The New Politics of the Welfare State*. Oxford: Oxford University Press.

Jaeger, Mads Meier (2006) What makes people support public responsibility for welfare provision: self-interest or political ideology? A longitudinal approach, *Acta Sociologica*, 49(3): 321–38.

Jallinoja, Riitta (1983) *Naisasialiikkeen taistelukaudet* (The Years of Feminist Struggles). Helsinki: WSOY.

Jallinoja, Riitta (1991) *Moderni elämä: Ajankuva ja käytännöt* [Modern Life: Images and Practices]. Helsinki: SKS.

Jameson, Fredric (1998) *The Cultural Turn: Selected Writings on the Postmodern, 1983–1998*. London: Verso.

Jaurès, Jean (1934) *Oeuvres de Jean Jaurès. Textes rassemblés, présentés et annotés par Max Bonnafous. IV: l'Armée nouvelle*. Paris: Editions Rieder.

Jensen, T.E. and Kjærnes, U. (1997) Political dilemmas of designing the good life: the case of nutrition and social democracy, in P. Sulkunen, J. Holmwood, H. Radner and G. Schulze (eds), *Constructing the New Consumer Society*. London: Macmillan.

Jessop, Bob (2002) *The Future of the Capitalist State*. Cambridge: Polity.

Johansson, L. (1992) *Brännvin, postillor och röda fanor* [Spirits, Pulpits and the Red Flag]. Växjö: Högskolan i Växjö.

Johansson, Lennart (2000) The controversy sources of the Nordic solutions, in P. Sulkunen, C. Tigerstedt and K. Warpenius (eds), *Broken Spirits: Power and Ideas in Nordic Alcohol Control*. Helsinki: NAD.

Johansson, Sten (1970) *Om levnadsundersökelsen* [On Research on the Standard of Living]. Stockholm: Allmänna förlaget.

Johansson, Sten (1971) *Politiska resursser* [Political Resources]. Stockholm: Allmänna förlaget.

Julkunen, Raija (1994) Suomalainen sukupuolimalli 1960-luvun käänteenä [Finnish gender model as a turning point of the 1960s], in Anneli Anttonen et al. (eds), *Naisten hyvinvointivaltio* [The Women's Welfare State]. Tampere: Vastapaino.

Julkunen R. and Pärnänen A. (2005) *Uusi Ikäsopimus*. Jyväskylä: Minerva.

Kangas, Risto (2001) *Yhteiskunta* [Society]. Helsinki: Tutkijaliitto.

Keane, John (1988) *Democracy and Civil Society*. London: Verso.

Kilpinen, E. (2009) 'The Habitual Conception of Action and Social Theory', *Semiotica* 173(1/4): 99–128.

Kim, P. (1992) Does advertising work?: a review of the evidence, *Journal of Consumer Marketing*, 9: 5–21.

Kornhauser, William (1960) *The Politics of Mass Society*. London: Routledge and Kegan Paul.

Korpi, Walter (1978) *The Working Class in Welfare Capitalism: Work, Unions and Politics in Sweden*. London: Routledge & Kegan Paul.

Kosonen, Pekka (1995) *Eurooppalaiset hyvinvointivaltiot. Yhdentymisiä ja hajaantumisia* [European Welfare States: Convergence and Divergence]. Helsinki: Gaudeamus.

Kotler, P. and Armstrong, G. (2006) *Principles of Marketing*, 11th ed. New Jersey: Pearson-Prentice Hall.

Krahl, Hans-Jürgen (1971) *Konstitution und Klassenkampf. Zur historischen Dialektik von bürgerlichen Emanzipation und proletarischen Revolution*. Frankfurt am Main: Verlag Neue Kritik.

Kriesi, Hanspeter (1989) New social movements and the new class in the Netherlands, *American Journal of Sociology*, 94(5): 1078–116.

Krovoza, Alfred (1976) *Produktion und Sozialisation*. Frankfurt am Main: Europäischer Verlagsanstalt.

Kuusi, Pekka (1961) *60-luvun sosiaalipolitiikka [Social Politics for the 1960s]*. Helsinki: WSOY.

Lalander, Philip (2003) *Hooked on Heroin: Drugs and Drifters in a Globalized World*. Oxford: Berg Publishers.

Lalander, Philip and Salasuo, Mikko (eds) (2005) *Drugs and Youth Cultures: Global and Local Expressions*. Helsinki: NAD.

Lambert, William R. (1983) *Drink and Sobriety in Victorian Wales, 1820–1895*. Cardiff: University of Wales Press.

Landowski, Eric (2004) *Passions sans nom*. Paris: PUF.

Landowski, E. (2005) Les interactions risquées, in *Nouveaux Actes Sémiotiques*. Limoges: Pulim, pp. 101–3.

Lasch, Christopher (1991) *The True and Only Heaven: Progress and Its Critics*. New York and London: Norton & Company.

Lash, Scott and Urry, John (1987) *The End of Organized Capitalism*. Cambridge: Polity Press.

Latour, Bruno (1988) *The Pasteurization of France*. Trans. Alan Sheridan and John Law. Cambridge, MA: Harvard University Press.

Latour, Bruno (1993) Ethnography of high tech: about the Aramis case, in P. Lemonnier (ed.), *Technological Choices: Transformation in Material Cultures since the Neolithic*. New York: Routledge.

Laval, Christian (2006) *L'homme économique. Essai sur les racines du néoliberalisme*. Paris: Gallimard.

Lawrence, David H. ([1910] 1990) *Democracy: Selected Essays*. Harmondsworth: Penguin.

Leroy, Anne-Marie (1999) Les réformes administratives dans les pays de l'OCDE: une tentative de synthèse, in *Etat et gestion publique. Actes du colloque du 16 décembre 1999*. Paris: Conseil d'Analyse Economique.

Lesnoff, Michael (1986) *Social Contract*. London: Macmillan.

Levine, Harry G. (1978) The discovery of addiction: changing conceptions of habitual drunkenness in America, *Journal of Studies on Alcohol*, 39(1): 143–74.

Levine, Harry G. (1992) Temperance cultures: concern about alcohol problems in Nordic and English-speaking cultures, in M. Lader, G. Edwards and C. Drummond (eds), *The Nature of Alcohol and Drug Related Problems*. New York: Oxford University Press.

Lévi-Strauss, Claude (1964) *Le cru et le cuit. Mythologiques I*. Paris: Plon.

Levi-Strauss, Claude (1965) Le triangle culinaire, *L' Arc*, 26: 19–29.

Levi-Strauss, Claude (1968) 'L'Origine des manières de table', *Mythologies III*. Paris: Plon.

Lindner, Rolf (1977) *Das Gefühl von Freiheit und Abenteuer. Ideologie und Praxis der Werbung.* New York and Frankfurt: Campus.

Lipovetsky, Gilles (1992) *La crépuscule du devoir. L'Éthique indolore des nouveaux temps démocratiques*. Paris: Gallimard.

Lipset, Seymour M. (1969) *The Political Man*. London: Heinemann.

Lockwood, David (1958) *The Black-Coated Worker*. London: George Allen and Unwin.

Longum, Leif (1997) Nordisk kulturradikalisme 1870–1980. Kritisk korrektiv og romantisk utopi (Nordic cultural radicalism, 1870–1980: Critical corrective and romantic utopia), in G. Bexell and H. Stenius (eds), *Värdetraditioner i nordiskt perspektiv*. Lund: Lund University Press.

Lovejoy, Arthur (1955) *Essays in the History of Ideas*. New York: George Braziller.

Lupton, Deborah (1995) *The Imperative of Health: Public Health and the Regulated Body*. London: Sage.

Maarse, Hans (2006) The privatization of health care in Europe: an eight-country analysis, *Journal of Health Politics, Policy and Law*, 31(5): 981–1014.

Määttä, Mirja and Kalliomaa-Puha, Laura (2005) Sopiva yhteiskunta? Koti, koulu ja uusi sopimuksellisuus [Contracting society? Home, school and the new contractualism], in Kati Rantala and Pekka Sulkunen (eds), *Projektiyhteiskunnan kääntöpuolia* [The Project Society Inside Out]. Helsinki: Gaudeamus.

Macpherson, C.B. (1977) *The Political Theory of Possessive Individualism*, 7th edn. Oxford: Oxford University Press.

Maffesoli, Michel (1994) *The Time of the Tribes: The Decline of Individualism in Mass Society.* London: Sage.

Maffesoli, Michel (1996) *Contemplation of the World Figures of Community Style*. Minneapolis: University of Minnesota Press.

Maffesoli, Michel (1997) The return of Dionysos, in P. Sulkunen, J. Holmwood, H. Radner and G. Schulze (eds), *Constructing the New Consumer Society*. London: Macmillan.

Magnusson, L. (1985) Orsaker till det förindustriella drickandet. Supandet i hantverkets Eskilstuna. [Reasons for pre-industrial drinking: the craftsmen of Eskilstuna]. *Alkoholpolitik*, 2: 23–9.

Mäkelä Klaus (1976) *Alkojolipolittisen Mielipideilmaston vaihtelut Suomessa 1960- ja 70-luvulla*. [Fluctuations in the Climate of Opinion Concerning Alcohol Control Measures]. Helsinki: Alkoholipoliittisen tutkimuslaitoksen tutkimusseloste.

Mandeville, Bernand ([1723] 1997) *The Fable of the Bees and Other Writings*, ed. E.J. Hundert. Indianapolis: Hackett Publishing Company.

Malthus, Thomas ([1798] 1993) *An Essay on the Principle of Population*. Oxford: Oxford University Press.

Mannheim, Karl ([1986] 1997) *Conservatism: A Contribution to the Sociology of Knowledge*. London and New York: Routledge and Kegan Paul.

Margolis, Stacy (2002) Addiction and the ends of desire, in J.F. Brodie and M. Redfield (eds), *High Anxieties: Cultural Studies in Addiction*. Berkeley, CA: University of California Press.

Martin, Bernice (1981) *Sociology of Contemporary Cultural Change*. New York: St Martin's Press.

Marx, Karl ([1850] 2003) *The Class Struggles in France*. London: Resistance Books.

Marx, Karl ([1859] 1973) *Karl Marx: Grundrisse*. Trans. Martin Nicolaus. London: Penguin Classics.

Mauss, Marcel ([1924] 1970) *The Gift: Forms and Functions of Exchange in Archaic Societies.* Trans. Ian Cunnison. London: Cohen & West Ltd.

McClay, William (1994) *Masterless: Self and Society in Modern America*. Chapel Hill, NC: The University of North Carolina Press.

McCracken, Grant (1988) *Culture and Consumption*. Bloomington, IN: Indiana University Press.

McKendrick, Neil, Brewer, John and Plumb, J.H. (1982) *The Birth of a Consumer Society: The Commercialization of Eighteenth-Century England*. Bloomington, IN: Indiana University Press.

Mehnert, Armin (1973) *Bedürfnisse – Manipulation – individuelle Konsumtion in der BRD*. Frankfurt am Main: Suhrkamp.

Mendel, Gerard (1968) *La Révolte contre le Père*. Paris: Payot.

Mendras, Henry (1988) *La Seconde Révolution Française, 1965–1984*. Paris: Gallimard.

Messu, Michel (1999) Solidarism and familialism: the influence of ideological conceptions on the formation of French social protection, in P. Abrahamson, D. Blanchet, A. Hatland, N. Lefaucheur, J. Palme and H. Uusitalo (eds), *Comparing Social Welfare Systems in Nordic Europe and France*. Paris: Collection MIRE.

Mills, C. Wright ([1951 1956]) *White Collar*. Oxford: Oxford University Press.

Mills, C. Wright (1959a) *The Sociological Imagination*. New York: Oxford University Press.

Mills, C. Wright (1959b) *The Power Elite*. New York: Oxford University Press.

Monjardet, Dominique and Benguigui, Georges (1982) L'utopie gestionnaire – les couches moyennes. *Revue française de sociologie*, XXIII(4): 605–36.

Montesquieu ([1748] 1989) *The Spirit of the Laws*. Trans., ed. Anne M. Cohler, Basia Carolyn Miller and Harold Samuel Stone. Cambridge: Cambridge University Press.

Montesquieu (1951) *Oeuvres complètes II*. Paris: Editions Gallimard.

Mukerji, Chandra (1983) *From Graven Images: Patterns of Modern Materialism*. New York: Columbia University Press.

Muller, Jerry (1993) *Adam Smith in His Time and Ours: Designing the Decent Society*. New York: The Free Press.

Myrdal, A. and Myrdal, G. (1935) *Kris i befolkningsfrågan* [The Crisis in the Population Question]. Stockholm: Albert Bonniers Förlag.

Negt, Oskar (1973) *Über das Verhältnis von Ökonomie und Gesellschaftstheorie bei Karl Marx*. Frankfurt am Main: Verlag O.

Newman, J. (2000) Beyond the New Public Management? Modernizing public services, in J. Clarke, S. Gewirtz and E. McLaughlin (eds), *New Managerialism, New Welfare?* London: Open University Press and Sage, pp. 45–61.

Nielsen, Nils Kayser (1997) Kritisk loyalitet – om kulturradikalisme i Norden [Critical loyalty – on cultural radicalism in Nordic countries], in G. Bexell and H. Stenius (eds), *Värdetraditioner i nordisket perspektiv*. Lund: Lund University Press.

Nieminen, Armas (1951) *Taistelu sukupuolimoraalista* [The War over Sexual Morality]. Turku: Uuden Auran osakeyhtiön kirjapaino.

Nourrisson, Philippe (1990) *Le buveur du XIXe siècle*. Paris: Albin Michel.

OECD (1995) *Governance in Transition: Public Management Reforms in OECD Countries*. Paris: OECD.

OECD (2002) *Public Sector Modernisation: A New Agenda. Exccecutive Summary*. GOV/PUMA 2002: 2. Paris: OECD.

Offe, Klaus (1985) *Disorganized Capitalism: Contemporary Transformations of Work and Politics*. London: Polity Press.

Olsson, Sven (1990) *Social Policy and Welfare State in Sweden*. Lund: Arkiv förlag.

Outhwaite, William (2005) *The Future of "Society"*. Oxford: Blackwell.

Paine, Thomas ([1791] 2003) *Common Sense, Rights of Man and Other Essential Writings*. London: Signet Classics.

Pakulski, Jan and Waters, Malcolm (1996) *The Death of Class*. London: Sage.

Parker, H., Measham, F. and Aldridge, J. (2001) *Dancing on Drugs: Risk, Health and Hedonism in the British Drug Scene*. London and New York: Routledge.

Paton, D.N. (1977) Drink and the temperance movement in nineteenth century Scotland, unpublished PhD thesis, University of Edinburgh.

Peel, J.D.Y. (1992) *Herbert Spencer: The Evolution of a Sociologist*, 2nd edn. Aldershot: Gregg Revivals.

Peltonen, Matti (1996) Olympiavuoden käytösopas [Good manners for the Olympic year], in M. Peltonen (ed.), *Rillumarei ja valistus. Kulttuurikahakoita 1950-luvun Suomessa* [Rillumarei and Enlightenment: Cultural Conflicts in Finland of the 1950s]. Helsinki: Suomen Historiallinen Seura.

Petersen, A. and Lupton, D. (1996) *The New Public health: Health and Self in the Age of Risk*. London: Sage.

Pettersen, Per Arnt (1995) Who wants economic transfers? in Stefan Svallfors (ed.), *In the Eye of the Beholder: Opinions on Welfare and Justice in Comparative Perspective*. Umeå: Impello.

Pierson, Christopher (1991) *Beyond the Welfare State?* Pennsylvania: Pennsylvania University Press.

Pieters, Danny (2003) Freedom of choice in Europe´s social security law, *European Journal of Social Security*, 5(4): 287–304.

Ploug, Niels (1994) The welfare state in liquidation? in N. Ploug and J. Kvist (eds), *Recent Trends in Cash Benefits in Europe*. Copenhagen: The Danish National Institute of Social Research.

Pohrt, Wolfgang (1976) *Theorie des Gebrauchswerts*. Frankfurt am Main: Syndikat.

Polanyi, Karl ([1944] 1957) *The Great Transformation: The Political and Economic Origins of Our Time*. Boston: Beacon Press.

Pollit, Christopher (1990) *Managerialism and the Public Services: The Anglo-American Experience*. Oxford: Basil Blackwell.

Putnam, Robert D. (2000) *Bowling Alone: The Collapse and Revival of American Community*. New York: Simon and Schuster.

Ragnarsson, Lennart (1993) *Från motbolk till snabbköp* [From Motbolk to Free Purchases]. Stockholm: Systembolaget.

Rantala, K. and Sulkunen, P. (eds) (2006) *Projektiyhteiskunnan kääntöpuolia* [The Flip-side of the Project Society]. Helsinki: Gaudeamus.

Raphael, D.D. and Macfie, A.L. (1984) Introduction, in Adam Smith ([1790] 1984) *The Theory of Moral Semtiments*, Glasgow edn, eds D.D. Raphael and A.L. Macfie. Indianapolis: Liberty Fund.

Rauch, Dietmar (2007) Is there really a Scandinavian social service model? A comparison of childcare and elderlycare in six European countries, *Acta Sociologica*, 50(3): 249–70.

Rawls, John (1993) *Political Liberalism*. New York: Columbia University Press.

Reichelt, Helmut (1970) *Zur Logischen Struktur des Kapitalbegriffs bei Karl Marx*. Frankfurt am Main: Europäischer Verlagsanstalt.

Riesman, David (1950) *The Lonely Crowd: A Study of the Changing American Character*. New Haven, CT: Yale University Press.

Rioux, J.-P. (1971) *La révolution industrielle*. Paris: Seuil.

Roberts, J. (1984) *Drink, Temperance and the Working Class in 19th Century Germany*. London: Allen and Unwin.

Roller, Edeltraud (1995) The welfare state: the equality dimension, in O. Borre and E. Scarbrugh (eds), *The Scope of Government*. Oxford: Oxford University Press.

Room, Robin (1984) A "reverence for strong drink": the Lost Generation and the elevation of alcohol in American culture, *Journal of Studies in Alcohol*, 45(6): 540–6.

Rosanvallon, Pierre (1990) *L'état en France de 1789 à nos jours*. Paris: Seuil.

Rose, K.D. (1997) *American Women and the Repeal of Prohibition*. New York: New York University Press.

Rose, Nikolas (1999) *Powers of Freedom: Reframing Political Thought*. Cambridge: Cambridge University Press.

Rosenzweig, R. (1983) *Eight Hours for What We Will: Workers and Leisure in an Industrial City, 1870–1920*. Cambridge: Cambridge University Press.

Roszak, Theodore ([1968] 1995) *The Making of a Counterp-Culture*. Berkeley, CA: University of California Press.

Rouhunkoski, Mauri (1949) Johdanto [Introduction], in *Väestöliiton Syntyvyyden Säännöstelyn Opas* [The Guide for Child Restriction]. Helsinki: Väestöliitto.

Rousseau, Jean-Jacques ([1755] 1998) *Discours sur l'origine et les fondements de l'inégalité parmi les hommes*. Paris: Nathan.

Sainsbury, Diane (2001) Welfare state challenges and responses: institutional and ideological resilience or restructuring? *Acta Sociologica*, 44(3): 257–66.

Sartre, Jean-Paul ([1948] 1975) *Presentation des Temps Modernes*. Paris: Gallimard.

Schanz, Hans-Jørgen (1974) *Til rekonstruktionen af kritikken af den politiske økonomins omfangslogiske status.* [Towards a Reconstruction of the Ontological Status of the Critique of Political Economy]. Århus: Modtryk.

Schanz, Hans-Jørgen (1996) *Karl Marx i tilbageblik efter murens fald* [Karl Marx after the Fall of the Wall]. Århus: Modtryk.

Scheffler, Samuel (1988) Agent-Centred Restrictions. Rationality and the Virtues', in S. Scheffler (ed.), *Consequentialism and its Critics.* Oxford: Oxford University Press.

Schiman, L.L. (1988) *Crusade Against Drink in Victorian England.* London: Macmillan.

Schmid Noerr, Gunzelin (2002) Editor's Afterword, in T.W. Adorno and M. Horkheimer, *The Dialectic of Enlightenment. Philosophical Fragments.* Ed. Gunzelin Schmid Noerr, trans. Edmund Jephcott. Stanford, CA: Stanford University Press.

Schulze, Gerhard (1992) *Erlebnisgesellschaft. Kultursoziologie der Gegenwart.* Frankfurt am Main: Campus Verlag.

Sicard, Jean-François (2004) Economie et philosophie chez Adam Smith. *Sens Public.* Available at: www.sens-public.org/article.php3?id_article=61. Accessed 29 July 2004.

Sillanpää, Miina (1925) Quoted in Sulkunen Irma (1986) *Raittius kansalaisuskontona. Raittiusliikkeen järjestäytyminen 1870-luvulta suurlakon jälkeisiin vuosiin* [Temperance as a Civil Religion: The Organization of the Temperance Movement between 1870 and the General Strike of 1906]. Helsinki: Societas Historica Finlandiae.

Simmel, Georg ([1900] 1990) *The Philosophy of Money,* 2nd edn. Trans. Tom Bottomore and David Frisby. London: Routledge.

Singer, Brian C.J. (2004) Montesquieu, Adam Smith and the discovery of the social, *Journal of Classical Sociology,* 4(1): 31–57.

Sjö, Fabian (2005) Drugs in Swedish club culture – creating identity and distance to mainstream society, in Philip Lalander and Mikko Salasuo (eds), *Drugs and Youth Cultures: Global and Local Expressions.* Helsinki: NAD, pp. 31–45.

Slagstad, Rune (1998) *De nasjonale strateger* [The National Strategies]. Oslo: Pax Förlag.

Smith, Adam ([1776] 1976) *Inquiry into the Nature and Causes of the Wealth of Nations,* Vol. 1, Glasgow edn, ed. R.H. Campbell, A.S. Skinner and W.B. Todd. Oxford: Clarendon Press.

Smith, Adam ([1778] 1982) *Lectures on Jurisprudence,* eds R.L. Meek, D.D. Rapahel and P.G. Stein. Indianapolis: Liberty Fund.

Smith, Adam ([1790] 1984) *The Theory of Moral Sentiments,* Glasgow edn, ed. D.D. Raphael and A.L. Macfie. Indianapolis: Liberty Fund.

Smout, T.C. ([1986] 1997) *A Century of Scottish People.* London: Fontana Press.

Sørensen, Aage (1998) On kings, pietism and rent-seeking in Scandinavian welfare states, *Acta Sociologica,* 41(4): 363–75.

Sorokin, T. (1974) *Society, Culture and Personality: Their Structure and dynamics.* New York and London: Harper and Brothers.

Spencer, H. ([1891] 1996) From freedom to bondage, in M. Taylor (ed.), *Herbert Spencer and the Limits of State.* Bristol: Thoemmes Press.

Spode, H. (1993) *Die Macht der Trunkenheit. Kultur- und Socialsgeschichte des Alkohols in Deutschland.* Opladen: Ledge and Budrich.

Stephens, John D. (1996) The Scandinavian welfare states: achievements, crisis and prospects, in Gøsta Esping-Andersen (ed.), *Welfare States in Transition: National Adaptations in Global Economies.* London: Sage.

Sulkunen, Irma (1986) *Raittius kansalaisuskontona. Raittiusliikkeen järjestäytyminen 1870-luvulta suurlakon jälkeisiin vuosiin* [Temperance as a Civil Religion: The organization of the Temperance Movement between 1870 and the General Strike of 1906]. Helsinki: Societas Historica Finlandiae.

Sulkunen, Olavi (2000) *Kansainväliset ammattiyhdistysoikeudet. Tutkimus niiden synnystä, sisällöstä ja systeemiyhteydestä* [International Trade Union Rights: A Study of their Origins, Normative Contents and Systemic Coherence in Public International Law and International Labour Law]. Helsinki: Suomalainen lakimiesyhdistys.

Sulkunen, Pekka (1982) Society made visible: On the cultural sociology of Pierre Bourdieu, *Acta Sociologica*, 25(2): 103–15.

Sulkunen, Pekka (1990) Isoäidin suolikaasut ja Jaguaarin tuli: Claude Lévi-Strauss ja sosiologinen kulttuuriteoria [Grandmother's flatus and Jaguar's fire: Claude Lévi-Strauss and the sociological theory of culture], *Suomen Antropologi*, 2: 17–27.

Sulkunen, Pekka (1992) *The European New Middle Class: Individuality and Tribalism in Mass Society*. Aldershot: Avebury.

Sulkunen, Pekka (1997) Problems of prevention: mundane speech and expert discourse on alcohol policy, in P. Sulkunen, J. Holmwood, H. Radner and G. Schulze (eds), *Constructing the New Consumer Society*. London: Macmillan.

Sulkunen, Pekka (2000) The liberal arguments, in P. Sulkunen, C. Tigerstedt, C. Sutton and K. Warpenius (eds), *Broken Spirits: Power and Ideas in Nordic Alcohol Control*. Helsinki: NAD.

Sulkunen, P., Alasuutari, P., Nätkin, R. and Kinnunen, M. (1997) *The Urban Pub*. Helsinki: Stakes.

Sulkunen, P., Tigerstedt, C., Sutton, C. and Warpenius, K. (eds) (2000) *Broken Spirits: Power and Ideas in Nordic Alcohol Control*. Helsinki: NAD.

Sulkunen, P. Rantala, K. and Määttä, M. (2004) 'The ethics of not taking a stand: dilemmas of drug and alcohol prevention in a consumer society—a case study', *International Journal of Drug Policy*, 15, (5–6): 427–344.

Sulkunen, P. and Törrönen, J. (1997a) The production of values: the concept of modality in textual discourse analysis, *Semiotica: Journal of the International Association for Semiotic Studies*, 113(1/2): 43–69.

Sulkunen, P. and Törrönen, J. (1997b) Constructing speaker images: the problem of enunciation in discourse analysis, *Semiotica: Journal of the International Association for Semiotic Studies*, 115(1/2): 121–46.

Sulkunen, P. and Warpenius, K. (2000) Reforming the self and the other: the temperance movement and the duality of modern subjectivity, *Critical Public Health*, 10(4): 423–38.

Svallfors, Stefan (1989) *Vem älskar välfärdstaten? Attityder, organiserande intressen och svensk välfärds politik* [Who Loves the Welfare State? Attitudes, Organized Interests and Swedish Welfare Policy]. Lund: Arvik.

Svallfors, Stefan (1996) *Välfärdsstatens moraliska ekonomi. Välfärdsopinionen i 90-talets Sverige* [The Moral Economy of the Welfare State: Welfare Opinions in Sweden in the 1990s]. Umeå: Boréa bokförlak.

Svallfors, S. and Taylor-Gooby, P. (eds) (1999) *The End of the Welfare State? Responses to State Retrenchment*. London: Routledge & Kegan Paul.

Sztompka, Pjotr (1993) *The Sociology of Social Science*. Oxford: Blackwell Publishers.

Tammi, Tuukka (2007) *Medicalising Prohibition? Harm Reduction in Finnish and International Drug Policy*. Helsinki: STAKES Research Report 161.

Taylor, Anya (1999) *Bacchus in Romantic England: Writers and Drink, 1780–1830*. London: Macmillan.

Taylor, Charles (1992) *The Ethics of Authenticity*. Toronto: Canadian Broadcasting Company.

Taylor-Gooby, Peter (1985) *Public Opinion, Ideology and State Welfare*. London: Routledge and Kegan Paul.

Taylor-Gooby, Peter (1995) Who wants the welfare state? Support for state welfare in European countries, in Stefan Svallfors (ed.), *In the Eye of the Beholder: Opinions on Welfare and Justice in Comparative Perspective*. Umeå: Impello.

Therborn, Göran (1989) States, populations and productivity: towards a political theory of the welfare states, in Peter Lassman (ed.), *Politics and Social Theory*. London: Routledge.

Therborn, Göran (1995) *European Modernity and Beyond: The Trajectory of European Societies, 1945–2000*. London: Sage.

Therborn, Göran (2004) *Between Sex and Power: Family in the World, 1900–2000*. London: Routledge.

Thompson, E.P. ([1963] 1980) *The Making of the English Working Class*. Harmondsworth: Penguin Books.

Thornton, Sarah (1996) *Club Cultures: Music, Media and Subcultural Capital*. London: Wesleyan University Press.

Tigerstedt, Christoffer (2000) Discipline and public health, in P. Sulkunen, C. Tigerstedt, C. Sutton and K. Warpenius (eds), *Broken Spirits: Power and Ideas in Nordic Alcohol Control*. Helsinki: NAD, pp. 93–114.

Tilman, Rick (1984) *C. Wright Mills. A Native American and His American Intellectual Roots*. University Park, PA: The Pennsylvania State University Press.

Timberlake, J.H. (1963) *Prohibition and the Progressive Movement, 1900–1920*. Cambridge, MA: Harvard University Press.

Titmuss, Richard (1976) *Commitment to Welfare*. London: George Allen and Unwin.

Touraine, Alain (1968) *Le mouvement du mai ou le communisme utopique*. Paris: Seuil.

Touraine, Alain ([1973] 1977) *The Self-Production of Society*, Trans. Derek Coltman. Chicago: University of Chicago Press.

Touraine, Alain (1978) *La voix et le regard*. Paris: Seuil.

Touraine, Alain ([1984] 1988) *The Return of the Actor*. Trans. Myra Godzich. Minneapolis: University of Minnesota Press.

Toynbee, Polly (2005) Cut binge drinking the easy way. *The Guardian*, 21 January 2005, p. 3.

Trosa, Sylvie (1999) Réinventer l'Etat, ici et ailleurs, in *Etat et gestion publique. Actes du colloque du 16 décembre 1999*. Paris: Conseil d'Analyse Economique.

Tuori, Kaarlo (2007) Rights, democracy and local self-governance: social rights in the Constitution of Finland, *Juridica international*, 2: 70–3.

Turner, B.S. (1992) *Regulating Bodies: Essays in Medical Sociology*. London: Routledge.

Valverde, Mariana (1998) *Diseases of the Will: Alcohol and the Dilemmas of Freedom*. Cambridge: Cambridge University Press.

Vandervelde, Emile (1910) *Les socialistes et les Bons Templars*. 2e mille. Cahors and Berne: Roggwill.

Veblen, Thorstein ([1899] 1961) *The Theory of the Leisure Class*. New York: The Modern Library.

Veblen, Thorstein ([1919] 2002) *The Vested Interests and the Common Man*. New Brunswick, NJ: Transaction Publishers.

Vigarello, G. (1985) *Le propre et le sale, l'hygiéne du corps depius le Moyen Age*. Paris: Seuil.

Vignon, Jérôme (1999) Leçons de l'action publique en Europe, in *Etat et gestion publique. Actes du colloque du 16 décembre 1999*. Paris: Conseil d'Analyse Economique.

Vincent, C. and Tomlinson, S. (1997) Home–school relationships: 'the swarming of disciplinary mechanisms', *British Educational Research Journal*, 23(3): 361.

Wagner, Peter (2001a) *A History and Theory of the Social Sciences*. London: Sage.

Wagner, Peter (2001b) *Theorizing Modernity*. London: Sage.

Wagner, Peter (2006) Social theory and political philosophy, in G. Delany (ed.), *Handbook of Contemporary European Social Theory*. London: Routledge.

Walby, Sylvia (1997) *Gender Transformations*. London: Routledge

Warde, Alan (1994) Consumption, identity-formation and uncertainty, *Sociology*, 28: 877–98.

Warpenius, K. and Sutton, C. (2000) The ideal of the alcohol-free society, in P. Sulkunen, C. Tigerstedt, C. Sutton and K. Warpenius (eds), *Broken Spirits: Power and Ideas in Nordic Alcohol Control*. Helsinki: NAD, pp. 45–66.

Weakliem, David L. (1991) The two lefts? Occupation and party choice in France, Italy and the Netherlands, *American Journal of Sociology*, 96(6): 1327–61.

Weber, Max ([1920] 2002) *The Protestant Ethic and the Spirit of Capitalism*. Trans. Hans Gerth, Wright Mills and Stephen Kalberg. Los Angeles: Roxbury Publishing Company.

Weeks, Jeffrey (1985) *Sexuality and its Discontents*. London: Routledge.

WHO (1986) Ottawa Charter for Health Promotion: Accessed 8 May 2004 http://www.who.int/hpr/archive/docs/ottawa.html

Wilensky, Harold (1975) *The Welfare State and Equality: Structural and Ideological Roots of Public Expenditure*. Berkeley, CA: University of California Press.

Williams, Raymond (1961) *The Long Revolution*. London: Chatto and Windus.

Williams, Rosalind (1982) *Dream Worlds: Mass Consumption in Late Nineteenth Century France*. Berkeley, CA: University of California Press.

Willis, Paul (1978) *Learning to Labour: How Working Class Kinds Get Working Class Jobs*. Farnborough: Saxon House.

Wilson, Elizabeth (1977) *Women and the Welfare State*. London: Tavistock.

Winch, Donald (1978) *Adam Smith's Politics: An Essay in Historiographic Revision*. Cambridge: Cambridge University Press.

Wolfe, Alain (1989) *Whose Keeper? Social Science and Moral Obligation*. Berkeley, CA: University of California Press.

Index